GREEK
HOMOSEXUALITY

K.J. Dover

Harvard University Press
Cambridge, Massachusetts
1978

Library of Congress Cataloging in Publication Data

Dover, Kenneth James.
  Greek homosexuality.

  Bibliography: p.
  Includes indexes.
  1. Homosexuality – Greece. 2. Homosexuality – Law
and legislation – Greece. 3. Homosexuality and art.
4. Homosexuality in literature. 4. Literature and
morals. I. Title.

HQ76.3.G8D68   1977   301.41'57'0938   77-22423
ISBN 0-674-36261-6

Printed in Great Britain

Illustrations

Thanks are due to the many museums holding vases reproduced in
this book (see List of Vases, pp. 205-226), who have been most
helpful in providing prints. Special permission is acknowledged from
the following: National Museum, Copenhagen for B16, R1027; the
Director of Antiquities and the Cyprus Museum for B65; Musée du
Louvre, Paris, and Chuzeville, Paris, for B166, B462, B470, B494,
C19,. R59, R348, R422, R454, R659; Museum of Fine Arts, Boston
for B342, B598a and b. R223, R456, R577, R603, R651, R783;
Antikenmuseum, Staatliche Museum Preussischer Kulturbesitz,
Berlin (West) for BB24, R196a, R259, R303, R970, R1127; Musée
du Petit Palais, Paris, and Etablissements Bulloz, Paris, for R414;
Mr Walter Bareiss and the Metropolitan Museum of Art, New York
for R462; Tony Raubitschek for R547; the Fitzwilliam Museum,
Cambridge for R684; the Fogg Art Museum, Harvard University
(David M. Robinson bequest) for R712a and b; Soprintendente alle
Antichità, Firenze for R867.

Contents

III   SPECIAL ASPECTS AND DEVELOPMENTS

IV   CHANGES

Preface

This book has a modest and limited aim: to describe those phenomena of homosexual behaviour and sentiment which are to be found in Greek art and literature between the eighth and second centuries B.C., and so to provide a basis for more detailed and specialised exploration (which I leave to others) of the sexual aspects of Greek art, society and morality.

In an article published seventy years ago Erich Bethe observed that the intrusion of moral evaluation, 'the deadly enemy of science', had vitiated the study of Greek homosexuality; and it has continued to do so. A combination of love of Athens with hatred of homosexuality underlies the judgments that homosexual relations were 'a Dorian sin, cultivated by a tiny minority at Athens' (J.A.K. Thomson, ignoring the evidence of the visual arts) or that they were 'regarded as disgraceful both by law and ... by general opinion' (A.E. Taylor, ignoring the implications of the text to which he refers in his footnote). A combination of love of Greek culture in general with an inability or unwillingness to recognise behavioural distinctions which were of great importance within that culture generates statements to the effect that 'homosexuality' *tout court* or 'pederasty' was forbidden by law in most Greek cities (Flacelière, Marrou). I know of no topic in classical studies on which a scholar's normal ability to perceive differences and draw inferences is so easily impaired; and none on which a writer is so likely to be thought to have said what he has not said or to be charged with omitting to say something which he has said several times. From personal knowledge I endorse Karlen's comment that 'Some (*sc.* public and academic experts on sex) are secret homosexuals, their "research" disguised apologetics. Other researchers and clinicians reveal in private a vengeful hatred toward sexual deviants that they would never display in print or in public.' Naturally, I cannot see my own blind spots or explain adequately why my own attitude is what it is, but I will describe it briefly, so that the reader may bear it in mind.

Established linguistic usage compels me to treat 'heterosexual' and 'homosexual' as antithetical, but if I followed my inclination I would replace 'heterosexual' by 'sexual' and treat what is called 'homosexuality' as a subdivision of the 'quasi-sexual' (or 'pseudo-sexual'; not 'parasexual'). Anyone who wishes to make an impression on me by ascribing my inclination to prejudice must first persuade me that he has made a serious attempt to distinguish between prejudice and judgment.

No argument which purports to show that homosexuality in general is natural or unnatural, healthy or morbid, legal or illegal, in conformity with God's will or contrary to it, tells me whether any particular homosexual act is morally right or morally wrong. I am fortunate in not experiencing moral shock or disgust at any genital act whatsoever, provided that it is welcome and agreeable to all the participants (whether they number one, two or more than two). Any act may be – to me, or to any other individual – aesthetically attractive or aesthetically repulsive. Any act may be committed in furtherance of a morally good or morally bad intention. Any act may have good or bad consequences. No act is sanctified, and none is debased, simply by having a genital dimension.

Some readers, especially if they are familiar with previous treatment of the subject, may be surprised by the distribution of emphasis in this book; I have dealt comparatively briefly with some famous people and places (Sappho, Socrates, Sparta) and more fully than is usual with such topics as graffiti, legal terminology and the details of bodily stimulus and response. The reason is that the question which I have tried to answer is not a question about the famous but about Greek society in general. Readers may also be surprised that I do not say very much explicitly about relations between men and women. I ask these readers to remember first, that the book is about a single element in Greek sexual life, and secondly, that my primary object is to describe what is most easily and clearly observed, offering such explanations as are prompted by everyday experience (in which what actually matters to people is often quite different from what 'ought' to matter) and attempting (not with uniform success) to restrain myself from speculation at more theoretical levels.

Originally it was intended that Professor George Devereux and I should write this book in collaboration. Pressure of other commitments made it impossible for Professor Devereux to contribute to the book, but I have invariably profited from discussing with him many of the problems which have arisen in writing it; I have not attempted to do myself what his great experience and learning in anthropology and psychoanalysis qualify him to do. Many classicists, at home and abroad, have given me helpful comment, criticism, advice and information; all errors are mine.

Corpus Christi College, Oxford   K.J. Dover

Abbreviations

1. Ancient authors and works:

Ar(istophanes) *Ach(arnians)*, *Eccl(esiazusae)*, *Lys(istrata)*,
  Thesm(ophoriazusae)
Dem(osthenes)
Eur(ipides)
H(ero)d(o)t(os)
Hom(er) *Il(iad)*, *Od(yssey)*
Lys(ias)
Pl(ato) *Ch(a)rm(ides)*, *Euth(y)d(emus)*, *G(o)rg(ias)*, *Lys(is)*, *Ph(ae)dr(us)*,
  Pr(o)t(agoras), *Rep(ublic)*, *S(y)mp(osium)*
Plu(tarch) *Dial(ogue on Love)*, *Lyc(urgus)*
Thuc(ydides)
Xen(ophon) *Anab(asis)*, *Cyr(opaedia)*, *Hell(enica)*, *(Constitution of the)*
  Lac(edaemonians), *Mem(orabilia)*, *S(y)mp(osium)*

2. Corpora of texts, inscriptions and vases:

CA = *Collectanea Alexandrina*, ed. Powell, J.U. (Oxford 1925)
CAF = *Comicorum Atticorum Fragmenta*, ed. Kock, Theodor
  (Leipzig 1880-8)
CGF = *Comicorum Graecorum Fragmenta*, ed. Austin, Colin,
  i (Berlin 1973)
CVA = *Corpus Vasorum Antiquorum*
DK = *Die Fragmente der Vorsokratiker*, ed. Diels, H., sixth
  edition, revised by Kranz, W. (Berlin 1951-2)
FGrHist = *Fragmenta Graecorum Historicorum*, ed. Jacoby, F. (Berlin,
  1923-30, Leiden 1943–)
HE = *The Greek Anthology*, ed. Gow, A.S.F., and Page, Denys,
  i: *Hellenistic Epigrams* (Cambridge, 1965)
IEG = *Iambi et Elegi Graeci*, ed. West, M.L. (Oxford 1971-2)
IG = *Inscriptiones Graecae*
PLF = *Poetarum Lesbiorum Fragmenta*, ed. Lobel, E., and Page,
  Denys (Oxford, 1955)
PMG = *Poetae Melici Graeci*, ed. Page, Denys (Oxford 1962)
SEG = *Supplementum Epigraphicum Graecum*

SLG = *Supplementum Lyricis Graecis*, ed. Page, Denys (Oxford 1974)

TGF = *Tragicorum Graecorum Fragmenta*, ed. Nauck, A. (Leipzig 1889, repr. Hildesheim 1964)

Wehrli = *Die Schule des Aristoteles*, ed. Wehrli, F. (Basel 1944-59)

3. Modern books:

LSJ = Liddell, H.G., and Scott, R., *Greek-English Lexicon*, revised by Stuart Jones, Sir Henry, and McKenzie, R., with Supplement (Oxford 1968)

RE   = *Real-Enzyklopädie der klassischen Altertumswissenschaft*

Details of the following are given in the bibliography on p. 227:

ABV = Beazley (1956)
AC   = Dover (1972)
ARV = Beazley (1963)
EG   = Boardman and La Rocca
GPM = Dover (1975)
IGD = Trendall and Webster (1971)
LCS = Trendall (1967b)
Par = Beazley (1972)
PhV = Trendall (1967a)
RCA = Metzger (1951)

4. Periodicals:

AA   = *Archäologischer Anzeiger*
ABSA = *Annual of the British School at Athens*
AJA   = *American Journal of Archaeology*
AJP   = *American Journal of Philology*
AK   = *Antike Kunst*
BICS = *Bulletin of the Institute of Classical Studies*
CP   = *Classical Philology*
CQ   = *Classical Quarterly*
CR   = *Classical Review*
HSCP = *Harvard Studies in Classical Philology*
JHS   = *Journal of Hellenic Studies*
MDAI = *Mitteilungen des deutschen archäologischen Instituts*
QUCC = *Quaderni Urbinati di Cultura Classica*
RM   = *Rheinisches Museum*
TAPA = *Transactions of the American Philological Association*
ZPE   = *Zeitschrift für Papyrologie und Epigraphik*

Note: any vase illustrated in this book is starred thus: R295*

I

Problems, Sources and Methods

1. *Scale*

For the purpose of this enquiry, homosexuality is defined as the disposition to seek sensory pleasure through bodily contact with persons of one's own sex in preference to contact with the other sex. There may well be other purposes for which this definition would be superficial and inadequate; but Greek culture differed from ours in its readiness to recognise the alternation of homosexual and heterosexual preferences in the same individual, its implicit denial that such alternation or coexistence created peculiar problems for the individual or for society,[1] its sympathetic response to the open expression of homosexual desire in words and behaviour, and its taste for the uninhibited treatment of homosexual subjects in literature and the visual arts. It therefore presents us with a mass of undisguised[2] phenomena, and we have little occasion, in considering the work of any Greek writer, artist or philosopher, to construct arguments in favour of a diagnosis of latent or repressed homosexuality.

How, when and why overt and unrepressed homosexuality became so conspicuous a feature of Greek life is an interesting subject for speculation, but we are sadly short of evidence, for there is no doubt that overt homosexuality was already widespread by the early part of the sixth century B.C. Analogies from other times and places and the identification of factors common to many dissimilar cultures have considerable suggestive value but still leave many alternatives open; a further complication is that biologists, anthropologists and historians

---

1. The Greeks were aware (cf. p. 62) that individuals differ in their sexual preferences, but their language has no nouns corresponding to the English nouns 'a homosexual' and 'a heterosexual', since they assumed (cf. pp. 60f.) that (*a*) virtually everyone responds at different times both to homosexual and to heterosexual stimuli, and (*b*) virtually no male both penetrates other males and submits to penetration by other males at the same stage of his life (cf. p. 87). Cf. Westwood 100-13.

2. That is not to say that *nothing* was concealed or suppressed (cf. p. 171 n.2), or that nothing was repressed in the individual consciousness.

differ in their axiomatic beliefs about the vulnerability of sexual behaviour and sexual emotion to initially trivial changes of fashion.[3] Why the Athenians of the fourth century B.C. accepted homosexuality so readily and conformed so happily to the homosexual ethos is a question which can be answered instantly at a superficial level: they accepted it because it was acceptable to their fathers and uncles and grandfathers. The interesting and important question in respect of the fourth century is: how did homosexuality really work? How was it integrated with heterosexuality, and how was the moral and aesthetic evaluation of good and bad homosexual behaviour related to the values of classical Greek society in general? The subject is richly documented, though it has one important deficiency: all Greek art, literature and archival material, with the exception of a little poetry surviving only in fragments and citations, was the work of males, and the evidence bearing upon female sexuality of any kind is exiguous by comparison with the superabundant evidence for male homosexuality. 'Male' must therefore be understood with the words 'homosexual' and 'homosexuality' throughout this book, unless 'female' is specified.

The evidence covers a long period of time and is of very many kinds; it includes, for example, primitive graffiti on the rocks of Thera, a wall-painting in a tomb at Paestum, scurrilous political jokes and slanders, Plato's formulation of an ideal philosophical education, and the products of ancient research into the institutions of Crete. Readers who do not know much about the Greeks and approach the subject of Greek homosexuality out of an interest in psychology or sociology – or out of ordinary human curiosity about other people's sexual behaviour – may wish for brief guidance on the compartments into which it is both customary and useful to divide Greek history and on the salient differences between those compartments. The earliest extant words inscribed in the Greek alphabet are datable to the eighth century B.C.; it is probable that the earliest known Greek work of literature, Homer's *Iliad*, took shape in that same century; and the close of the century saw the beginnings of representation (as opposed to decoration) in the visual arts. It is therefore between 800 and 700 B.C. that the Greeks become articulate for us.[4] The lower terminus of the ancient Greek world is the sixth century A.D., in which the overt

3. Cf. D.J. West 45-7, 114 on the power of culture and society to determine sexual behaviour, and Devereux (1967) 69-73 on the important distinction between behavioural patterns and fundamental orientations of the personality.

4. In saying this I ignore the Mycenean documents, partly because they are not the sort of material from which we learn much about people's thoughts and feelings, but mainly because of the cultural discontinuity created by the half-millennium of illiteracy which separated the Mycenean world from the invention of the alphabet.

expression of explicitly pagan thought and feeling was extinguished. In this period of one thousand three hundred years there are four critical moments. The first is the decisive defeat of the Persian attempt in 480 B.C. to bring the Greek mainland into the Persian Empire; this is the boundary between the 'archaic' and 'classical' periods. The second crisis is the latter half of the fourth century B.C., in which the Greek mainland and the Aegean islands became subordinated to the kingdom of Macedon, the Macedonian king Alexander conquered the Persian Empire, and Greek-speakers and Greek culture and institutions were thereby disseminated throughout the Middle East. The third crisis is the second century B.C., when increasing Roman intervention in the Balkans and the Aegean culminated in the incorporation of the Greek mainland into the Roman Empire as a province (146 B.C.). The last crisis was the progressive disintegration of the western half of the Roman Empire in the fourth and fifth centuries A.D., from which the Greek-speaking eastern half, with its capital at Byzantium (Constantinople), emerged as the enduring link between the ancient Greek world and later ages. In the archaic and classical periods the sovereign state was the city, often ludicrously small by modern standards but making its own laws, observing its own institutions and rituals and fighting wars or making treaties with its neighbours. Big cities drew many small cities into 'alliances' which were often empires rather than associations of equals; but imperial power of this kind ebbed and flowed, and it is vital to remember, whenever one is tempted to generalise about the Greeks, that in the archaic and classical periods the term 'the Greeks' covers hundreds of sovereign city-states, distributed throughout Greece, the Aegean and coastal areas of (mainly) Turkey, the Black Sea, Sicily and South Italy, constituting a linguistic and cultural continuum but nevertheless admitting of striking differences in political structure and social ideals.

Classical Greek literature is predominantly Attic ('Attica' was the territory of the city-state of Athens), and in the classical period Attica is also represented by more documentary inscriptions than the whole of the rest of the Greek world. Archaic literature, on the other hand, was almost entirely non-Attic, and this fact makes it difficult to define ways in which (say) Athens in 350 B.C. differed either from the Ionian cities at the same date or from the Athens of two centuries earlier. The cultural dominance which Attica established during the classical period, especially in literature, ensured that the Attic dialect became the basis of standard Greek in the subsequent period and the ancestor of the medieval and modern Greek dialects, but in the 'Hellenistic' age, which began at the end of the fourth century B.C., Athens ceased to be politically powerful. As a cultural term, 'Hellenistic' can be applied to the Greeks right down to the end of paganism, but it is usual to apply it in a more restricted sense, denoting the last three centuries B.C., and to refer thereafter to the 'Roman' or 'imperial' period.

The beginnings of Greek cultural nostalgia can be detected as early as the fourth century B.C., at least at Athens, when no tragic poet of genius had appeared as heir to Sophokles and Euripides, and it was undoubtedly in part a product of the Athenians' regret at the loss of the imperial power which they had exercised over the Aegean for much of the fifth century. Nostalgia was diffused and reinforced by the submergence of the city-states in Macedonian and Greco-Macedonian monarchies, and further reinforced by the absorption of the Greek-speaking world into the Roman Empire. One consequence of this process was a tendency to venerate the literature of the classical period as canonical; by-products were the development of strong antiquarian interests on the part of many educated people and a desire to maintain in literature the conventions, of form and style and social usage, which belonged to the classical past. For this reason writers of late date – particularly of the first two centuries A.D. – contain much which is directly relevant to the classical period; they were, after all, able to read and use a mass of Greek literature which is lost to us, and it often happens that our only access to a writer of the fourth century B.C. is through references, paraphrases and quotations in works composed during the Roman Empire. Since, however, the distinctive features of Greek civilisation were fully developed before the end of the classical period, I have not judged it useful to accumulate evidence which shows only that characteristically Greek attitudes and behaviour survived for a long time as ingredients of a Greco-Roman cultural amalgam, nor have I said anything about characteristically Roman elements in that amalgam.

2. *The visual arts*

Many hundreds of Greek vase-paintings[5] depict older males

5. In the course of working on this book I have looked at most of the published photographs of Greek vases. My generalisations may need to be modified in the light of new material or by rectification of errors caused by negligence and inexperience on my part in the interpretation of existing material, but I should be surprised if any of them can actually be replaced by contrary generalisations. I am far from claiming expertise in the interpretation of pictures, but I am fortified by seeing that experts sometimes err, e.g. in describing a typical pair of males engaged in intercrural copulation as 'wrestlers' or in taking a scene of homosexual courtship, in which hares

conversing with younger males, offering them gifts, cajoling or entreating them, titillating or embracing them. A high proportion of these pictures are of such a kind that if a representative sample survived from some alien culture of which we knew little there would be no good grounds for interpreting them as depictions of homosexual relationships. One may, after all, talk to a boy or offer him a present without being motivated by lust; one may embrace one's own son or nephew, and one may lay restraining hands on a thief or a runaway. In the case of the Greek pictures, however, even if we take into account no evidence other than the totality of the pictures themselves, every point on a scale of intimacy is fully represented. At one end of the scale, apparently relaxed and thoughtful conversation; at the other end, a man thrusting his erect penis between the thighs of a youth; at intermediate points, a boy indignantly refusing the offer of a present, or a man putting out his hand to touch the genitals of a youth. Close analogies with scenes in which one of the participants is a woman are also instructive; we may see in one picture a man offering a gift to a half-naked woman, while in another a man in the same pose may be offering the same gift to a boy, and the boy's expression and gesture may be the same as the woman's. Some gestures are 'culture-bound', and it is possible to make bad mistakes in interpreting them; others make sense when treated as common to us and the Greeks, as when (R52) a youth is arming for departure on military service and his father wags a forefinger in offering advice. Facial expressions which manifest anger, grief or pleasure are normally what we would expect them to be if we put ourselves in the place of the people depicted. The same is true of stance, though alternatives are more often open; thus in R841 a youth standing in a pose of embarrassment and indecision while his companion converses with a woman may be either jealous of the claims of the other sex on his bosom-friend or wishing that he had taken the initiative himself, and the man in R344 who looks pensively at a youth and a boy in conversation may either be a rival of the youth in courting the boy or a relative of the boy disquieted by the turn the conversation is taking. The boy in R381 is almost certainly under homosexual siege from three youths, but the man in R684*, thoughtfully stroking his beard while talking to a boy, may be a teacher to whom the boy has put a difficult question.[6] Even pointing

---

are offered as gifts, as a 'discussion of the day's hunting'. Such errors may underlie the incorrect statement of Robinson and Fluck 14 (repeated in *GPM* 214 and, with a large-scale misprint, in Dover [1973a] 67) about the rarity of scenes of homosexual copulation in vase-paintings.

6. Cf. G. Neumann 109.

and display may be ambiguous; we could hardly misinterpret R647, where a woman in conversation with a man lifts her skirt slightly with one hand and points to her breasts with the other, but it is hard to know whether the youth in B258, who turns round towards a man following him and points to his own buttocks, is issuing a serious invitation or making a gesture of insolent mockery, and there is a possibility that the resemblance of the position of his arm and hand to a pointing gesture is accidental.

Many other features help us to decide whether or not a picture is erotic. In R636 the end of a bed appears in the background of a conversation between a man and a woman. Sometimes a small figure of Eros, the divine personification of heterosexual and homosexual passion, flies above or between the participants in a scene, e.g. B478 (men and boys), R168 (women, with breasts bared, embracing youths). Often a boy or youth receives from an older male a gift (e.g. a cockerel or hare) of the kind held by the passive partner in a scene of homosexual copulation. Occasionally the painter gives words to one or other of the participants in a conversation between an older and a younger male, e.g. (R463) 'Let me!' and 'Stop it!'[7] Our knowledge of mythology is also useful; when we see a bearded male dropping a sceptre in order to seize a struggling youth or boy, we know that we are witnessing not a domestic brawl or a political dispute, but the manifestation of Zeus's irresistible passion for Ganymede, for we can compare such scenes with others in which a winged female (Dawn) lays violent hands on Tithonos, for whom she conceived a passion.

Representations of Ganymede and Tithonos, legendary persons whose beauty aroused even deities, enable us to define the criteria of male beauty, and we can observe that the same criteria are satisfied by portrayals of eternally youthful gods (notably Apollo) and of the boys or youths depicted as pursued, courted or embraced by everyday human lovers. From this we can derive a justification for categorising as 'pin-ups' the great number of youths portrayed in a variety of poses on vessels of all kinds, particularly the typical isolated youth (usually naked, sometimes dressing or undressing) who occupies the interior surface of a shallow vessel. We cannot fail to notice how greatly the male pin-up outnumbers the female at the beginning of the classical period, and how the balance is somewhat redressed later.[8] The positive evidence of these pictures is reinforced by the negative evidence of pictures in which the painter intends to depict what is

7. It is possible that *eāson* here means not 'Let me!' but 'Leave me alone!', in which case both *eāson* and 'Stop it!' are uttered by the boy.

8. Cf. Webster 226-43.

ugly, disgusting or ridiculous: satyrs (cf. Xen. *Smp.* 4.19, 'If I weren't better-looking than *you*, I'd be uglier than all the silenoi[9] in the satyr-plays!'), 'comasts' (drunken revellers dancing and losing all their inhibitions),[10] shrivelled old men, actors dressed for comic burlesques on mythical themes, Asiatics and slaves in degrading situations, or – identifiable through their combination of features characteristic of these other categories – simple comic caricatures. Contrast between the pin-ups and the uglies enables us to say what the Greeks admired and despised in the shape and size not only of the facial features and torso but also of the genitals.

We must not imagine, however, that the vase-paintings directly 'illustrate' the literature available to us or that this literature is any kind of 'commentary' on the vase-paintings. Most of the vases which portray homosexual relations, and a great many of those which portray anything relevant to the questions which arise out of a consideration of homosexuality, were made between 570 and 470 B.C.; the great age of erotic vase-painting was therefore at an end half a century before the birth of Plato and the earliest plays of Aristophanes. Except for some citations from the poems of Solon, we have no Attic literature earlier than the *Persians* of Aiskhylos (472 B.C.). When the evidence of Attic literature becomes abundant, erotic vase-painting is already severely inhibited (cf. pp. 152 f.), and vase-painting as a whole declines to vanishing-point in Attica during the fourth century. Much interesting material can be found in the vases produced from the middle of the fifth century to the end of the fourth in the Greek cities of southern Italy and Sicily, but that is a long way from Athens. It should be added that down to the mid-sixth century Corinth was a major centre of production of painted pottery, and much was also produced during the archaic period in (e.g.) Lakonia, Euboia and the eastern coasts of the Aegean; the Athenian 'monopoly' of this art-form is not in evidence until the latter part of the sixth century, and our literary evidence for the sexual behaviour and attitudes of (e.g.) archaic Corinth is negligible (cf. p. 195).[11] Equally, there is very little literary evidence relating to Boiotia, where certain genres of vase-painting maintained themselves throughout the period of Athenian cultural and artistic dominance.

9. 'Silenos' is the name of the father and leader of the satyrs (on whose characteristic appearance and behaviour cf. pp. 71, 99), but (like 'Pan' and 'Eros') the name can be applied to a genus.

10. Cf. Greifenhagen (1929) 26, 43f., 47f.

11. Here and elsewhere the reader is asked to note that I do not use 'negligible', 'very little', etc., as synonyms of 'no' and 'none'; nor do I use 'seldom' to mean 'never', or 'essentially' and 'fundamentally' to mean 'entirely' or 'exclusively'.

Despite the limitations, imposed by uneven distribution of the material in time and place, on our use of vase-painting as if it were contemporary illustration of literary references to homosexual behaviour, we may nevertheless find that a vase-painting and a passage of literature separated by two hundred years or more contribute significantly each to the understanding of the other even when either of the two in isolation would be open to a variety of interpretations. This is not as surprising as it might seem, for the rate of change of Greek attitudes, practices and institutions, although faster than that of older civilisations – and faster at Athens than elsewhere in the Greek world – was still very slow compared with anything to which we are accustomed in our own day. The most important reservation in the use of vase-painting for the interpretation of Greek literature or society concerns not the time-scale or the diversity of regional cultures but the autonomy of the visual arts in general and the autonomy of each artistic genre. If at a certain date we find a great increase in the depiction of a certain type of behaviour, it does not follow that this type of behaviour had actually increased. It may be that its depiction is peculiarly well adapted to the shape of the surface used by the painters, or that it was a predilection of an individual painter who was greatly admired and imitated, or even that by some trivial accident it became a subject associated with, and therefore expected from, a particular style of painting. It is worth remembering in this connection that the story that Herakles tried to carry off the tripod from the sanctuary of Apollo at Delphi, a story illustrated by more than 150 vases and by some important sculpture at Delphi and elsewhere, is known in extant classical literature only from a single oblique allusion in Pindar (*Olympian Odes* 9.32f.). Stories about violent conflicts between deities were undoubtedly less acceptable to the classical period than to the archaic, but it is also true that the configuration of the struggle for the tripod made it an ideal subject for vase-painting[12] or for a pedimental sculpture. Similarly, the fact that vase-painters most commonly represent heterosexual intercourse as penetration from the rear, the man standing and the woman bending over, does not in itself tell us that the Greeks preferred that position, for it is a configuration which can have evolved from the 'processional' character of the earliest Greek figure-painting;

12. Whether or not the tripod itself is made the focus of the picture, the two figures in the tension of conflict seize our attention, and if they are flanked by the comparatively relaxed figures of Artemis and Athena the scene forms a characteristic and effective upright-cross-upright. On the effect of shape and configuration on the depiction of youths, cf. p.72.

we need later literary evidence (and in fact we have some) to sustain the inference that it was indeed a favoured posture.

Many vase-paintings include short inscriptions, of which the commonest single type is an exclamation about the beauty of a named or unnamed boy or adolescent youth. Exclamations about female beauty are much less common; this fact accords with the predominance of male over female nudes in the paintings, and it is an independent fact, since the inscription often conveys a message not apparently related to any figures, objects or motifs in the picture itself. Vase-inscriptions should not be considered in isolation from graffiti painted[13] or incised on vases after firing, or on broken fragments, rocks or walls, and there are types of graffiti to which allusion is made in literature (cf. III A.). Consideration of all these categories indicates that expression of admiration for the beauty of a male was much commoner than the expression of personal and political malice and ridicule, but it also warns us that the range of significance of any given vase-inscription or graffito can be very wide; the Greeks were often arbitrary, impulsive, frivolous, cynical, witty or jocular, and they are not always well served by too earnest or solemn a temperament in a modern interpreter.

3. *Literature*

The five most important sources of material on homosexuality are: (*a*) late archaic and early classical homosexual poetry; (*b*) Attic comedy, particularly Aristophanes and his contemporaries; (*c*) Plato; (*d*) a speech of Aiskhines, the *Prosecution of Timarkhos*; (*e*) homosexual poetry of the Hellenistic period. The questions raised by this material can sometimes be answered by reference to comparatively brief allusions and comments in other authors, especially Xenophon (whose activity as a writer spanned the first half of the fourth century) and the authors of speeches made in the Athenian lawcourts at various times in the fourth century.[14]

(*a*) The chief concentration of homosexual poetry before Hellenistic times is the last 164 verses ('Book II') of the corpus of verses ascribed to Theognis of Megara. It is a succession of short poems (some consist

---

13. Archaeologists distinguish between incised 'graffiti' and painted 'dipinti', but in ordinary usage the distinction is no longer observed.

14. What is very widely known or aesthetically striking or attractive is not always and necessarily as important for the purpose of the present enquiry as aesthetically unimpressive but unambiguous passages of uninspiring and little-read authors. Hence the absence of some distinguished names from my 'five most important sources'.

of only one elegiac couplet) predominantly of homosexual character, addressed to boys or expressing feelings about boys. Its segregation from the work of Theognis as a whole ('Book I' contains 1220 verses) was probably effected in the early Middle Ages, when sensibilities were jolted by the juxtaposition of extravagant expressions of homosexual emotion with stern exhortations to honesty and truthfulness.[15] There is room for controversy both about the date of Theognis himself and about the authenticity of much of the poetry ascribed to him. An Attic red-figure vase of the early fifth century (R1053) depicts a man at a dinner-party singing the words 'O most handsome of boys', which (in Greek; English word-order is different) are the opening words of Theognis 1365f., 'O most handsome and desirable of all boys', but the phrase is not a remarkable one and may well have been a poetic cliché. However, quotations of Theognis in Plato suggest that there was a substantial degree of coincidence between the text of Theognis known to Plato and at any rate the first third of what we call 'Theognis'. Since the great age of moralising elegiac poetry extended approximately from the middle of the seventh century B.C. to the middle of the sixth, at least one passage of Theognis (1103f.) makes a historical allusion for which a date at the end of the seventh century is most appropriate, and several others may plausibly be considered to point to the same period, the core of the body of poetry ascribed to Theognis may take us well back into the archaic period;[16] but the accretions may be strung out over a long time, perhaps even extending to the Hellenistic age.

(*b*) Homosexuality afforded good material for humour to Aristophanes, whose eleven extant plays run from 425 to 388 B.C., and to the many other comic poets whose plays are known to us through fragments and citations (comparatively few of these can be dated with assurance earlier than the 430s, and overtly sexual humour declined in popularity[17] after the mid-fourth century). It was not the business of the comic poets to present scholars of later times with a judicious delineation of Athenian society, but to make their audiences laugh, and in particular to afford those audiences temporary vicarious release from the constraints imposed by law, religion and social

---

15. Cf. M.L. West (1974) 43-5.

16. Cf. *ibid.* 65-71.

17. Cf. Aristotle *Nicomachean Ethics* 1128[a] 22-5; his generalisation is supported by what we can read of late fourth-century and early third-century comedy, but its validity is not as absolute as we might have imagined if we had known nothing at all of the lost plays of his period.

convention. Characters in Aristophanes therefore realise outrageous ambitions, often by means which belong to the world of fairy-tale rather than to our familiar world of cause and effect, and in the process they may insult, trick and triumph over generals, politicians, administrators, intellectuals and deities.[18] This kind of comedy is characterised by lavish use of the Greek equivalents of our 'four-letter words', a feature which it shares with iambic poetry of the archaic period (Arkhilokhos and Hipponax) but not with other literary genres; the language of serious Greek literature, poetry and prose alike, is euphemistic and its allusions to processes of the genito-urinary system tend to be imprecise. The comic poets also inherited a tradition which accorded poets the right to admonish and upbraid the community, and this conjunction of a didactic role with a liberating role produces the comic world in which people are (in the words of Aristotle, *Poetics* 1448[a]16-18) 'not as good' as we find them to be in life.[19] Comedy tends to assume that we all want to cheat our neighbours and evade our obligations; and it translates both heterosexual and homosexual relations into the most explicit physiological terms, with little regard for their 'romantic' aspects (cf. III C.). The comic poet would perhaps have claimed that through the medium of his choruses and his shrewd, robust, somewhat philistine and cynical characters he rescues us from deception and self-deception, but the interpreter of comedy must remember that there are many things in life with which Aristophanic comedy does not try to cope. It is often hard to decide just what the evidence of a comic passage proves, but fortunately not so hard to detect usages and attitudes which must be accepted as the background of a joke or comic idea if an audience is to get the point.

(*c*) Plato, who was born in 428 B.C. and died in 347 B.C., treated the love which is aroused by the stimulus of visual beauty as a special case, operative at a low level, of the force which impels humanity to seek understanding of the eternal, immutable 'form' or 'idea' of 'the Beautiful itself'. Since Plato experienced, and was not able to reject, a craving[20] to believe both that the ultimate order of the universe is accessible to human reason and that the ultimate cause of its being what it is is good, and since our response to good is love and desire (for that is what we mean[21] when we call something good), it follows that for

18. Cf. *AC* 30-48.

19. Literally, 'worse than those now'; 'worse than ...' is normal Greek in the sense 'not as good as ...' (so too e.g. 'uglier than ...' = 'not as good-looking as ...').

20. Cf. Nygren 166 'philosophy ... in the sense of a philosophy of life built up partly on a religious basis'.

21. Cf. Pl. *Smp.* 204e-205a.

Plato a philosopher, as he frees himself from concern over the body and the material world of particulars, progressing ever 'upwards' by reason, becomes increasingly aware that reason and love are convergent upon a point at which they must in the end fuse together. In two works above all, *Symposium* and *Phaedrus*, Plato takes homosexual desire and homosexual love as the starting-point from which to develop his metaphysical theory; and it is of particular importance that he regards philosophy not as an activity to be pursued in solitary meditation and communicated in *ex cathedra* pronouncements by a master to his disciples,[22] but as a dialectical progress which may well begin in the response of an older male to the stimulus afforded by a younger male who combines bodily beauty with 'beauty of the soul'.[23] Cause and effect are not easy to disentangle in the interpretation of Plato's philosophical method. An Athenian aristocrat, he moved in a section of society which certainly regarded strong homosexual desire and emotion as normal, and Athenian society in general entertained a low opinion of the intellectual capacity and staying-power of women.[24] Plato's philosophical treatment of homosexual love may have been an outcome of this ambience. We must however leave open the possibility that his own homosexual emotion was abnormally intense and his heterosexual response abnormally deficient. He may therefore present a somewhat exaggerated picture of the homosexual orientation of his own time, place and class. In any case, Plato does not speak *in propria persona*, but represents Socrates and others discussing moral and philosophical questions; Socrates himself left nothing in writing, and the other participants in the Socratic dialogues which Plato composed express a variety of views.[25] We might go badly wrong if, for example, we simply assumed that all the statements about Athenian sentiment put into the mouth of 'Pausanias' in Plato's *Symposium* must be objective statements of fact or even Plato's own considered opinion on a question of fact; they may prove to be so in the light of other evidence (and I think they are), but we cannot dispense with that other evidence, and the difference between 'the Athenians thought ...' and

22. Cf. however n. 24 below.

23. I use inverted commas since (*a*) 'soul' as a translation of *psūkhē* (in antithesis to *sōma*, 'body') often has positive religious connotations which are not necessarily present in *psūkhē*, and (*b*) I do not use the words 'beauty' and 'beautiful' except with reference to form, colour and sound, so that for me 'beautiful soul' is a senseless expression.

24. On the exceptional case of Diotima in the *Symposium* cf. p.161 n.11.

25. The voice of Plato in old age is heard from the anonymous Athenian who is the expositor in Plato's *Laws* (not a Socratic dialogue); cf. John Gould 71-130.

'Plato represents Pausanias, in such-and-such a context and for such-and-such a purpose, as saying that the Athenians thought ...' is a very important difference indeed, not least because Pausanias was a real person whose disposition, we have some reason to think (cf. p. 84), was more exclusively homosexual than was common in the Greek world. It is even more important to distinguish between what was characteristically and peculiarly Platonic and what was generally thought and felt in fourth-century Athens, let alone in the Greek world as a whole. Plato differed from most Athenians of his time in possession of wealth and leisure, in boundless zeal for the study of philosophy and mathematics, in a suspicious and censorious attitude to the arts,[26] and in contempt for democracy (to which it is fair to add that he differed from them also in his ability to write in a way which combines to a unique degree dramatic power, convincing characterisation, vitality and elegance). Modern readers of *Phaedrus* and *Symposium*, which they may well have seen in the pornography section of a bookshop, are apt to believe that what they find therein is the quintessential doctrine of the Greeks on the whole topic of homosexuality, expressed in definitive terms by their acknowledged spokesman. Yet Plato's right to speak even for Greek philosophy – to say nothing of a right to speak for Greek civilisation – was not conceded by other pupils of Socrates, and although Plato gave great impetus to philosophy, neither his own pupils nor the philosophical schools which arose in the two following generations accorded his teaching the status of revelation.

(*d*) In 346 B.C. an Athenian politician, Timarkhos, was prosecuted under a law which provided that an Athenian citizen who had prostituted himself to another male – that is to say, had accepted money or goods in return for the homosexual use of his body – should be debarred from participation in political life. Aiskhines' *Prosecution of Timarkhos* (number 'i' in modern editions of the surviving speeches of Aiskhines) is a written version of the principal speech for the prosecution, and its peculiar value is twofold. It is the only surviving work of Greek literature on a substantial scale (45 printed pages in a modern edition) which is entirely concerned with homosexual relationships and practices; and just as the original speech was designed to persuade a jury of several hundred ordinary citizens, so

26. Many excuses can be made for Plato, and some initial impressions are modified on reflection, but he can still be described as 'suspicious and censorious' by contrast with the numerous Greeks whose aesthetic response to art and literature was strong enough to mitigate their anxiety about moral implications.

the written version is designed to persuade the reader that the prosecutor is of value as a politically active member of the community and the defendant unworthy to exercise the normal functions of a citizen. There was no judge in an Athenian court of law, no one to give the jury skilled and objective guidance, no one to rule evidence inadmissible or to restrain a speaker who introduced narrative, comment or allegations irrelevant to the point of issue.[27] Each of the speakers had to try to convince the jury that he, and not the opposing party, was the person to be trusted, the good citizen whose exemplary record in public and private life created a presumption that he was in the right; and each had to try to impose the contrary *persona* on his adversary. Accordingly, a speaker could not take the risk of expressing sentiments which, in his judgment, were likely to be suspect or repugnant to the average juror. If we want to discover the social and moral rules which the average Athenian of the fourth century B.C. treated with outward respect and professed to observe, we cannot do better than study the sentiments and generalisations which the forensic orators make explicit, the implications of their allusions, boasts or reproaches, and the points at which they introduce, or omit to introduce, evaluative terms into a narrative.[28] Aiskhines i is thus the only surviving text which gives us access to the sentiments which it was prudent to profess in public on the subject of homosexuality in Athens during the classical period; Plato, by contrast, was writing for readers interested in philosophy, who could put a book down if it angered, shocked or bored them, not for a jury which could deprive him of his life or citizenship or property if he failed to conciliate them, and the humorous treatment of homosexuality in Aristophanes' plays was a seasoning, not a central motif which could seriously affect his chances of winning first prize at a dramatic festival. We must however remember, in making use of Aiskhines i, that the sentiments of 346 B.C. were not necessarily the same as those of (say) 446; for the mid-fifth century we entirely lack the evidence of forensic speeches.

(*e*) A considerable number of 'epigrams', i.e. short poems (mostly of two to five elegiac couplets), were composed on homosexual themes from the third century B.C. onwards. They were incorporated in a succession of anthologies, of which the earliest and most important was the *Garland* of Meleagros, *c.* 100 B.C.; as one would expect, each

---

27. Irrelevance was open to criticism, and procedural rules attempted to restrain it (Harrison ii 163), but to judge from the speeches which we read the restraint was not very effective.
28. Cf. *GPM* 5-14.

anthologist drew heavily on his predecessors, discarded some of their items, and added fresh material. What we call the 'Greek Anthology' was compiled by Konstantinos Kephalas in the tenth century A.D.; it survives in the 'Palatine Anthology', near to Kephalas in date, in the 'Planudean Anthology', compiled by Maximos Planudes in 1301, and in some minor collections of later date.[29] Homosexual epigrams, to the number of some three hundred, are collected in book xii of the Greek Anthology, and heterosexual epigrams in book v; some slight carelessness in classification is shown by a scatter of misplaced epigrams. Those epigrams which are later in date than Meleagros tell us little or nothing of importance about Greek sentiment and practice in homosexual relations which we do not already know from earlier material.[30] What we find in the *Garland*, on the other hand, is often of considerable value when taken in conjunction with allusions in comedy or details in vase-paintings, thanks to the numerous constants (cf. p. 112) in the history of Greek culture.

The chapters which follow do not take the evidence in chronological order; they begin not at the beginning, but at the centre of things, where the evidence is most abundant and most detailed. The number of different issues relevant to homosexuality raised by Aiskhines i is considerable, and I propose to explore each of them far enough to make what Aiskhines said to the jurors in 346 B.C. intelligible in terms of the jurors' attitudes and assumptions. For this reason Chapter II is the mainstay of the book, and it will be followed by an exploration of what I regard as special cases and side-issues.

4. *Vocabulary*

It will be necessary later (II B. 2-3) to discuss the Greek words for love, sexual desire and various acts and emotions which are related to love, to desire or to both. But three other problems of translation will be with us almost from the first and will stay with us to the end. One of these is constituted by the word *kalos*, which means 'beautiful', 'handsome', 'pretty', 'attractive' or 'lovely' when applied to a human being, animal, object or place, and 'admirable', 'creditable' or

29. Cf. *HE* i xiii-xxi, xxxii-xlv.

30. For example: Straton, a Greek poet of Roman imperial times, regards young males of 16-17 as more exciting than those of any other age; if this view was held (as I think it probably was) by the Athenians of the classical period, Straton tells us nothing new, and if it was not held by them, Straton is irrelevant to the subject of this book. Flacelière 55f., in keeping with his general disregard of chronology, gives no hint of Straton's date.

'honourable' when applied to actions or institutions. It must be emphasised that the Greeks did not call a person 'beautiful' by virtue of that person's morals, intelligence, ability or temperament, but solely by virtue of shape, colour, texture and movement. The English distinction between 'handsome', applied to males, and 'beautiful', applied to females, has no corresponding distinction in Greek; only the grammatical form can show whether a given instance of *kalos* has a masculine, feminine or neuter reference, and translation is sometimes complicated by the use of the masculine plural to mean 'handsome males and beautiful females' and the use of the neuter plural to mean 'beauty in people, attractiveness in things and conspicuous virtue in actions'. In translating passages I have tended to keep 'beautiful' even on occasions when it does not sound quite right in English, and when I have used a different word I have indicated in brackets, in cases where misunderstandings might arise, that the original has *kalos*.

The second problem concerns the 'active' (or 'assertive', or 'dominant') and 'passive' (or 'receptive', or 'subordinate') partners in a homosexual relationship. Since the reciprocal desire of partners belonging to the same age-category is virtually unknown in Greek homosexuality (cf. p. 85), the distinction between the bodily activity of the one who has fallen in love and the bodily passivity of the one with whom he has fallen in love is of the highest importance. In many contexts, and almost invariably in poetry, the passive partner is called *pais*, 'boy' (plural *paides*), a word also used for 'child', 'girl', 'son', 'daughter', and 'slave'. The *pais* in a homosexual relationship was often a youth who had attained full height (the vase-paintings leave us in no doubt about that); in order to avoid cumbrousness and at the same time to avoid the imprecision of 'boy', I have consistently adopted the Greek term *erōmenos*, masculine passive participle of *erān*, 'be in love with ...', 'have a passionate desire for ...'. I have however retained 'boy' in translating a Greek passage which says *pais*, and I use 'boy' or 'youth' in describing any relationship in which the approximate age of the junior partner is known. For the senior partner I have adopted the Greek noun *erastēs*, 'lover', which is equally applicable to heterosexual and homosexual relations but (being, like *erōmenos*, derived from *erān*) is free (cf. II B sections 2-3) from the ambiguities inherent in the English word 'love'. From now on 'erastes' and 'eromenos' will be printed as if they were English words. The Greeks often used the word *paidika* in the sense 'eromenos'. It is the neuter plural of an adjective *paidikos*, 'having to do with *paides*', but constantly treated as if it were a masculine singular, e.g. 'Kleinias was the *paidika* of Ktesippos'. I shall use this word in discussing passages of Greek which use it, and shall print it in roman.[31]

The third problem arises from the readiness with which people extend an originally precise term for a specific type of sexual behaviour to all sexual behaviour of which they disapprove and even to non-sexual behaviour which is for any reason unwelcome to them. *Porneiā*, for example, means 'prostitution' in classical Greek (cf. p. 20), but in later Greek (e.g. I Cor. 5.1) it is applied to any sexual behaviour towards which the writer is hostile. We do not normally interpret instances of modern colloquial usage, e.g. 'wanker', or 'motherfucker', as conveying precise charges of sexual deviation, and we should be no less cautious in the interpretation of comparable Greek words, whether they are to some extent etymologically analysable (e.g. *katapūgōn*; cf. pp. 142f.) or etymologically mysterious (e.g. *kinaidos*). Conversely, we must be prepared for the possibility that words which we could not recognise as sexual by inspecting them in isolation (e.g. the compound stem *aiskhropoi-*, literally 'do what is ugly/disgraceful/shameful') had a precise sexual reference (cf. 'unnatural' in English).

---

31. In two quotations from fifth-century comedy, Kratinos fr. 258 and Eupolis fr. 327, *paidika* refers to a girl, but in both the language may very well be humorous and figurative; at any rate, the word never has a feminine reference thereafter. The adjective is found in the sense 'boyish', 'childish', and also 'sportive', 'frivolous', the antonym of 'serious', as if it functioned as an adjective of *paidiā*, 'fun', 'relaxation'. I suspect that *paidika* = 'eromenos' originated as a pun, the assumption being that a man spent his leisure-time in keeping company with a boy whom he hoped to seduce (cf. modern idioms such as 'He's got himself a smashing bit of homework'). The word occurs in the obscure title (apparently 'You'll scare <the> paidika') of a mime by Sophron in the fifth century.

II

The Prosecution of Timarkhos

A. The Law

1. *Male prostitution*

In the early summer of 346 B.C. the city of Athens made a peace-treaty with Philip II of Macedon. Dissatisfaction with the terms of the treaty, and in particular with aggressive action by Philip in the last days before he actually swore to its observance, was such that the envoys whose task it had been to go to Philip's court and receive his oath were threatened on their return with a prosecution which, if successful, might cost them their lives. This prosecution was instigated by Demosthenes, who had been one of the envoys but dissociated himself from the rest on their return; acting with Demosthenes, and perhaps designated as leading prosecutor, was a certain Timarkhos. The envoys were able to counter this threat by recourse to a law which debarred from addressing the assembly, and from many other civic rights, any citizen who had maltreated his parents, evaded military service, fled in battle, consumed his inheritance, or prostituted his body to another male; this law provided for the denunciation, indictment and trial of anyone who, although disqualified on one or other of these grounds, had attempted to exercise any of the rights forbidden to him. It was believed that Timarkhos, who had certainly been active in the assembly and had held public office, could be shown, at least to the satisfaction of a jury (lacking, as all Athenian juries lacked, the guidance of a professional judge), to have prostituted himself in his youth. This belief was justified, for Aiskhines, one of the threatened envoys, brought Timarkhos to court and won the case. Timarkhos was disenfranchised (Dem. xix 284), and thereby Demosthenes and his political associates suffered a reverse; three years were to pass before Aiskhines was prosecuted for misconduct on the embassy, and then he was acquitted. Since the greater part of our evidence for the events of 346 B.C. comes from highly partisan sources, it is hard to assess the balance of Athenian opinion on issues of foreign policy at any given moment, and it would be unwise to suppose that the revelation of Timarkhos's squalid past was enough in itself to convince the citizenry that Aiskhines must be right about Philip II and Demosthenes wrong. The demonstration that Timarkhos was attempting to exercise political rights from which he was legally debarred, whatever the reason for the debarment, will have weighed more heavily with the Athenians; and the diminution of his social and political standing by the jurors' acceptance of Aiskhines' vilification and ridicule as justified, whatever the quality of the evidence, may have been the most important factor of all in frustrating the political efforts of the group to which Timarkhos belonged.

According to the law which Aiskhines describes in §§ 29-32, with selective verbatim citation, a citizen who was *peporneumenos* or *hētairēkōs* was debarred from the exercise of his civic rights:

> because the legislator considered that one who had been a vendor of his own body for others to treat as they pleased (*lit.* 'for *hubris*'; cf. Section 4) would have no hesitation in selling the interests of the community as a whole.[1]

The two categories of conduct which the law explicitly named are in fact two distinct species of the genus 'sale of one's own body'. *Peporneumenos* is the perfective participle of the verb *porneuesthai*, 'behave as a *pornē* or *pornos*'. *Pornē*, cognate with *pernanai*, 'sell', was the normal Greek word (first attested in the seventh century B.C. [Arkhilokhos fr. 302]) for a woman who takes money (if a slave, on her owner's behalf) in return for the sexual use of her body, i.e. 'prostitute'. We find also a masculine form *pornos* applied to men or boys who submit to homosexual acts in return for money (Xen. *Mem.* i 6.13, Ar. *Wealth* 153-9; first in an archaic graffito on Thera, *IG* xii. 3. 536). *Hētairēkōs* is the perfective participle (infinitive *hētairēkenai*) of the verb *hetairein*, cognate with *hetairos*, the normal word for 'companion', 'comrade', 'partner'. *Hetairā*, the feminine form of *hetairos*, often[2] denoted a woman who was maintained by a man, at a level acceptable to her, for the purpose of a sexual relationship without formal process of marriage, implicit promise of permanence or intention of raising a family, but not without hope on the man's part that she might love

---

1. On this type of argument cf. *GPM* 41, 298f., 302.
2. But not always; a woman could refer to a female friend of hers as 'my *hetairā*', (e.g. Ar. *Lys.* 701), just as a man could refer to 'my *hetairos*' without any homosexual connotation. If a woman said 'my *hetairos*', on the other hand (e.g. Ar. *Eccl.* 912), or a man 'my *hetairā*', the connotation would be erotic.

him; hence it is sometimes nearer to 'mistress' than to 'prostitute'. In the classical period the verb *hetairein* and the abstract noun *hetairēsis* do not seem to have been used of a hetaira, but exclusively of a man or boy who played a homosexual role analogous to that of a hetaira.

Whether a woman was regarded as a common prostitute or as a hetaira depended to some extent on the number of different men with whom she had intercourse and on the duration of her relationship with each man. Plainly a woman in a brothel, dealing with a queue of customers every day, was a *pornē*, and equally plainly a woman who was kept in luxury by a wealthy man for a year or more, during which time she never (well, hardly ever) had intercourse with anyone else, was a hetaira, but the dividing line between the two categories could not be sharp; how, for instance, should one classify a woman who had intercourse with four different men in a week, hoped on each occasion to establish a lasting and exclusive relationship, and succeeded in doing so with the fourth man? Moreover, whether one applied the term *pornē* or the term 'hetaira' to a woman depended on the emotional attitude towards her which one wished to express or to engender in one's hearers.[3] Anaxilas fr. 21 draws a distinction in terms of loyalty and affection, but fr. 22, an indignant vilification of the greed and deceitfulness of women who sell themselves, begins and ends (lines 1, 31) by calling them hetairai but in the middle (line 22) calls them *pornai*. Perikles had children by Aspasia, who was certainly distinguished and accomplished, probably fastidious and probably also faithful to Perikles; but Eupolis fr. 98 represents one of these sons, Perikles the younger, as shamed by the appellation 'the whore's son'.

The law cited by Aiskhines, in saying '... or *peporneumenos* or *hētairēkōs*', implies a distinction in respect of homosexual conduct analogous to the distinction between the *pornē* and the hetaira, and §§51f. make this plainer:

> Now, if Timarkhos had remained with Misgolas and had not gone on to anyone else, his conduct would have been less improper (*lit.*, 'more *metrios*'), if there is anything proper in behaviour of the kind we are considering; and, for my part, I would have had no hesitation in bringing against him only the charge which the legislator names so bluntly, *hētairēkenai*; for anyone who acts in that way in relation to one man, but takes pay for his activity, is liable, in my opinion, to that charge alone. But if I remind you (*sc.* of the facts) and prove – passing over those gross (*lit.*, 'wild') creatures, Kedonides and Autokleides and Thersandros, in whose houses he has found a welcome – that he has earned money by the use of his body not only in Misgolas's keeping but

3. Cf. Hauschild 8f.

in someone else's, and then in another's, and that he has gone from that
to a new one, there is not much doubt by then that he is not simply
hētairēkōs but – by Dionysos! I don't see how I can go on beating about
the bush all day – actually *peporneumenos*. Anyone who acts in this way
indiscriminately, in relation to many men, for pay, is liable, in my
opinion, to precisely that charge.

From now on, all parts of the verbs *porneuesthai* and *hetairein* will be
translated 'prostitute ... -self', but the original word will be indicated
in each instance by adding '(*porn.*)' or '(*het.*)'.

The 'facts' of which Aiskhines 'reminds' the jury have in part been
retailed in §§37-44. To give an impression of magnanimity, Aiskhines
says (§39) that he will pass over in silence 'all the offences which
Timarkhos committed against his own body when he was a boy' and
begin with the period at which he was an adolescent youth (*meirakion*)
and spent his days at a doctor's surgery, ostensibly to learn medicine
but in reality to pick up homosexual custom (§40). A certain
Misgolas, a distinguished citizen but a man of 'extraordinary
enthusiasm for this activity', took Timarkhos home to live with him,
having made an advance payment (§41). A further series of allegations
follows in §§53ff.; turned out by Misgolas, who could no longer afford
him, Timarkhos went to live in turn with Antikles, Pittalakos and
Hegesandros. The 'wild men' whom Aiskhines 'passes over' in §52 are
not mentioned again, nor should we expect them to be; 'I will say
nothing about ...' is a common orator's way of making a damaging
allegation while at the same time trying to secure the credit for not
making it (this technique is used again in §§106, 107, 109, 170). Rules
of evidence in Athenian courts were, by modern standards, very lax;
Aiskhines speaks with great complacency of the fact that the
defendant's history is well known to many of the jurors (§44, 'that I
am telling the truth is known to all those who were acquainted with
Misgolas and Timarkhos at that period'), and in §§92f. he urges the
jury not to attend solely to the evidence produced in court, but to take
into account all the rumours and gossip they have ever heard about
Timarkhos (cf. §§48, 73, 80-5, 89f., 121f., 127, 130). There was, of
course, a strong tactical reason for taking this line: the extreme
difficulty, in the absence of any written contract, of proving beyond
doubt that Timarkhos received money from the men with whom he
lived.

Let us at this point pause to list certain questions prompted by
what has been said so far:

(*a*) The law cited by Aiskhines referred to the sale, not the gift, of one's body. It said nothing of 'unnatural practices', 'gross indecency', and the like, and thus it appears not to have imposed any penalty on those who submitted to homosexual acts for love or for fun. Was that in fact the law's intention? Were there other laws which penalised non-commercial homosexuality?

(*b*) The law penalised the seller; did it not penalise the buyer?

(*c*) Aiskhines evinces hesitation and embarrassment at having to utter the word *peporneumenos* in court, and he speaks (§51) of the law's 'bluntness' in using even the word *hētairēkōs*. What was the extent of Athenian inhibition in speaking of homosexual conduct, and what were the reasons for it?

2. *Penalties*

It was possible for any Athenian to vilify and ridicule any other Athenian for any conduct whatsoever, real or alleged, which could be represented as disadvantageous in the community as a whole, and to found his attack on moral principles generally professed, however imperfectly observed, by the citizen-body. Evidence of an unusual degree of enthusiasm for heterosexual or homosexual intercourse afforded manifold grounds for moral censure: the enthusiast was more likely than other people to commit crimes such as rape and adultery, and more likely to be tempted to acquire money dishonestly as a means to purchased sexual enjoyment; more likely to consume his inheritance on hetairai and prostitutes, instead of preserving it as taxable capital or devoting it to purposes welcome and useful to the community; more likely also to choose pleasure or comfort in circumstances which called for the soldierly virtues of self-sacrifice, endurance and resistance to pain.[4] Also, anyone who could be regarded as abetting another's delinquency, and thereby as bringing about a hypothetical disadvantage to the community (this could be said, for example, of the person who had caused another to prostitute himself and had thus deprived the community of that other person's counsel in the future), was vulnerable to attack. It is hard to think of any act upon which a sufficiently determined and ingenious adversary, adept at moralising, cannot put a sinister interpretation; but this is quite a different matter from the precise question whether the client of a male prostitute incurred a penalty prescribed by law.

---

4. On Greek moral arguments in favour of chastity cf. Dover (1973) 61-5 and *GPM* 178-80, 208f., 210.

It proves curiously difficult to discover from Aiskhines' speech the answer to this question, and we have to remind ourselves that if a speaker in court thought it helpful to his case to confuse the issue while professing to clarify it, he would do his best to confuse it. The same is true of a modern advocate, and it is the business of the judge to dispel confusion. In an Athenian court, if the case was of an unusual kind and rested upon laws with which the jurors were unfamiliar (considerations which apply [§132; cf. §17] to the case of Timarkhos), a speaker had a better chance at least to create in the jury a frame of mind favourable to him, even if he could not wholly succeed in misleading them on questions of legal fact.

It is to be presumed that a speaker could not expect to get away with plain misrepresentation of the law's actual words, especially when – as was normal practice – the relevant law itself had been read out by the clerk of the court at the moment when the speaker needed it for the purposes of his argument. Hence statements of the form 'the law says ...' have a claim to be considered true unless there is good evidence to the contrary. If the words quoted from the law are archaic, elliptical or otherwise hard to interpret, and are explained by the speaker, the probability that his statement of the text is true approximates to certainty, but the correctness of his explanation is a different matter; it would be a mistake to treat such an explanation, whether offered by prosecutor or by defendant, as the Greek equivalent of a jurist's considered opinion. It is also noticeable that on occasion the clerk of the court is instructed by the speaker to begin reading the law from a certain point in the text or to stop before reading the whole text, for the speaker may wish to mislead the jury by expounding part of the law in a way which would be absolutely precluded if the preceding or following part were read out.[5] Moreover, in summarising a law the speaker may combine verbatim quotation with comment and interpretation of his own. §19 provides a good example:[6]

> 'If any Athenian,' he (*sc.* the legislator) says, 'has prostituted (*het.*) himself, let it not be open to him to become one of the nine archons' – because, I imagine, that office is one in which a crown is worn – 'or to carry out a priestly function' – as not even being clean in body – 'or act as an advocate,' he says, 'in the state's interest, or hold any office whatsoever at any time, in Attica or abroad, allotted or elected, or serve

5. E.g. Dem. xxiv 71. It is possible that the difficulty of following Aiskhines' argument in iii 30-3, 47 and the rebuttal of it in Dem. xviii 120f. arises in part from selective quotation by both sides.
6. Cf. Merkelbach (1975) and Wankel 73f.

as a herald, or go on an embassy' – or bring to trial men who have been on an embassy, or take money for threatening false accusations – 'or deliver an opinion on any occasion in council or assembly,' however accomplished an orator he may be.

Classical Greek script did not possess equivalents of the inverted commas, dashes and brackets which are required in translating such a passage into English, so that any reader (from 346 B.C. to the present day) who did not actually hear Aiskhines utter these words and had no access to people who had heard him was compelled to exercise his own judgment in separating quotation from comment. It is not hard to see that 'because, I imagine ...' is comment; 'as not even being ...' is a comment on 'priestly function' analogous to the preceding comment on 'nine archons', though without the first person singular which clarifies the distinction between text and comment, and recurs, in slightly different form, in §188. The repetition of 'he says' after 'or act as an advocate' is designed to renew, after those two comments, the impression that what we are hearing is essentially a quotation of the law. 'Or bring to trial ...' might pass, with a very inattentive or slow-witted hearer, as quotation, but in fact it is inserted because Timarkhos had embarked on a prosecution of the envoys; prosecuting envoys did not differ juridically from any other kind of prosecution, and the law affecting prostitution will naturally not have specified disqualification from just one out of the whole range of possible prosecutions. 'Or take money ...' implies that Timarkhos has been bribed to bring a false charge against Aiskhines; it cannot possibly be part of the law, for blackmail and corrupt practice – unlike the holding of administrative and religious offices – were not privileges left open by the law to those innocent of prostitution. Finally, 'however accomplished ...' is a qualification exceedingly improbable in an actual law (we have enough of the Athenian laws to justify statements about what is or is not legal style) but exactly in accord with a litigant's usual allegation that his opponent attempts to conceal dishonesty of purpose under meretricious rhetoric (cf. Aiskhines' sneers against Demosthenes' technical expertise, §§94, 119, 125, 166, 170).[7]

Aiskhines seems to have composed on behalf (though certainly not at the behest) of Misgolas (§§45f.) and Hegesandros (§67) testimony which, he hoped, they would formally acknowledge as theirs by appearing in court when it was read out.[8] In the case of the testimony

---

7. Cf. Dover (1968) 155-8 and *GPM* 25f.; and on bribery, cf. Dem. xxiv 66.
8. On procedure over testimony in court cf. Harrison ii 139f.

composed for Misgolas, whose goodwill he is evidently anxious to retain, if possible (§41, 'a fine man in every other respect, and in no way open to criticism, but possessed of an extraordinary enthusiasm for this activity [*sc.* homosexual relations]'),[9] he claims not to have named the true relationship between Misgolas and Timarkhos, 'nor anything else which makes a truthful witness liable to legal penalty,' but only what is 'without danger or disgrace for the witness'. How he managed this we do not know, since the document inserted in our text of the speech (§50), purporting to be the testimony of Misgolas, is betrayed as a later forgery by the erroneous patronymic and demotic given therein to Misgolas,[10] but presumably, once Misgolas had deposed that Timarkhos had lived in his house for such-and-such a period, Aiskhines could then hope (with justification, as the outcome of the case showed) to 'demonstrate' the nature of the relationship by appeal to rumour and gossip and the fact (if it was a fact) that Timarkhos, when young and exceptionally good-looking, had a great deal of money to spend while living in Misgolas's house (§§41f., 75f.). Aiskhines describes the testimony he has composed for Hegesandros as 'a little plainer' (§67) than that composed for Misgolas (presumably good relations with Hegesandros were not so important to Aiskhines politically); but again, the putative document (§68) is not reliable evidence for the actual wording.

Aiskhines' reference to 'penalty' and 'danger' (cf. §98) is expanded in §72:

> I do not suppose that you (*sc.* the jurors) are so forgetful as not to recall the laws which you heard read out a little while ago, in which it is laid down that anyone who has hired an Athenian for this practice, or anyone who has hired himself out, is liable to the greatest penalties, the same for both. What man, then, is in such a desperate plight that he would be willing to give plain testimony of a kind which involves his showing himself – if his testimony is true – to be liable to the severest (*lit.*, 'last', 'extreme') penalties?

9. Compare the strikingly cautious manner in which Demosthenes criticises Euboulos in xxi 206f.; it suggests that just at that time Demosthenes was anxious not to alienate him. The word used by Aiskhines for 'enthusiasm' is that used by Alkibiades in Pl. *Smp.* 217a for what he imagined, as an adolescent, to be Socrates' homosexual interest in his beauty.

10. Some speeches undoubtedly contained documents or documentary excerpts from the first, but it was more usual for the written version of a speech to give only a heading (e.g. 'decree') indicating the point at which a document was read out in court. At a much later date many of these deficiencies were repaired by fabrication of documents; it is quite common for a fabricated document to contain demonstrable historical errors and late linguistic features.

By 'the greatest penalties' (cf. §§20, 90) or 'the severest penalties' Aiskhines means execution, as is clear from an analogy drawn with the bribery of jurors (§87):

> On that basis, it was absolutely necessary that the man who offered the bribe should give evidence that he did so, and the other man that he received it, when the penalty laid down by the law for both of them is death, as in the matter which concerns us now, if anyone hires an Athenian to use as he pleases, and again, if any Athenian voluntarily offers the shaming of his body for hire ... (§88) ... Those put on trial (*sc.* for bribery) ... were sentenced to death ...

That an offence other than treason or homicide should incur the death penalty is no matter for surprise, since the Athenians executed people for a wide range of offences, though in many cases it was open to the court to impose a ruinous fine instead. What is striking is that the laws which were read out and expounded in the earlier part of Aiskhines' speech do not in fact support the statements which he makes in §72 and §87. It was not the case that the law prescribed the death penalty both for a male prostitute and for his client. Its provisions were:

(*a*) If a man who has prostituted himself thereafter addresses the assembly, holds an administrative office, etc., *then* an indictment, entitled 'indictment of *hetairēsis*', may be brought against him, and if he is found guilty, he may be executed. The relevant passages are §§20, 32, 40, 73, 195.

(*b*) If the father or guardian of a boy has hired him out for homosexual use, both the father (or guardian) and the client are liable to punishment. See further §§13f.

(*c*) Acting as the procurer of a woman or boy of free status (i.e. not a slave) incurs the severest penalty (§§14, 184).

(*d*) *Hubris* committed against man, boy or woman, of free or slave status, also incurs severe penalties (§§15f.).

The nature of *hubris* will be discussed in Section 4 below; provisionally, we may interpret it as assault for the purpose of doing as one pleases.

The law cited under (*c*) has no bearing whatever on the case of Timarkhos, since Aiskhines does not assert that he procured anyone else or that he was the beneficiary of procurement. But mention of the fact that procurement could incur the death penalty serves rhetorically to establish an association of prostitution with punishment in the minds of the jury, and there may be an underlying implication (cf. p. 38 below on '*hubris* against oneself') that Timarkhos was, as it were, his own procurer; so Ar. *Clouds* 979f. speaks of a flirtatious boy as 'playing the pimp (*proagōgeuōn*) for himself with his eyes'.

The law cited under (*b*) again has no bearing on the case of Timarkhos, for it is not alleged that Timarkhos hired out a son or ward of his own, nor that he made homosexual use of anyone so hired. Here too mention of the law contributes to the association of homosexuality with punishment; since Aiskhines says more about this law than about the law against procuring, we may suspect that he has a stronger rhetorical point, and consideration of the details shows our suspicion to be justified. Indeed, Aiskhines makes use of the law in order to mislead the jury on an important question. When he states in §72 that the laws which have been read out to the jury prescribe 'the greatest penalties' for anyone who hires an Athenian for homosexual use, he is guilty of double falsehood. The laws which have been read out (§§12, 16, 21, 35) say no such thing; and the law which prescribed punishment for the client of a boy hired out by father or guardian was not read out, but only summarised by Aiskhines in his own words (§13). The fresh statement in §87 that 'anyone who hires an Athenian to use as he pleases' is liable to punishment again omits the essential specification of 'an Athenian' as a boy hired out by father or guardian.

It is evident from what Aiskhines says about that situation that the law did not envisage execution as a normal punishment for the father or guardian, for it went on to provide that when such a boy grew up he was absolved from the customary obligation to maintain his father. In two passages Aiskhines makes it sound as if a boy forced into prostitution by his father was not himself penalised:

§13: If anyone is hired out for prostitution by his father ... the law says that there should be no indictment of the boy himself ...

§18: Here the legislator is not yet speaking to the person (*lit.*, 'body') of the boy ... but when he is enrolled on the register (*sc.* as an adult citizen) ... thereafter the legislator speaks not to anyone else, but to Timarkhos[11] himself.

Yet we read in §14:

11. We expect 'the boy himself', and it is possible that that is what Aiskhines wrote; but see Kaimakis 35f. and Wankel 72.

The law (*sc.* which exempts the prostituted boy from maintaining his father) deprives the father during his lifetime of the benefits of begetting children, just as the father (*sc.* deprived) the boy of his freedom of speech.

This implies that when the boy grows up he suffers the disabilities imposed by the law (deprivation of the right to speak in public) even though his prostitution had not been of his own choosing; 'no indictment' in §13 therefore means no indictment at the time (and none [cf. p. 27] at any time provided that the boy does not attempt, when grown up, to exercise the rights from which he is now automatically debarred). The rhetorical purpose of asserting that in the case of a prostituted boy the punishment at the time fell on the father or guardian, not on the boy, is simply to emphasise that Timarkhos chose his own way of life when he was already grown up.

The wording of the law under (*a*) carries two implications of the greatest importance. One (to be discussed more fully in Section 3 below) is that since foreigners visiting or residing at Athens had no right in any case to hold office or address the assembly, they were free to prostitute themselves as much as they pleased, without incurring any penalty or any disability greater than that which their status as non-citizens already imposed on them. The second implication is that if an Athenian citizen made no secret of his prostitution, did not present himself for the allocation of offices by lot, declared his unfitness if through someone's inadvertence he was elected to office, and abstained from embarking on any of the procedures forbidden to him by the law, he was safe from prosecution and punishment. The validity of this second implication is sustained by a series of passages:

§3: It will be shown that ... Timarkhos alone has brought this whole case on himself. The laws laid down that because of his shameful life he should not address the assembly; in saying that, they issued a command, in my judgment, by no means difficult to comply with, but extremely easy.

§§19f.: 'If any Athenian,' says the legislator, 'has prostituted himself (*het.*), let him not be permitted to ... hold any office ever ... or to deliver an opinion in council or assembly ...' And if anyone acts contrary to these (*sc.* prohibitions) the legislator has provided indictments of prostitution (*het.*) and imposed the greatest penalties.

§32: These, then, he (*sc.* the legislator) debars from the rostrum, these he forbids to speak in the assembly. And if anyone, in contravention of those (*sc.* prohibitions) ... speaks ... , 'Let any Athenian who wishes,' he says, 'proclaim (*sc.* the need for) an official scrutiny' (cf. §46).

§40: ... earning money for that very thing of which the law says that those who do it may not address the assembly (*lit.*, 'which the law forbids to do or not also address the assembly').

§73: The reason why Timarkhos is on trial is that after behaving as he did he addressed the assembly, contrary to the law.

§195: Tell those who are guilty of crime against their own bodies not to inflict themselves upon you, but to cease addressing the assembly; for the law too investigates not those who live simply as private citizens but those who take part in political life.

Aiskhines refers in §74 to male prostitutes, recognised as such by the public, who plied their trade by waiting for customers in or in front of their houses or rented rooms. The reference does not suffice to prove that the practice was legal, any more than the continued existence of pimps could 'prove' that it is legal nowadays to live off a prostitute's earnings, but another passage (§§119f.), in which Aiskhines forestalls arguments likely (he says) to be used by Demosthenes on Timarkhos's behalf, is decisive:

He (*sc.* Demosthenes) expresses great surprise if you do not all remember that each year the Council farms out the prostitution tax; those who have bought (*sc.* the right to collect) the tax do not (*sc.*, Demosthenes says,) conjecture, but know precisely, those who follow this trade ... He says that (*sc.* proof of) the activity requires not (*sc.* simply) a prosecutor's accusation but testimony from the tax-farmer who collected this tax from Timarkhos.

Clearly the state would not have made regular provision for the taxation of an activity which it had forbidden.

Then in §158 Aiskhines tells a curious story. An orphan, he says, Diophantos by name, lodged a complaint with the magistrate whose duties included the care of orphans, alleging that a foreigner had failed to pay him the four drakhmai which he owed him for homosexual use of his body. Aiskhines' introduction of the story with the words 'Who among you does not know ...?' is unpromising, since 'You all know ...' was commonly used by a speaker in court to lend conviction to an audacious falsehood, but Aiskhines specifies the magistrate ('whose assessor was Aristophon or Azenia', an eminent politician, still active in 346), and a false story of which the very basis is implausible serves little useful purpose.

Again, Aiskhines imagines (§163) someone who had hired Timarkhos for homosexual use as suing him for breach of contract:

Will not the man who hires an Athenian contrary to the law be stoned, and leave the court after incurring not only the (*sc.* fine of) one obol in the drakhme but maltreatment (*hubris*) into the bargain?

The fine of one obol in the drakhme, i.e. one sixth of the sum claimed, was imposed on a plaintiff if more than four fifths of the jury found in favour of the defendant. Stoning was not a punishment actually prescribed by law, but traditions about the Persian invasion of 480 (Hdt. ix 5, Dem. xviii 204) told of men who had been stoned to death, together with their wives and children, by reason of conduct (advocacy of surrender to Persian demands) arousing in the whole community a spontaneous horror and indignation which burst the bonds of law. Aiskhines therefore means not that the plaintiff in the hypothetical case would incur a legal penalty – indeed, he would have the letter of the law on his side – but that he would kindle in the jurors an indignation which would vent itself in violence. The phrase 'contrary to law' in §163 begs the question; it is plain from the evidence discussed so far that the use of a homosexual prostitute was not always or necessarily contrary to law, but only in certain specific circumstances.

3. *Status*

It is noticeable that the law paraphrased in §19 says not 'if anyone has prostituted himself ...', but 'if an Athenian (*lit.*, 'someone of the Athenians') has prostituted himself ...', and similarly in §72, 'if anyone hires an Athenian for this practice', §90, 'he who has shamed (*sc.* by homosexual use) one of the citizens', and §163, 'the man who hires an Athenian'. We have already had occasion to remark that since no one but an Athenian citizen could hold administrative office at Athens or make a proposal in the assembly, foreigners were not affected by the law which imposed penalties on men who sought to exercise these functions after prostituting themselves; we have also seen good reason to believe that homosexual prostitution *per se* did not incur a penalty. We should expect in consequence that boys and men who made a living from homosexual prostitution would be predominantly non-Athenian, and this expectation is borne out by a section (§195) of Aiskhines' peroration:

Tell those who are hunters of such young men as are easily caught to turn to foreign visitors or resident foreigners, so that they may not be denied the pursuit of their inclinations and you (*sc.* the people of Athens) may come to no harm.

The male prostitutes who plied their trade in brothels and paid the tax levied on their profession (§§119f., 123f.) were presumably for the most part foreigners. §195 implies that no law was concerned to deny satisfaction to homosexual 'inclinations' (*prohairesis*, i.e. 'choice', 'preference', 'way of life')[12] on a commercial basis, provided that no Athenian was procured for the purpose; and on the implication of 'easily caught' – a criterion of distinction between submission for money and submission for reasons of sentiment – see further pp. 88ff.

It happens that in the period before the Timarkhos case the one contractual homosexual relationship for which we have detailed evidence involved a youth who had at best marginal citizen status and may in fact have been regarded as being, for all practical purposes, a foreigner. In Lysias iii (*Defence against Simon*) the speaker (we do not know his name) has been accused by a certain Simon of wounding him with murderous intent. The speaker explains (§5):

> We (*sc.* Simon and I) conceived a desire for Theodotos, a Plataean youth. I was good to him and expected him to be fond of me, but Simon thought that he would compel him by illegal force to do whatever he (*sc.* Simon) wished.

So far as concerns the rights and wrongs of the violence which erupted when each of the two men thought that Theodotos should be with him and not with the other, we can hardly form an opinion, for only one side of the case is available to us, and we have no control on the colourful allegations made therein. The speech was composed some years later than 394 (as appears from the reference in §45 to the battle of Koroneia) and the date may have some bearing on the status of Theodotos. Those Plataeans who escaped in time from the Peloponnesian capture of Plataiai in 427 were given Athenian citizenship (Dem. lix 103f.; cf. Thuc. iii 55.3, 63.2), and though some remained at Athens, with membership of Athenian demes, for nearly a generation after the end of the Peloponnesian War, Plataiai was re-established as an independent city-state in or soon after 386 (Paus. ix 1.4; cf. Isok. xiv 11-14). Moreover the decree of 427, cited and discussed in Dem. lix 104-6, did not give Athenian citizenship indiscriminately to anyone who claimed, then or subsequently, to be a Plataean, but provided that every claim should be scrutinised (with reference, *inter alia*, to the claimant's political record as a friend of Athens), and that the offer should be closed when the fugitives of 427 had been dealt with. Thirdly, a limit was set to the range of religious

12. Cf. *GPM* 151f.

and administrative offices which should be open to these new citizens, and it was provided that the limitation should apply to those of their issue whose birth did not satisfy Athenian criteria of legitimacy. Given these facts, it is quite possible that the young Plataean Theodotos did not possess Athenian citizen status at all; and even if he did, he could never have been regarded by Athenians in the same light as a youth of pure Athenian ancestry.

When the speaker confesses in §5 that he hoped to secure the affection of Theodotos by 'being good to him' (*lit.*, 'doing him well', i.e. being his benefactor), he is coming as near as makes no matter to declaring a relationship of *hetairēsis*. He shows embarrassment (§§4, 9) at having to admit to a degree of infatuation which ill-wishers will think foolish and contemptible in a man of his age,[13] but no sign of apprehension that his relations with Theodotos might incur any legal penalty. What is more important, he makes certain statements (§§22-4) about Simon's plea which are unlikely to be false, since Simon, as prosecutor, has already addressed the court:

> He (*sc.* Simon) went so far as to say that he himself had made a contract with Theodotos and had given him 300 drakhmai, and that I got the youth away from him with deliberate dishonest intent. But surely, if that was true, he should have got as many witnesses as possible to speak for him and tried to get the case decided according to law … Consider how impossible it is to believe what he has said. He set a valuation of 250 drakhmai on the whole of his own estate. Rather remarkable if he hired someone for prostitution (*het.*) for a larger sum than he in fact possesses!

The basis of the case presented by Simon, it seems, resembled that which Aiskhines (§163) regards as likely to end in the plaintiff's fleeing the court under a rain of missiles, blows and insults. But it differs in one vital respect: in the case imagined by Aiskhines the prostituted man is Athenian.

We do not know when the law imposing political disqualification on male prostitutes was originally made, and for that reason we cannot be sure of the reasons for making it (cf. pp. 103-9). Aiskhines would not have been displeased if his audience took his reference to 'the legislator' in §19 as a reference to Solon, who codified a body of law at Athens in the early sixth century; but even if that was his intention, and even if the intention reflected sincere belief, it does not help us much, for Athenians in the fourth century tended to commit

13. He does not suggest that he would have been less vulnerable to criticism if the object of his desire had been female; cf. p.63.

anachronisms in speaking of 'the laws of Solon' in cases in which we would say more cautiously 'Athenian law'. The law must antedate 424, since Ar. *Knights* 876-880 is a clear reference to a successful prosecution under it. Once the law had been made, homosexual prostitution will naturally have become the special preserve of foreigners. A foreigner at Athens was regarded as being of lower worth than a citizen, so that any event which adversely affected the prosperity or character of a foreigner was less important than it would have been if it had adversely affected a citizen in the same way and to the same extent.[14] It was easy to arouse indignation at injury done by a foreigner to a citizen, and judgment in a lawsuit between a citizen and a foreigner was apt to go against the foreigner in circumstances where the outcome would have been less predictable if both parties had been citizens. A character in Aristophanes (*Knights* 347) ridicules one who thinks himself a capable speaker just because 'you presented some piddling case against a foreign resident'. An incident described in Aiskhines (§43) is instructive, and the issue of its truth or falsity matters much less than the assumption which underlies it:

> They (*sc.* Misgolas and Phaidros) found him (*sc.* Timarkhos) having lunch with some visiting foreigners. They threatened the foreigners and told them to come along to the prison, because they had corrupted a youth of free status; the foreigners were frightened and disappeared, leaving the party that had been prepared.

Misgolas and Phaidros were bluffing, and the bluff is made all the more remarkable by saying not 'an Athenian youth' but 'a free youth' (*sc.* of any nationality). Even if the foreigners had been apprehended at the climax of an erotic tangle with Timarkhos, provided that Timarkhos had said that he was doing it because he liked it, no one had broken the law; but the foreigners were not prepared to face citizen accusers.

4. *Hubris*

Hubris is a term applied to any kind of behaviour in which one treats other people just as one pleases, with an arrogant confidence that one will escape paying any penalty for violating their rights and disobeying any law or moral rule accepted by society, whether or not such a law or rule is regarded as resting ultimately on divine sanctions. Together with the derived verb *hubrizein*, which can be

14. Cf. *GPM* 279-83.

transitive or intransitive ('commit hubris [against ...]'), and the noun *hubristēs*, 'man inclined to hubris', the word is attested in Homer, and the classical period added the adjective *hubristikos*, 'characteristic of a *hubristēs*'. Speakers in Athenian courts made lavish use of this group of words in castigating what they wished to portray as outrageous, arrogant or contemptuous behaviour, for the words carry a high emotive charge; the young Demosthenes, for example, applies *hubrizein* (xxvii 65) to his guardians' shameless misappropriation of his estate.[15]

There was however a specific offence called 'hubris' in Attic law. Anyone who stuck, pushed, pulled or restrained another person might put himself in danger of a prosecution for hubris. This prosecution was not a private lawsuit for damages, but an indictment for an offence against the community as a whole, and it was open to a jury to concur in a prosecutor's demand for the infliction of the death penalty. Indictments for hubris coexisted with private claims for damages arising out of simple assault, but to establish that an act of violence was hubris rather than assault it was necessary to persuade the jury that it proceeded from a certain attitude and disposition on the part of the accused: that is to say, from a wish on his part to establish a dominant position over his victim in the eyes of the community, or from a confidence that by reason of wealth, strength or influence he could afford to laugh at equality of rights under the law and treat other people as if they were chattels at his disposal. Dem. xxi 180 relates the case of a certain Ktesikles who in a religious procession struck a personal enemy with a whip and was not saved from execution by the excuse that he was drunk. Ktesikles in fact 'treated free men as if they were slaves', says Demosthenes, and (§72) 'it is not a blow in itself that men fear and resent, but a blow *eph' hubrei*', i.e. 'in furtherance' (or 'in satisfaction', 'in expression') 'of hubris', for this inflicts 'dishonour' on them, demoting them in social status and subordinating them to the aggressor until they can redress the situation by a successful indictment.

When an offence contains a sexual ingredient, or when some aspect of the sexual life of a man prosecuted for a non-sexual offence can be exploited maliciously, the hubris-group of words can be applied by an adversary both generically and specifically, in order to create a

15. Cf. *GPM* 54f., 110f., 147. In a wider context, hubris is over-confident violation of universal or divine laws, and so characteristic of successful kings and conquerors. The word can also be used indulgently, as in Pl. *Euthd.* 273a (Ktesippos is *hubristēs* 'because he is young'), or jocularly, as when Agathon calls Socrates *hubristēs* in Pl. *Smp.* 175e ('Why, you old so-and-so!'). Xen. *Cyr.* vii 5.62 uses *hubristēs* of an unmanageable horse.

profitable confusion in the jurors' minds. A man of strong sexual appetites, more shameless, importunate and headstrong in pursuit of their satisfaction than society regarded as acceptable, was *hubristēs*, and the man of opposite character, inclined to stop and think before acting in furtherance of his own short-term interests or appetites, was *sōphrōn*, an invariably complimentary word which can be translated, according to context, as 'sensible', 'careful', 'disciplined', 'law-abiding', 'moral', 'chaste', 'frugal', etc.[16] This was general and popular usage; but when the subject of the verb *hubrizein* is an adult male and the object a woman or boy, hubris implies, unless the context gives a clear indication to the contrary, that the offence is the commission of sexual or homosexual assault. Such assault is the subject of the law cited in Aiskhines i 15. It appears that the rape of a woman, in so far as it could be regarded as proceeding from an uncontrollable and unpremeditated access of sexual excitement, did not necessarily incur a charge of hubris.[17] Rape of a fully-grown youth by the simple exercise of superior strength is hardly a practical proposition, and the disparity of strength even between a man and a boy may not have been as great in Greek society as the disparity between man and woman which social convention assumed and helped to ensure; it would certainly not be assumed that the boy's resistance would be weakened by sexual arousal.[18] It may therefore be the case that unwilling homosexual submission was held to be the product of dishonest enticement, threats, blackmail, the collaboration of accomplices, or some other means which indicated premeditation, precluded the excuse of irresistible excitement, and automatically put the aggressor in danger of indictment for hubris.

But when every allowance is made for the extension of the term 'hubris' beyond simple physical assault. Aiskhines' use of the term and its cognates is intended not to make a serious legal point but to implant in the jurors an attitude of mind helpful to the prosecution. He applies the word to the acts to which Timarkhos submitted: 'such misdeeds and acts of hubris upon the body of Timarkhos' (§55), and

16. Cf. *GPM* 110, 116, 119-23.

17. Cf. Harrison i 19 n. 2, 34.

18. I do not countenance the strange notion that women 'really want' to be raped, but I am acquainted with a case in which, according to her own private testimony, a woman violently resisting rape became aware that her immediate desire for sexual intercourse had suddenly become much more powerful than her hatred of her attacker. The Greeks, given their presuppositions about female sexuality (cf. *GPM* 101f.), may have thought that such an occurrence was common; they did not expect the passive partner in a homosexual relationship (cf. p. 52) to derive physical pleasure from it.

'he thought nothing of the hubris committed upon his own body' (§116). Since, however, Timarkhos prostituted himself voluntarily – as Aiskhines elsewhere emphasises, in order to paint the man's character as depraved (§87, 'if an Athenian voluntarily earns money for shaming his body'; §188, 'voluntarily prostituted'; cf. §40, 'having chosen to sell himself') – no one who made use of Timarkhos could be regarded as exercising upon him the intimidation, deception or constraint which would justify a charge of hubris. It is one thing to say (§137) that 'violation of decency by hiring someone for money is the behaviour of a *hubristēs* who does not know right from wrong', for, as we have seen, anyone who attached the highest importance to the satisfaction of his own bodily desires could reasonably be called *hubristēs*; it is quite another matter to speak of a contractual agreement as if it were a hubris-relationship between aggressor and victim. But Aiskhines prepares the way for this argument unobtrusively, though confidently, by the terms in which (§15) he summarises the law on hubris:

> ... in which it is explicitly laid down that if anyone commits hubris against a boy – and hubris is committed, surely, by the man who hires him – or a man, or a woman ...

'Surely' here represents *dēpou*, a particle sometimes used to suggest that it would be unreasonable on the part of the hearer to question the observation offered or the conclusion drawn by the speaker; it may be almost an apology for insulting the hearer's intelligence by drawing his attention to the obvious, and it can therefore be used to deceive him into treating as obvious what is not so.[19] We see here the same technique at work as in § 19 (p. 25); Aiskhines has smuggled into his statement of the law an idiosyncratic and illegitimate interpretation of its intention. He does not seem to have felt himself on quite strong enough ground to argue outright for an equation of hire with hubris, as (for example) Dem. xxxv 26 argues that failure to repay a loan can fairly be called *sūlē*, 'plunder', since it entails depriving others of their money *biāi*, a word which sometimes means 'by physical force' and at other times 'against the will of ...'.[20]

The 'wild men' to whom Aiskhines refers in §52 are presumably the same kind of people as 'the son of Xenophantos' (i.e. Hieronymos) in Ar. *Clouds* 347-9, who is 'long-haired', 'wild' (*agrios*) and 'shaggy', and

19. Cf. Denniston 267.
20. Cf. *GPM* 53-6.

is compared to a centaur because of his 'craziness' (*maniā*).[21] Centaurs (with the honourable exception of the wise Khiron) were regarded, like satyrs, as creatures of ungovernable lust, given to pouncing on anyone, of either sex, whose beauty aroused them. Hieronymos seems to have had a thick head of hair, and hairiness, being suggestive of animality, was popularly regarded as an indication of lack of control over the appetites; the pseudo-Aristotelian *Problemata* discusses (iv 31) the question: 'Why are birds and hairy men lecherous?' *Long* hair has very varied associations; cf. p. 78. The particular 'craze' of Hieronymos may have been the shameless pursuit of boys, and this interpretation was followed by the ancient commentators on Aristophanes; it is reflected also in the scholion on Aiskhines i 52 and in part of the entry under 'céntaur' in the lexicographer Hesykhios (κ 2223-7): 'crude', 'wild', 'brigand', 'pederast' and 'arse'. The other part of the entry is not to be discounted, and in Ar. *Frogs* 38 *kentaurikōs*, 'like a centaur' (with reference to knocking on a door) means 'loudly', 'violently'. There was no law against 'wildness', and in Aiskhines i 52 we are concerned with social opprobrium directed against hybristic behaviour. Similarly the gangs or clubs of randy and combative young men to whom a certain Ariston, the speaker of Dem. liv, refers with distaste and indignation were proud to earn such names (§§14, 39) as 'Triballoi' (a Thracian tribe, proverbially uncivilised; the scholion on Aiskhines i 52 gives this too as a name for the 'wild men') or *ithuphalloi* ('with phallos erect').

Aiskhines' purpose in confusing the issue in respect of hubris is not to secure the punishment of any of Timarkhos's clients but to represent Timarkhos as himself guilty of hubris, and this he tries to suggest by means of a sophistic distinction between the legal personality and the body. There are two degrees of this argument: the first is that Timarkhos was ultimately responsible for the (so-called) hubris committed by the clients (§29, 'vendor of his own body for hubris'; §188, 'vendor of the hubris of his body'), and the second treats Timarkhos as the actual agent (§108, 'he who is *hubristēs* not only against others but also against his own body'; §185, 'he who has committed hubris against himself'). It is possible that a passage in §17 is intended to prepare the way for this argument. Aiskhines there draws attention to the fact that even hubris against slaves is punishable, and explains that it was the legislator's intention to discourage 'the man who is *hubristēs* against anyone whomsoever'; but since the same point is made by Demosthenes xxi 46 in quite a

---

21. *Maniā* and its cognates, like the equivalent terms for insanity in English and other modern languages, could be used to express 'craze', 'just crazy about ...', etc.

different connection, we should perhaps reserve judgment on the function of §17 in Aiskhines' design.

If anyone doubts whether Aiskhines can really have expected to persuade a jury (and subsequent readers of the speech) that Timarkhos was 'really' guilty of hubris, and that its victim was the agent's own body, he should reflect on the data discussed in Section 2 above, and in particular on Aiskhines' misrepresentation of the law in §§72, 87.[22] It must also be remembered that the Greeks did not take kindly to the idea that a man of bad character should be acquitted on a technicality or through a deficiency in explicit testimony; on the contrary, they were quite willing to try and to sentence people whose offence was to behave in ways which aroused resentment but could not easily be subsumed under precise legal prohibitions. The question to which our own courts address themselves is 'Has the defendant done what he is alleged to have done, or has he not?' and 'If he has done it, is it forbidden by law?' An Athenian court seems rather to have asked itself 'Given this situation, what treatment of the persons involved in it is most likely to have beneficial consequences for the community?' Both plaintiffs and defendants show, by the techniques of persuasion and criteria of relevance adopted in the speeches which are extant, that they are well aware of the question in the jurors' minds.[23]

B. Manifestations of Eros

1. *Defences against a charge of prostitution*

All we know for sure about Timarkhos's defence is that it was unsuccessful and that Demosthenes spoke on his behalf. If Aiskhines is even half right about the gossip occasioned by Timarkhos's association with Misgolas, and if any truth underlies the anecdotes which he tells about allusions and laughter in the assembly (§§80-4, 110) and the audience's interpretation of a reference in comedy to 'grown-up *pornoi* like Timarkhos' (§157), we can infer that Timarkhos would not have been on strong ground if he had tried to prove popular belief to be false. Refutation of rumour and gossip is hard enough at the best of times, and refutation of statements about the existence of

22. Montuori 12f. in fact concludes from the Timarkhos speech that anyone who had prostituted a male slave could be indicted for hubris. This conclusion is not compatible with Section 3 above.

23. Cf. *GPM* 146-50, 156-60, 292-5.

rumour and gossip is virtually impossible. A juror, assured that 'everyone knows' something of which he himself has never heard a word, is more likely to acquiesce, a little ashamed of his own unworldly ignorance, than to reject the statement in the confidence that he knows it to be unjustified. Timarkhos's hopes must have lain in asserting that his relationship with Misgolas and other men was not commercial but emotional, and in challenging his adversaries to produce any evidence that he had received payment in return for participation in homosexual acts.

When Aiskhines turns to examine possible lines of defence, with the intention of denigrating them in advance,[1] we find that he deals with two of them by enlarging on presuppositions which are important to the prosecution throughout; the third line of defence, however, turns out to be a counter-attack which involves Aiskhines in a defence of his own reputation and way of life.

(*a*) (§§119-24) Demosthenes will suggest that Timarkhos cannot have prostituted himself, since his name is not recorded among those from whom the tax on prostitutes (male or female) is levied. Aiskhines retorts: a decent citizen should be in a position to appeal to the community's knowledge of his life and conduct, and should not find himself compelled to rest his defence on a squalid quibble (§§121ff.).

(*b*) (§§125-31) 'I gather,' says Aiskhines, 'that another argument composed by that same sophist (*sc.* Demosthenes)[2] will be offered', to the effect that rumour is notoriously unjust and unreliable. Aiskhines meets this argument in part by citing what poets have said about Rumour (a contemptible evasion, since the integrity of Rumour, not her power, is the point at issue), in part by allegations about Demosthenes' boyhood (which, of course, could be testimony in favour of Rumour only if independently known to be true).

(*c*) The third argument is introduced as follows (§§132f.):

> I hear that one of the generals[3] will get up and speak in defence of Timarkhos, with languid air, conscious of the impression he is making,

1. It cannot have been difficult, in a community such as ancient Athens, to pick up gossip about an intended line of defence, and even in the absence of gossip it is possible for an intelligent and experienced prosecutor to foresee likely defences. In addition, the written version of a forensic speech was put into circulation after the hearing and modified to take account of what had been said, while preserving formal appearances to the contrary; cf. Dover (1968) 167-70.

2. On 'sophist' cf. p. 25 n.7.

3. An Athenian general was not a professional, but a citizen elected, on an annual basis, to high military command.

as being thoroughly conversant with wrestling-schools and educated society.[4] He will try to make out that it is ridiculous that this case should ever have been brought at all, claiming that I have not so much instituted a new kind of proceedings[5] (*lit.*, 'invented a judgment') as opened the way to an objectionable philistinism.[6] He will put before you first of all the example of your benefactors, Harmodios and Aristogeiton ... and ... sing the praises of the love (*philiā; see Section 3*) of Patroklos and Achilles which is said to have come into being through *erōs* ...

Harmodios and Aristogeiton killed Hipparkhos, the brother of the tyrant Hippias, in 514 B.C., and were regarded in popular tradition as having freed Athens from tyranny, though Hippias was not in fact expelled until 510. Both Harmodios and Aristogeiton perished in consequence of their act; Harmodios was the eromenos of Aristogeiton, and Hipparkhos's unsuccessful attempt to seduce him was the start of the quarrel which had such a spectacular political outcome (Thuc. vi 54-9). The peculiar features of Achilles' devotion to Patroklos, as portrayed in the *Iliad*, were not only the insane extravagance of his grief at Patroklos's death but his decision to stay on at Troy and avenge Patroklos even though he knew that by so doing he doomed himself to an early death when he could have gone home and lived to a peaceful old age. The defence envisaged by Aiskhines as likely to be offered on Timarkhos's behalf by the unnamed general amounts to this: a homosexual relationship can engender the most heroic self-sacrifice (cf. p. 191); Athens benefitted by the resolve of Harmodios and Aristogeiton to risk death in slaying the tyrant; Timarkhos's relations with his lovers were similar in kind to the great homosexual loves of history and legend; and if men involved in such relations are going to be attacked as prostitutes by mean and ignoble upstarts who do not know what they are talking about,[7] the spirit of Athens will be impaired.

4. The wrestling-school (on which see also Section 4 below) was a characteristic feature of upper-class education; cf. Ar. *Frogs* 729, 'brought up in wrestling-schools and choral dancing and music', characterising citizens of good old families. *Diatribai*, which I have translated 'educated society', most commonly denotes ways of spending one's time, whether in study or the arts or chit-chat, which are a matter of choice and not of economic compulsion.

5. It may have been a very long time since anyone was prosecuted for the offence committed by Timarkhos (cf. p. 141), and in that case it may have been believed that no one had ever been so prosecuted.

6. 'Formidable' (or 'extraordinary') 'lack of education (*apaideusiā*)'; Aiskhines' reference to Homer's 'educated hearers' (§142, cited on p. 53) is an indirect rebuttal of this slur.

7. It might seem irrational to argue simultaneously that (i) Aiskhines does not understand the homosexual eros of cultured society, and (ii) Aiskhines himself is

Moreover, says Aiskhines (§135), this general will ask

> if I am not ashamed, when I too make myself a nuisance in the gymnasia (*sc.* by hanging around handsome boys) and have been erastes of many ... and he says he will read out all the *erōtikos* poems which I have addressed to some (*sc.* eromenoi), and that he will produce evidence of some hard words and blows in which I have been involved, arising out of this activity.

Aiskhines' reply (§136) to these allegations may come as a surprise to a modern reader:

> For my part', I do not criticise *dikaios erōs*, nor do I assert that those of exceptional good looks have (*sc.* necessarily) prostituted themselves, nor do I deny that I myself have been *erōtikos* and remain so to this day; I do not deny that I have been involved in the contentions[8] and fights which arise from this activity. On the poems which they say I have composed, I admit to the poems, but I deny that they have the character with which my opponents will, by distortion, invest them.

So far from denying that decent boys, however good-looking, are ever involved in a homosexual relationship, Aiskhines implies that if a boy is good-looking he will necessarily have erastai;[9] [Dem.] lxi l indicates that encomia recited by an erastes might be more productive of embarrassment (*aiskhūnē*, 'shame') than of honour to such a boy. He distinguishes (unlike the comic poets;cf.pp.146f.) between prostitution and another kind of erotic relationship in which he declares that he himself is a participant. §133, two-thirds of the way through the speech, is the first moment at which we hear the word *erōs*; hitherto everything has been treated in terms of prostitution, with one mention (§57) of 'desire'. We now have to consider what Aiskhines means by attaching *dikaios* ('legitimate', 'honest', 'law-abiding') to *erōs*, and what exactly he is admitting when he accepts *erōtikos* as a characterisation of himself.

2. *Eros and desire*

From now on 'eros' will be printed as an English word, on a par with

---

incorrigibly *erōtikos*; but if that really was the argument (cf. n. 1 above), its point will have been that Aiskhines judges true eros by the standard of his own debased version of it.

8. *Philonīkiā*, 'desire to win', is a derogatory word after the earlier part of the fourth century B.C.; cf. *GPM* 233f.

9. Eros is not a reciprocal relationship; cf. p. 52.

'erastes' and 'eromenos'. The earliest words of the eros-group which we encounter in Greek are:

(*a*) *eros* (with a short *o*), which in Homer means 'desire' for a woman (*Il.* xiv 315), for food and drink (*Il.* i 469 and elsewhere, in the formula 'when they had expelled [*i.e.* satisfied] their eros of food and drink') and for other things for which one may feel a desire capable of satisfaction (e.g. *Il.* xxiv 227, 'when I have expelled my eros of lamentation'), and in Hesiod is personified as one of the first divine beings to come into existence (*Theogony* 120-2, 'most beautiful among the immortals').

(*b*) The adjectives *erannos, erateinos, eratos, eroeis*, 'lovely', 'attractive', applied to people, places, objects and activities.

(*c*) The seventh century B.C. adds the verb *erān* (also *erasthai*), 'desire (to ...)', 'be in love (with ...)', of which the aorist aspect is *erasthēnai*, 'conceive a desire (for ...)', 'fall in love (with ...)'. Throughout the classical and Hellenistic periods the connotation of this group of words is so regularly sexual that other uses of it can fairly be regarded as sexual metaphor. The god Eros, depicted in the visual arts as a young winged male,[10] is the personification of the force which makes us fall in love willy-nilly with another person.

Prodikos in the late fifth century defined eros as 'desire doubled', using for 'desire' the very general word *epithūmiā* (of which the verb is *epithūmein*) and adding that 'eros doubled is insanity' (B7). So too Xen. *Mem.* iii 9.7:

> (And he said) that those whose aberrations are slight are not regarded by most people as insane, but just as one calls strong desire 'eros', so one calls substantial distortion of a person's thinking 'insanity'.

Frequently eros and *erān* are treated as synonymous with *epithūmiā* and *epithūmein*;[11] so in Xen. *Smp.* 8.2, 8.8 the changes are rung on *epithūmiā*

10. Cf. Greifenhagen (1957), especially the illustrations (28-31) of R667.

11. When Socrates makes a speech in *Phaedrus* on the same premises as the speech which Phaidros has recited, he treats eros as desire which induces hubris and is in conflict with reason (*Phdr.* 237cd, 238bc); his own exposition of eros approaches the problem from a different angle altogether. Hyland 33f., in basing a distinction between *erān* and *epithūmein* on (e.g.) Pl. *Lys.* 221b, seems to me not to take sufficient account of Plato's readiness to say '*x* and *y*' instead of '*x*' or '*y*' whenever he is preparing the ground for a 'proof' of something about either *x* or *y* (cf. 'happiness' and 'success' in *Euthd.* 280b-d and 'knowledge', 'intelligence' and 'wisdom' *ibid.* 281a-d). Moreover, since Plato's concept of eros differed from everyone else's, no evidence relating to his use of *erān* and *epithūmein* tells us anything about Greek usage in general.

and words of the eros-group, with homosexual reference, and *ibid.* 4.62-4, in a jocular figurative passage on 'procuring' enthusiastic pupils and teachers for their mutual intellectual benefit. Simon's opponent (Lys. iii 39) says, 'when other people fall in love and are deprived of the object of their desire …'.

Plato's *Phaedrus* contains a remarkable passage (230e-234c) which purports to be composed by Lysias, addressed to an imaginary boy and urging him to 'grant his favours' to someone who is not in love with him rather than to someone who is. In those respects which have so far been analysed the style of the passage is Lysias's, not Plato's, but Plato was a skilful parodist (as we can see from *Smp.*) and perfectly able to imitate Lysias at a superficial level; the question of authorship must therefore remain open.[12] We find in the passage no explicit anatomical or physiological word, but rather such expressions as *kharizesthai*, 'grant a favour (to …)', 'do what one is asked to do', 'do what … want(s)' (233de, 234b; cf. Phaidros's summary in 227c), the same word as is used (231c) of generous and accommodating behaviour on the part of the man towards the boy; we find also 'succeeded in doing what they wanted' (232d) and 'fail to get what I want' (231a), a circumspectness of language which helps us to understand why Aiskhines professed such reluctance (§52) to utter such a word as *peporneumenos* in public. In the context, where the man makes it plain that he is not in love with the boy, there is no room for doubt about the nature of the 'favour' which he wants. No linguistic distinction is drawn here between the desire of the non-erastes for bodily satisfaction divorced from eros and the obsessive, more complex desires of the erastes. It is assumed that the erastes is initially aroused by the sight of the boy's beauty, even if he knows nothing of the boy's character (232e). The erastes 'follows' (*akolouthein*, 232a) the boy conspicuously and 'begs' from him (implied in 233e, by the analogy of a beggar at the door; cf. Xen. *Mem.* i 2.29), but will one day 'cease from his desire' (234a). The word *kharizesthai* is used frequently in the speech of Pausanias in Pl. *Smp.* (e.g. 182a) to denote a boy's surrender to' or 'gratification of' an erastes (cf. *Smp.* 217a, 218d); this surrender can also be denoted by *hupourgein*, 'render a service (to …)' and *hupēretein*, 'serve … as a subordinate' (used elsewhere of a ship's crew, staff officers, and a wide range of other services). So in Xen. *Hiero* 1.37:

> Whenever the eromenos renders a service (*hupourgein*) to a private citizen, that is in itself evidence that he is granting the favour

12. Cf. Dover (1968) 69-71.

(*kharizesthai*) out of affection, because the citizen can be sure that he (*sc.* the eromenos) is subordinating himself (*hupēretein*) without the imposition of any constraint; but a tyrant can never be sure that he is loved.

Cf. ibid. 7.6:

It was clear to us (*sc.* in our earlier discussion) that services (*hupourgiai*) rendered by those who do not reciprocate affection are not (*sc.* true) favours, and that sexual intercourse achieved by constraint is not pleasurable. Similarly services (*sc.* of any kind) rendered by those (*sc.* subjects) who are afraid is not an honour (*sc.* to the tyrant).

Hupourgein too is used in Pausanias's speech in Plato (*Smp.* 184d), of the submission of an eromenos to what his erastes wants.

Introducing the subject of the Lysianic composition, Phaidros speaks (227c) of 'one of the handsome (*sc.* eromenoi) being attempted'. *Peirān*, 'make an attempt on ...', 'make trial of ...', i.e. (in a sexual context) 'find out what ... is good for' (with the intention of following up any promising development) is used in Xen. *Hiero* 11.11 with reference to the response which a generous and just tyrant may expect from his subjects (and let us not, here or elsewhere, underrate the Greeks' sense of humour):

People wouldn't simply love (*philein*) you, they'd be in love (*erān*) with you; and you wouldn't have to make any attempt (*peirān*) on the beautiful – you'd have to put up with *their* attempts on *you*!

All the words considered in relation to homosexual dealings are equally applicable in heterosexual contexts. *Peirān* occurs in Lys. i 12, in a wife's jocular accusation that her husband has been making a pass at a slave-girl (cf. Ar. *Wealth* 150, of negotiating with hetairai); *kharizesthai* is used (e.g. Ar. *Eccl.* 629) of a woman's yielding to a man (cf. *kharis*, Plu. *Dial.* 751c); and Anaxilas fr. 21.2 uses *hupourgein* of a woman's compliance 'as a favour' with those who 'want something' from her.

The application of the same terminology to the feelings and actions which are manifested in heterosexual desire, homosexual eros and homosexual desire divorced from eros sharpens the question posed at the end of Section 1: what is the distinction between 'legitimate eros' and the relationship in which one partner pays the other for the provision of homosexual satisfaction? The term was not novel when Aiskhines used it; two generations earlier, Demokritos (B73) defined 'legitimate eros' as 'aiming, without hubris, at the beautiful'. That eros, as an intense, obsessive desire, should on occasion induce hubris is in no way alien to Greek thought.[13] In conjunction with Aiskhines i 136, Demokritos's definition suggests that

> *either* (a) Legitimate eros is one species of the genus eros, and 'prostitution' is another name, or a sub-species, of the species 'non-legitimate eros',

> *or* (b) eros and prostitution are two species of a genus and also either (i) legitimate eros is a sub-species of the species eros or (ii) eros is the name of the legitimate species of the genus, prostitution being always and necessarily illegitimate.

If (b) (ii) is correct, the word 'legitimate' is pleonastic in the expression 'legitimate eros'. A passage in a speech of Aiskhines delivered three years after the Timarkhos case (ii 166) favours (b) (ii):

> You (*sc.* Demosthenes) came into a prosperous house, the house of Aristarkhos, son of Moskhos, and ruined it. You received a deposit of three talents from Aristarkhos when he went into exile, in shameless contempt for the story you had put about, to the effect that you were an admirer[14] of his youthful beauty. You certainly were not; for in legitimate eros there is no room for dishonesty (*ponēriā*, 'badness')[15].

Aiskhines does not say here that Demosthenes, though an erastes of Aristarkhos, was a dishonest one, and that his behaviour manifested 'non-legitimate eros'; he denies that Demosthenes felt any eros for Aristarkhos at all. It looks as if Aiskhines is willing to apply the term 'eros' only to those homosexual relationships from which what is not *dikaios* is excluded: rape, fraud and intimidation are obviously excluded, and the trend of the whole speech shows that prostitution is also excluded. In ii 166 Demosthenes is denied the status of erastes because he did not behave towards Aristarkhos as we behave towards those whose well-being we sincerely seek to promote – that is to say, towards those whom we love. In i 171, with reference to the same relationship, Aiskhines says 'he pretended to be his erastes, and

13. In Xen. *Cyr.* vi 1.31-3 Araspas, 'seized with eros' for Pantheia, the wife of Abradatas, threatens to rape her when persuasion has failed, telling her 'if she wouldn't do it willingly, she'd do it unwillingly'.

14. *Zēlōtēs*; the verb *zēloun* is originally (and often) 'emulate', but may also be used of erotic emotion.

15. *Ponēros* is the most general Greek word for 'bad', denoting sometimes incompetence and uselessness, sometimes dishonesty; cf. *GPM* 52f., 64f.

having invited the youth into this *philanthrōpiā* ...'. *Philanthrōpos*, analysable as 'affectionate towards human beings', is invariably a complimentary word in Aiskhines' time, denoting the person who is kindly, compassionate and unselfish.[16] In i 137 Aiskhines enlarges on the subject of eros:

> To be in love with those who are beautiful and chaste (*sōphrōn*) I define as an emotion (*pathos*) experienced by a soul which is affectionate (*philanthrōpos*) and sympathetic (*eugnōmōn*);[17] but gross misbehaviour for monetary payment is the act of a *hubristēs* and uneducated man.[18] And in my view it is honourable (*kalos*) to be the object of eros without being corrupted (*adiaphthorōs*), but disgraceful to have prostituted oneself through greed for payment.

Eros is treated here as characteristic of the sensitive man – 'susceptible', one might say, to use a word which has common erotic connotations in English – and sensitivity is linked, naturally enough, with education and culture,[19] both here (in the contrast implied by 'uneducated') and in what Aiskhines says (§142) about the 'educated hearers' of Homer. A generalisation by Simon's adversary (Lys. iii 44) is also relevant; defending himself against the allegation that his charge is false, he says:

> A man in love is not, in my opinion, the sort of man who brings false charges. Those who are inclined to be *euēthēs* fall in love, but the most *panourgos* bring false charges.

Euēthēs, analysable as 'having a good character', denotes a person who is easily deceived or imposed upon because he does not or cannot apply enough intelligence to understanding the motives of people who are not as nice as he is; hence it may be complimentary ('ingenuous' in Pl. *Euthd.* 279c; *euēthikos* is 'impressionable' in Pl. *Chrm.* 175c), but it tends to be derogatory, 'foolish', 'simple'. *Panourgos*, sometimes coupled with words for 'clever', describes an immoral and shameless trickster. The speaker, like Aiskhines, needs to win the jurors' sympathy as a mortal smitten by homosexual Eros, though his admitted contract with a male prostitute is more concrete, and less

16. Cf. *GPM* 201-3.
17. Cf. *GPM* 140 n. 13.
18. Aiskhines here says 'man', not 'boy', because Timarkhos is a mature man at the time of the prosecution.
19. On the relevance of education and culture to moral discernment cf. *GPM* 89-93.

easily elevated to the plane of romantic sentiment, than Aiskhines' reputation as an *erōtikos* who expressed his emotions in poetry.

The question to which a modern reader may wish to get an answer is: does eros, as Aiskhines conceives it, entail or preclude bodily acts? Does the 'uncorrupted' eromenos resist all seduction and persuasion, of whatever kind, and withhold all 'favours', or does he only refuse gifts and promises which might lead to insinuations that he had prostituted himself? *Diaphtheirein*, with which *adiaphthorōs* is cognate, is 'spoil', 'destroy'; it is used, when it has a personal object, of causing people to behave, feel or think in ways which impair their performance of their roles in the community, and so of seducing a married woman (e.g. Lys. i 16), bribing a judge or official, or (in the famous case of Socrates) making young men heedless of tradition and authority. Aiskhines may wish to suggest that the good eromenos is never seduced; his second antithesis, between 'being the uncorrupted object of eros' and 'prostituting oneself', might even imply a refusal to use the term 'eros' of a relationship in which there is 'corruption', i.e. bodily contact, on any pretext. Yet the importation of the word 'payment' into both antitheses, coupled with the financial associations of *adiaphthorōs* ('uncorrupted' by promises and prospects of gain, in Dem. xviii 298), throws into prominence his silence about submission for reasons other than gain, and his abstention from an evaluation of the erastes, who naturally seeks accomplishment of his desires, is also significant. His problem was to adopt, in creating hostility to Timarkhos, the most austere standards compatible with the way in which he himself was known to have behaved as an erastes.

The composer of the erotic speech attributed to Demosthenes ('Dem. lxi') says (§1) that a *dikaios* erastes 'will neither do nor demand anything shameful'; but this leaves unresolved the problem of what makes an act shameful (cf. p.91 on Pl. *Smp.* 185b).

Quoting from a law which debarred slaves from the use of gymnasia and from 'being in love with a boy of free status, or following him', (§§138f.), Aiskhines argues that the legislator, by implication, positively encouraged citizens towards the good things which were forbidden to slaves. The form of the argument is: (i) slaves are forbidden *x*; (ii) slaves are also forbidden *y*; and (iii) we all know that the law encourages *x*; therefore (iv) the law encourages *y*.

> He did not say that the free man must not be in love (*sc.* with boys) and follow (*sc.* them), and he regarded such an occurrence not as harm to the boy but as affording evidence of (*sc.* the boy's) chastity.

– that is to say, as putting the boy's chastity to the test; it is assumed that the boy passes the test.

But since the boy is not responsible and not yet able to distinguish between the man of genuine good will and the contrary, he (*sc.* the legislator) chastens the man who is in love and postpones talk of *philiā* to the age at which the boy has a more mature intelligence; that an erastes should follow a boy and keep an eye on him he (*sc.* the legislator) regarded as the greatest guard and protection of (*sc.* the boy's) chastity.

Here the speaker's prescription is exact: to follow a boy because one is in love with him is permissible, but to express one's emotions overtly in any other way is not permissible until the boy is old enough to judge one's character. How old is that, and who decides in each case when the boy is old enough? And what relationship is denoted by 'talk of *philiā*'?

3. *Eros and Love*

Philiā is 'love' in general; the verb is *philein*, the adjective *philos* is 'dear (to …)', shading into 'own', 'close (to …)', and when *philos* is used as a noun it is 'friend' (anything on a scale from casual but agreeable acquaintance to intimacy of long standing) or 'relative', one of the 'loved ones' or 'nearest and dearest' with whom one is regarded as having a nexus of exceptional obligations and claims. This group of words is applied to love between parents and children, e.g. Ar. *Clouds* 79-83:

STREPSIADES: Now, I wonder how can I wake him up in the nicest way? (*Nervously*) Pheidippides! Pheidippi-deeees! PHEIDIPPIDES (*waking*): What is it, father? STREPSIADES (*solemnly*): Kiss me and give me your hand. PHEIDIPPIDES (*complying*): There! What is it? STREPSIADES: Tell me, do you love (*philein*) me? PHEIDIPPIDES: I swear I do!

The same question can be put in a sexual context, as in Xen. *Smp.* 9.6, where a pair of dancers, performing at a private party, are enacting the legend of Dionysos and Ariadne:

They heard Dionysos ask her if she loved (*philein*) him, and (*sc.* heard) her swear (*sc.* that she did), so that … everyone there swore too that the boy and girl really did love (*philein*) each other. They were not like (*sc.* dancers) who had been taught their movements, but like people given the chance to do what they had long been desiring. In the end the guests saw them embracing each other and going off as if to bed …

The question 'Do you love me?' can indeed be asked in circumstances in which 'Are you sexually aroused by me?' would be as otiose as it is stilted, but its significance varies according to whether it is put by the male to the female or by the female to the male. Strong sexual desire reinforces love, normally generates love, and is sometimes generated by love; cf. Pl. *Lys.* 221b, and the *philoi* of a boy in Pl. *Euthd.* 282b are treated as including 'those who say that they are his erastai'. It is not to be expected that Greek should always distinguish explicitly between eros and love;[20] Homer in fact uses the noun *philotēs* (*philiā* is a post-Homeric word) in seemly expressions for sexual intercourse, '*philotēs* and bed' and 'be joined in *philotēs*', as well as to denote friendly or affectionate relations between states, families and individuals. Homosexual poems, archaic and Hellenistic alike, profess love in abundance; since the noun *paiderastēs* and the verb *paiderastein* will not fit into the elegiac metre which was almost invariably favoured for this genre of poetry, the poets replace it by *paidophilēs* and *paidophilein* (e.g. Theognis 1345, 1357, Glaukos 1, Meleagros 80.2). *Agapān*, 'be content (with ...)' and *aspazesthai*, 'welcome', 'be glad of ...', are often linked with *philein* (e.g. Pl. *Lys.* 215d, 217b, 220d); *agapē*, the abstract noun corresponding to *agapān*, was later appropriated by Christian writers for love from which sexuality is absent,[21] but in R20 a half-naked woman on a bed bears the name 'Agape', and in the classical language there is no word for 'love' which precludes sexuality in cases where a sexual element in a relationship is socially acceptable. In [Dem.] lxi *agapān* denotes the attitude of erastes to eromenos (§6) and of deities to Ganymede and Adonis (§30).

A heterosexual love-affair, in romantic literature or in real life, may begin with a momentary glimpse of a graceful movement and culminate in the manifestation of that love than which there is no greater. The long-standing Western European assumption that homosexual eros is essentially diabolical may be responsible for a certain reluctance, even on the part of those who would immediately reject moral condemnation of homosexuality *per se*, to recognise that

20. In Anaxilas fr. 22.24, 'They (*sc.* prostitutes) don't say outright ... that they *erān* and *philein* and will enjoy intercourse', three different aspects of one emotional condition are specified, but the second and third are entailed by the first. Plato handles eros very mistrustfully in *Laws* 836e-837d, as an inexplicable mixture of the *philiā* which amounts to need and desire and the *philiā* between those who are attracted by their affinity; the passage is strikingly unlike those in his earlier works, and a stage more remote from ordinary Greek attitudes to eros and love.

21. Nygren 30, 'In Eros and Agape we have two conceptions which have originally nothing whatsoever to do with one another' presumably refers to the concepts denoted by those words in Christian writers. Armstrong 105f. and Rist 79f. criticise Nygren for taking too narrow a view of the 'egoism' of Eros as conceived by Plato.

homosexual eros can inspire as much unselfish devotion as heterosexual.[22] It was certainly exploited for military purposes, and to good military effect, the erastes and eromenos displaying to each other their readiness to endure pain and death (cf. p. 192), and in late antiquity we encounter stories of grand gestures (e.g. Plutarch *Dial.* 761c: a certain Theron chopped off his own thumb and challenged a rival erastes to do the same).[23] The most remarkable anecdote of this kind, however, comes from the early fourth century B.C.; Xen. *Anab.* vii 4.7 tells of a man willing to die for a youth about whom he knew no more than the visual stimulus of bodily beauty could tell him:

> A certain Olynthian, Episthenes, a *paiderastēs*, saw a handsome boy just in the first years of maturity ... about to be executed. He ran to Xenophon and begged him to intervene in defence of a handsome boy. Xenophon approached Seuthes and asked him not to execute the boy, explaining Episthenes' inclination (*tropos*[24]) and adding that when on one occasion he had put together a company with an eye solely to the beauty of its members Episthenes had been a brave fighter at their side. Seuthes asked 'Episthenes, would you be willing to die on behalf of this boy?' Episthenes stretched out his neck and said, 'Strike, if the boy says so and if he is going to be grateful'. Seuthes asked the boy if he should strike Episthenes instead of him. The boy would have none of it, but begged him not to slaughter either of them. Then Episthenes put his arm round the boy and said, 'Now, Seuthes, you've got to fight me for him, because I won't let him go!' Seuthes laughed and pursued the matter no further.

Episthenes' appeal to Xenophon was founded not on the boy's desert as a moral agent, but upon the awfulness of destroying a beautiful object, in this case human and alive. It is a way of thinking often conducive to ruthlessness, insensitivity and manipulation,[25] but Episthenes, expecting only gratitude after his death, can hardly be accused of offering payment for homosexual favours, unless perhaps he gambled on the realisation of a boyish fantasy of his own: beautiful princess is threatened with death, dreamer bravely offers own throat

---

22. Some responsibility is also borne by the further (incorrect) assumption that any male involved in a homosexual relationship is effeminate and that effeminacy entails timidity.

23. Suicide plays a conspicuous role in these stories, e.g. Konon Fl.16 (the eromenos kills himself because the erastes, weary of the exacting tasks imposed on him and never rewarded, publicly shows his preference for another youth). So does murder, e.g. Plu. *Dial.* 768f. and *Love Stories* 2, 3.

24. On this wording cf. p.63.

25. Cf. *GPM* 159f., 240-2, 296-8.

to cruel king, king's heart is touched, no one dies, beautiful princess sinks into dreamer's arms, bound to him by eternal gratitude – only in this case the princess was male.

If a man is in love with a woman and she reciprocates his eros, she is said to *anterān* (Xen. *Smp.* 8.3, with reference to a young husband and wife), and the eros which she feels generates love;[26] cf. the argument in Pl. *Smp.* 179b that Alkestis so surpassed the parents of her husband Admetos 'in love because of her eros' that she, unlike them, was willing to die in his place. In a homosexual relationship, however, the eromenos is not expected to reciprocate the eros of the erastes; the word *anterastēs* means 'rival erastes', not one who returns eros for eros, and it is noteworthy that in Pl. *Smp.* 192b the predominantly homosexual male, when not *paiderastēs*, is *philerastēs* (i.e. 'fond of his erastes'). The distinction may on occasion break down in late Greek (e.g. Suda μ 497, where an erastes commits suicide in despair and his hard-hearted eromenos, at last 'reciprocating his eros' [*anterastheis*], follows his example), but the classical usage is illustrated by Pl. *Phdr.* 255d, where the nature of eros is being explained in metaphysical terms:

> He (*sc.* the eromenos) is in love; but with what, he is at a loss to know ... He possesses an *anterōs*[27] which is a replica of (*sc.* the erastes') eros; but he calls it, and believes it to be, not eros but love (*philiā*).

The difference between the emotions of the two partners is emphasised by Xen. *Smp.* 8.21:

> Also, the boy does not share in the man's pleasure in intercourse, as a woman does; cold sober, he looks upon the other drunk with sexual desire.

In crude terms, what does the eromenos get out of submission to his erastes? The conventional Greek answer is, no bodily pleasure (cf. Pl. *Phdr.* 240d); should he do so, he incurs disapproval as a *pornos* (cf. p. 103) and as perverted (cf. p. 169). There is no particular good humour in Asklepiades 46, on the theme 'Now you're getting past it, you're asking for it!'; epigrams on the theme 'Soon you'll be too old, and it'll be too late!' (Alkaios of Messene 7, 8, Phanias 1, Thymokles 1) imply

26. Naturally a man hopes that even if a woman does not fully reciprocate his eros she will nevertheless love him; what is said in Xen. *Hiero* 1.37, 7.6 with a primarily homosexual reference (cf. p. 45) applies equally to heterosexual relations. Cf. p. 50 on *agapē*.

27. In Plu. *Lyc.* 18.9 *anterān* means 'be a (*sc.* hostile) rival in eros'.

'You won't have the satisfaction of being desired and admired'.

What the erastes hopes to engender in the eromenos is not eros but love; that is clear from the use of *antiphilein*, 'love in return', in the passage from Xen. *Hiero* cited above and from *ibid.* 1.34f., *Mem.* ii 6. 28, *Smp.* 8.16, 8.19, Pl. *Phdr.* 255d-256a, *Smp.* 217a, 218c. It clearly emerges also from Pl. *Smp.* 182c on 'the eros of Aristogeiton and the (*sc.* resultant) love (*philiā*) of Harmodios (*sc.* for Aristogeiton)'. Love inspired by admiration and gratitude towards the erastes, coupled with compassion, induces the eromenos to grant the 'favours' and perform the 'services' which the erastes so obviously and passionately desires; in that case, there is indeed love on both sides, but eros on one side only – and of course it is possible for an eromenos to hate his erastes (Pl. *Lys.* 212b), as a woman may hate a man who is obsessed with her and never gives her a moment's peace. Aiskhines i 133 represents the general defending Timarkhos as praising the 'love (*philiā*) of Patroklos and Achilles which is said to have come into being through eros', and in §142 he enlarges on this theme:

Homer has many occasions to speak of Patroklos and Achilles; but he maintains silence on their eros and the specification (*epōnumiā*, 'additional name') of their love (*philiā*), judging that the extraordinary degree of their affection (*eunoia*, 'benevolence', 'goodwill') was obvious to sensitive (*lit.*, 'educated', 'cultured') hearers. There is a passage in which Achilles says ... that he has unwillingly broken the promise he made to Patroklos's father Menoitios; for he had declared that he would bring him back safe to Opus if Menoitios sent Patroklos to Troy with him and entrusted him to his care. It is obvious from this that it was through eros that he took charge of Patroklos.

('Obvious' only on the assumption that the eromenos was in some sense dependent on the erastes and the erastes responsible for him; Pl. *Smp.* 179e-180b represents Patroklos as the erastes and Achilles as the eromenos whose sacrifice of his own life was inspired by devoted admiration).[28]

So long as the language of eros was imprecise (and it seems, from what Aiskhines says of Homer, that reticence was *de rigueur*), and so long as behaviour in public was decorous and circumspect (in Xen. *Smp.* 1.2 Kallias invites his eromenos Autolykos to dinner not alone, but with Autolykos's father, and is praised [8.11] for doing so), the substance of any given homosexual relationship could only be, for everyone but the erastes and eromenos themselves, a matter of

28. On the vicissitudes of the legend of Achilles and Patroklos, and in particular its treatment by Aiskhylos, cf. p.197.

conjecture. Was the 'service' or 'favour' that A desired from B a kindly smile, a readiness to accompany him to watch a race, or what? In Xen. *Smp.* 8.24 Socrates apologises for his 'coarseness' in mentioning homosexual bodily contact in a generalisation, even though he speaks only of kissing and caressing; he apologises in exactly the same terms in 8.41 for being over-serious at a party where people wish to feel at their ease. When Alkibiades tells the guests at Agathon's party about his own attempt, long ago, to seduce Socrates, he makes it plain (Pl. *Smp.* 217b, 217e) that he is breaking the rules of polite conversation in a very striking way. We do not and cannot know whether there were erastai and eromenoi who abstained from bodily contact; perhaps they would always have said they did, if asked,[29] but in educated society convention protected them from direct questioning; in most heterosexual cultures, after all, it is not common form to ask A, 'Yes, but haven't you screwed B yet?', no matter how greedily the question may be discussed by C and D.

4. *Following and fighting*

Two of the three specific allegations which Aiskhines expects to encounter (§135) are 'making myself a nuisance in the gymnasia' and involvement in 'hard words and blows arising out of this activity'. The second allegation he accepts as true (§136), with so little sign of shame that we can easily imagine the words spoken in a tone of pride; the judgment implicit in the first allegation he naturally rejects by silence while accepting and repeating its substance, 'I myself have been *erōtikos* and remain so' (~ §135, 'that I have been erastes of many').

The gymnasium as a whole or the wrestling-school (*palaistrā*) in particular[30] provided opportunities for looking at naked boys, bringing oneself discreetly to a boy's notice in the hope of eventually speaking to him (for the gymnasium functioned as a social centre for

29. The non-erastes in Pl. *Phdr.* 234a implies that an erastes who has had his way with a boy will boast of it afterwards, naming the boy, to his friends. The speaker is however deploying every argument he can think of in order to turn the boy against erastai; on the analogy of heterosexual societies in which even the busiest fornicators refrain from naming women, we may doubt whether boasting was at all common, and we cannot suppose that it met with social approval. When Xenophon (*Hell.* v 3.20) says that Agesipolis shared with Agesilaos 'talk which was youthful and to-do-with-hunting and to-do-with-horses and *paidikos*' he would probably be taken by his Greek readers to mean '... and talk about *paidika*', but he may possibly have meant (cf. p. 17 n.31) 'boyish chat'.

30. The wrestling-school was sometimes part of a gymnasium (as implied by Aiskhines' use [§138] of 'gymnasia' in commenting on the words 'in the wrestling-schools' in the law quoted), sometimes a separate establishment; cf. Oehler 2009f.

males who could afford leisure), and even touching a boy in a suggestive way, as if by accident, while wrestling with him (cf. Pl. *Smp.* 217c 'I often wrestled with him, and no one else was there ... but I didn't get any further'). Ar. *Peace* 762f. refers to 'hanging around *palaistrai* trying to seduce boys', and in *Birds* 139-42 a character envisages an encounter with a handsome boy who has 'left the gymnasium, after a bath' as an occasion on which steps towards homosexual seduction might be taken. Certain introductory scenes in Platonic dialogues convey a lively impression of the situations created by the presence of exceptionally good-looking boys in wrestling-schools. In *Chrm.* 154a-c Socrates, having arrived at the wrestling-school of Taureas after a long absence from Athens, has asked Kritias who among the young is now 'outstanding in accomplishment (*sophiā*) or beauty or both':

> Kritias glanced towards the door, where he had seen some young men coming in, quarrelling with one another, and a crowd following behind them.
> 'So far as the good-looking (*kalos*) ones are concerned', he says, 'I think you'll soon know. The people coming in are the advance party, the erastai of the one who is regarded as the best-looking of all at the present time.'

When the youth – Kritias's nephew Kharmides – has come in (154c):

> I marvelled at his stature and beauty, and I felt everyone else in the room was in love (*erān*) with him; they were thrown into such amazement and confusion when he came in, and there were many other erastai following after him too.

Similarly in *Euthd.* 273a the young Kleinias is followed in by a 'great many erastai, including Ktesippos'; Ktesippos at first sits at a distance while the boy talks to the sophists Euthydemos and Dionysodoros, but comes nearer when Euthydemos keeps on leaning forward and obscuring his view of his eromenos (274bc). In *Lysis* 206e we find that boys and youths are standing around together in the wrestling-school of Mikkos; the handsome Lysis comes and sits with Socrates and Ktesippos only when a boy of the same age, Ktesippos's nephew Menexenos, has already done so, and the youth Hippothales, hopelessly infatuated with Lysis, takes up an inconspicuous position on the edge of the ground, 'afraid of annoying Lysis' (207b).

An erastes who formed part of a group such as Plato describes could not expect his sentiment to remain unremarked for long. We have seen (p. 48) that 'following' a boy is recognised as overt erotic behaviour in a law cited by Aiskhines (§139), which he interprets as permitting the erastes, even encouraging him, to watch the object of his eros in silence from a discreet distance. This may have conformed to an ideal pattern of behaviour, an element in the ritualisation of homosexual eros, but the boundary between silent and vocal importuning is ill-defined and easily crossed. The non-erastes in Pl. *Phdr.* 232ab recognises no such boundary:

> It is unavoidable that many people should know of erastai (*i.e.* identify the erastai of a given eromenos) and see them following those with whom they are in love and devoting their time to that; so that when they (*sc.* erastes and eromenos) are seen conversing, it is assumed that the (*sc.* erastes') desire that they should be together[31] has been realised, or is about to be.

The young men who came ahead of Kharmides into the presence of Socrates were 'quarrelling'. About what? Perhaps Plato refers only to the brutal badinage of the young, though *loidoreisthai*, 'vilify', 'abuse', is a strong word. But what were Aiskhines' 'contentions and fights' about? The jurors would hardly have accepted from him a protestation that his only object was to rescue modest and virtuous boys from the lust of 'wild men'; fighting over eromenoi, or women, or both, had familiar enough associations for everyone, such as are indicated by a passage of Xenophon (*Anab.* v 8.4), in which Xenophon addresses some soldiers who have complained of his rough handling:

> Did I ask you for something and hit you when you wouldn't give it to me? Did I demand anything back from you? Fighting over paidika? Did I get drunk and beat you up?

These words recall the quarrel which was the occasion of Lysias's *Defence against Simon*, where the rival claims of Simon and the speaker on the young Plataean were of a very earthy nature. There is a heterosexual analogue in Lysias iv, the outcome of a brawl in which, it seems, the speaker secured a woman for whom he and his adversary had paid jointly (§9):

> He is not ashamed to call his black eyes a 'wound', and be carried about on a couch, and pretend to be at death's door, all because of a prostitute – whom he can keep, so far as I'm concerned, if he'll pay me back my money.

---

31. Given the context, this must be (as it is sometimes elsewhere) a euphemism for copulation.

Indeed, Lys. iii 43 treats the fight with Simon as coming into the same category as a commonplace fight over a woman:

> It would be intolerable if, whenever people get hurt through drunkenness or horseplay or hard words or through fighting over a' hetaira ... you are going to impose such insupportably heavy penalties.

Compare also Dem. liv 14, much closer in date to Aiskhines:

> And he'll say: there are in this city plenty of good men's sons, who get up to the sort of mischief that young men do ... and some of them are in love with hetairai; and his son is one of them, and he's often given and taken blows over a hetaira; and that's the way young men behave.

This sounds like the kind of fighting which involves people who are rivals for possession of a sexual object; the mauling and pulling of a slave-girl, with the imminent intervention of someone who wants to take her to a different destination, is not an infrequent motif in late archaic and early classical vase-painting, and the end which the energetic males in these pictures are pursuing is not philosophical discussion. An eromenos of citizen status, protected from treatment of this kind by the law restraining hubris (cf. pp. 34-9), is in the position of a female animal or bird which waits with apparently patient indifference for the outcome of noisy conflict between males; precisely the fact that it is perilous to lay hands on him without his consent, and even self-defeating to thrust oneself into his company without positive encouragement, perpetuates the conventional uncertainty about what exactly will happen if in the end he goes off with one erastes rather than with another.

5. *Homosexual poetry*

We do not possess any of the *erōtikos* poems which Aiskhines composed, but it is possible to infer their character from such poetic material as we do possess, principally 'book ii' of Theognis and the *Garland* of Meleagros (the encomia in verse and prose with which Hippothales, in love with Lysis, bored his friends to distraction [Pl. *Lysis* 204cd] seem to have been of Pindaric type, commemorating the boy's ancestors [*ibid.* 205cd]). The Theognidean collection contains some poems which may have no sexual reference at all (e.g. 1381ab), some which could just as well refer to heterosexual as to homosexual eros (1231, 1275, 1323-6, 1386-9), and many more which speak in terms of friendship and enmity, loyalty. and treachery, or good and bad advice (1238a-40, 1243-8, 1257f., 1295-8, 1311-18, 1351f., 1363f., 1377-80), verses which would not be out of place in didactic, moralising or political poetry. Some which could otherwise be given a non-sexual interpretation reveal their character only through brief but explicit mention of the boy's beauty (1259-62, 1279-82) or of the poet's eros[32] (1337-40, 1341-4, 1345-50, 1357-60 [the 'fire of eros']). The couplet 1327f. is more specific in declaring that the poet will never cease to 'fawn on' the boy so long as the boy's cheek is hairless. The poet demands that the boy should 'listen' to him (1235-8, 1319-22 [for 'eros is hard to endure'], 1365f.); he 'asks' in the hope that the boy will 'give' (1329-34); he expects 'gratitude' or 'favours' in return for benevolence or benefaction (1263-6). The boy flees, the poet pursues: 1287-94, where the boy's flight is compared to that of the legendary Atalante, who shunned marriage but yielded in the end; 1299-1304, where the boy is reminded that his beauty will not last long (cf. 1305-10, a reminder to a 'cruel boy' that he, like the poet now, will one day meet with refusal of 'the works of Aphrodite', i.e. love-making); 1353-7, where 'pursuit' may or may not issue in 'accomplishment' (cf. 1369f.). 'Accomplishment' is expressed figuratively in 1278cd:

> A lion trusting in its strength, I seized in my claws a fawn from under a hind, but did not drink its blood.[33]

This is also the first couplet of 949-54, which continues in similar vein ('I mounted the high walls but did not sack the city ... '). Evidently the editor who segregated the homosexual poems of Theognis into 'book ii' did not think 949-54 homosexual. Closer attention to the poems which follow (955-62) might have changed his mind (note 959-62, on drinking no more from a spring which is 'now muddied' [cf. Kallimakhos 2.3]).

Felicitation of an erastes who can 'sleep all day with a handsome boy' (1335f.) is unusually direct for Theognis. There are however a few poems which would have sounded to a fifth-century Athenian, and probably also to Greeks of other times and places, heavily charged with allusions to copulation, e.g.: 1249-52, where a boy is compared to a horse which, 'sated with barley', has 'come back to our

---

32. By 'the poet' I mean the *persona* adopted for the purpose of composition; we do not know which poems, if any, express the feelings of their composers for actual boys at any given time.

33. In Kydias fr. 714, cited by Pl. *Chrm.* 155d, the handsome boy is the lion and the susceptible adult is the fawn smitten and devoured by desire.

stable wanting a good charioteer';³⁴ 1267-70, complaining that a boy, who 'loves (*philein*) him who is present' (i.e. the erastes of the moment), is like a horse which cares nothing for the charioteer cast in the dust but 'bears the next man, sated with barley'; 1361f., in which the poet tells the boy who has 'strayed from my *philotēs*' that he (the boy) 'ran aground' and 'took hold of a rotten cable'.³⁵ 'Barley' (*krūthai*) is comic slang for 'penis';³⁶ 'rotten (*sapros*) rope' is used figuratively in Ar. *Wasps* 1343, where Philokleon tells a girl to take hold of his aged penis; and the imagery of horse, reins and rider is familiar with reference to heterosexual intercourse from Anakreon fr. 417.³⁷ Moreover, 1270, 'he loves the man of the moment' is echoed in 1367f.:

A boy shows gratitude, whereas a woman has no steady companion; she loves the man of the moment.

Among the epigrams attributed in antiquity (though not unanimously)³⁸ to Plato, one (10) addresses the dead Dion in extravagant terms, 'O Dion, who drove my heart insane with eros!', and another (3) represents the poet as all but expiring with joy when he kissed Agathon (not the dramatist) on the mouth (cf. p. 94). Some of the Hellenistic poems are more blatantly physiological than anything which preceded them, but the majority deal with love, desire, pain, gratitude and the emotions generally in terms which are strictly – lexicographically, one might say – compatible with the supposition that the erastes desires absolutely no more than to monopolise the presence and converse of the eromenos whose beauty he admires. It is only when we insist, as we must, on translating such words as 'pursue' and 'accomplish' into concrete realities that the extent of the disguise which convention imposed upon the expression of homosexual eros becomes apparent. This convention left it open to Aiskhines to deny (§136) that his own poems meant what his detractors said they meant.

34. *Hēniokhos*, lit., 'rein-holder', denotes a charioteer (horses 'bear' [*pherein*] a chariot and therefore the man in it); *epembatēs* (Anakreon's word) can denote either a charioteer or a rider on a horse's back.

35. 'You ran aground ... and you took hold ...' does not make it clear whether taking hold of a rotten rope was a cause or a consequence of shipwreck.

36. Cf. Henderson 119f.

37. Although Anakreon's word *epembatēs* almost certainly means 'rider' in his poem; cf. n.34.

38. Cf. Aulus Gellius xix 11.1 on the Agathon couplet: 'Quite a number of early writers assert that these verses are by Plato.' Many Greek epigrams have alternative ascriptions, or none at all, or sometimes historically impossible ascriptions.

C. Nature and Society

1. *Natural impulse*

There is one passage in Aiskhines, and one only, which suggests that heterosexuality is natural and homosexuality unnatural; this comes (§185) after he has recited details of the law's debarment of adulterous women from public festivals and sanctuaries:

> Now, when your ancestors distinguished so firmly between shameful and honourable conduct, will you acquit Timarkhos, when he is guilty of the most shameful practices? Timarkhos, who is a man and male in body, but has committed a woman's transgressions (*lit.*, 'errors')?[1] Who among you will then punish a woman caught in wrongdoing? Will it not deserve a charge of insensitivity, to deal harshly with her who transgresses according to nature, yet listen to the advice (*sc.* in council or assembly) of him who has outraged (*hubrizein*) himself contrary to nature?

It looks straightforward; yet if Aiskhines really means that homosexual relations in general are unnatural, he is adopting a standpoint otherwise expounded only in one strand of the Socratic-Platonic philosophical tradition (cf. p. 167) and contradicting what is implicit in many unphilosophical utterances of his time (including his own in §136). What is more important, he is contradicting the view which he adopts in §138, where he leads up to the conclusion (cf. p. 48) that the law positively encourages the 'following' of a handsome boy by a male citizen:

> Our ancestors, in making laws on the subject of practices and the compulsions of nature (*lit.*, 'those [*sc.* things] which are necessary from nature'), forbade slaves to do what, in our ancestors' view, free men ought to do.

There follows the reference to the debarment of slaves from gymnasia, and then the clause which prescribes punishment for a slave who falls in love with a boy of free status. An expositor of Aiskhines in late antiquity or the early Middle Ages added the words 'goods and evils' to 'compulsions of nature', in order to make the passage refer to moral choice at the most general level, and the interpolated words appear in

---

1. On 'error' cf. *GPM* 152f.

one branch of the manuscript tradition.[2] But 'those goods and evils which are compulsory' (or 'inevitable', 'necessary', etc.) 'by nature' is not an expression which reflects Greek ways of talking and thinking about good and evil; another meaning which could be attached to the words in isolation, 'bare minimum goods and evils', does not make sense with reference to gymnasia and homosexual eros; whereas 'compulsions of nature' can be paralleled from classical Attic if it refers to the sexual instinct and the universal impulse to possess beautiful people. In Ar. *Clouds* 1075-82 the immoralist Wrong embarks on the subject of 'the compulsions of nature' and illustrates it by the example of a man who falls in love with a married woman and commits adultery with her. 'Nature willed it', says a character in Menander (*Epitrepontes* 1123, quoting Euripides [fr. 265a]) in extenuation of a rape, 'and she cares nothing for law'; in Eur. fr. 840 Laios, referring to his own homosexual rape of Khrysippos, says helplessly, 'I have understanding, but nature forces me'. It is difficult in these circumstances to explain Aiskhines' 'compulsions of nature' except on the assumption that he regards the homosexual response of one male to the beauty of another as natural.

If that was his view, Xenophon would have agreed with him. In a passage of *Hiero* (1.31-3) the poet Simonides is represented as conversing with the tyrant Hieron:

> 'How do you mean, Hieron? Are you telling me that eros for paidika does not grow (*emphuesthai*) in a tyrant (*sc.* as it does in other people)? How is it then that you are in love with Dailokhos ...?' Hieron said ... 'My passion (*erān*) for Dailokhos is for what human nature perhaps compels us to want from the beautiful, but I have a very strong desire to attain the object of my passion (*sc.* only) with his love and consent.'

This 'perhaps' must be understood in the light of a view, put forward by the earnest young Araspas in Xen. *Cyr.* v 1.9-17, that to speak of being 'compelled' to eros by beauty is an immoral evasion; it is doubtful whether Xenophon entirely shared this view, for he describes later how Araspas, put in charge of a beautiful woman, 'was overcome by eros, hardly surprisingly' (*ibid.* 1.19) and in consequence (vi 1.31) 'was compelled to try to persuade her to have intercourse with him'. It must be remembered that *anankē*, 'compulsion', 'necessity', and its adjective *anankaios* do not always denote what is absolutely inevitable

---

2. The interpolation of words and phrases intended as clarification is not uncommon in the textual tradition of Demosthenes and Aiskhines; it is more conspicuous in some manuscripts than in others.

and inescapable, but sometimes forces which can be defeated by resolute resistance or predicaments from which resilience and intelligence provide an escape.[3] This does not, however, affect the point that the terms in which reference is made to heterosexual and to homosexual emotion are the same. Simon's adversary (Lys. iii 4), embarrassed at having to describe his homosexual entanglement at an age of which discretion would be expected, says 'It is in all men to have a desire'.

Apart from the 'nature' (*phusis*) of the human species, each human being has his own 'nature', i.e. the way in which he has developed mentally and physically; and whatever characteristic anyone has, he is likely to have it more than some people and less than others. Greek recognition that some people are more homosexual than others need not surprise us. It is clearest in the story put into the mouth of Aristophanes by Plato in *Smp.* 189c-193d: human beings were originally double, each with two heads, four legs, two genital systems, and so on, but Zeus ordered their bisection, and ever since (as commonly in the folktale genre, the time-scale is ignored and the distinction between species and individual is blurred)[4] each of us goes round seeking his or her 'other half' and falling in love with it when we find it. In this story the products of an original double male are homosexual males (191e-192c), who marry and beget children 'under the compulsion of custom, without natural inclination' (192b); the products of an original double female are homosexual females (191e); and the rest are heterosexual, the products of an original male-female. The variability of people in respect of their sexual orientation (genetically determined, in Aristophanes' story) is incidentally recognised in Aiskhines' reference to the 'extraordinary enthusiasm' of Misgolas for homosexual relations (§41) and in Xenophon's use of *tropos* – 'way', 'character', 'disposition', 'inclination' – in describing the behaviour of the extravagant *paiderastēs* Episthenes (cf. p. 51); cf. also Aiskhines' use of *prohairesis* (p. 32). Aiskhines contemplates (§140) substituting *tropos* for 'eros' as the appropriate word for the emotion which inspired Harmodios and Aristogeiton (it is, of course, to his advantage if he can deprive the defence of such support as it might gain from the magic names of the tyrannicides):

> Those whose valour has remained unsurpassed, Harmodios and Aristogeiton, were educated by their chaste and law-abiding – is 'eros' the right word, or 'inclination'? – to be men of such a kind that anyone

---

3. Cf. Dover (1973a) 65. On sexual 'compulsion' cf. Schreckenburg 54-61.
4. Cf. Dover (1966) 41-5.

who praises their deeds is felt never to do justice, in his encomium, to what they accomplished.

(It should however be mentioned that Aiskhines may have written 'law-abiding eros, or however one should call it, to be men ...').[5]

Aphrodite and Eros are both, in somewhat different ways, personifications of the forces which make us desire people and fall in love with them. In so far as the term *aphrodīsia*, lit., 'things of Aphrodite', denotes sexual intercourse, and the verb *aphrodīsiazein* is 'have sexual intercourse', there is some justification for the generalisation that genital activity as a whole is the province of Aphrodite and the obsessive focussing of desire on one person, which we call 'falling in love', the province of Eros. Not surprisingly, the distinction, though implicit in much Greek literature, is nowhere made explicit, nor was there a consistent Greek view of the relation between Aphrodite and Eros as personal deities; in the archaic period Eros is regarded as having come into being at a much earlier stage of the world's history than Aphrodite, the classical period tends to treat him as her minister or agent, and in Hellenistic literature he is often her spoilt and unruly son. Moreover, the notion that the female deity inspires heterosexual passion and the male deity homosexual appears only as a Hellenistic conceit, in Meleagros 18:

> Aphrodite, female (*sc.* deity), ignites the fire that makes one mad for a woman, but Eros himself holds the reins of male desire. Which way am I to incline? To the boy or to his mother? I declare that even Aphrodite herself will say: 'The bold lad is the winner!'

In Theognis 1304, 1319f. the beauty of the eromenos is a 'gift of Aphrodite', and among the Hellenistic epigrams we find several (e.g. Asklepiades 1, Meleagros 119) in which it is Aphrodite who has caused a man to fall in love with a boy.

Aphrodīsia can denote homosexual copulation, as in Xen. *Hiero* 1.29 (contrasting *paidika aphrodīsia* with 'child-begetting *aphrodīsia*'), 1.36, *Mem.* i 3.8. Indeed, a general reference to *aphrodīsia* may be followed by a homosexual exemplification and by no other. So Xen. *Ages.* 5.4, speaking of the superhuman self-restraint which characterised the Spartan king Agesilaos in respect of *aphrodīsia*, chooses as his example an occasion on which the king avoided kissing a certain young

---

5. 'Whatever *tropos*' means 'however', and the insertion of 'whatever' was suggested by Baiter and Sauppe in 1840, to give the sense '... law-abiding eros, or however one should call it, to be men ...'. This emendation, however, is not required by grammar, style or sense.

Persian, despite the offence given by this failure to comply with Persian custom,[6] because he had fallen in love with the youth and feared to take any step which might arouse his emotion further. If Agesilaos thought homosexual relations wrong, evidently Xenophon did not think the impulse to those relations a blemish in a character for which he had an unreserved admiration. Compare Xen. *Oec.* 12.13f.:

> 'In my opinion,' said Iskhomakhos, 'those who are distraught over sex, (*duserōtes tōn aphrodīsiōn*, 'in love, to their misfortune, with sexual intercourse') 'cannot be taught to care about anything more than that. It is not easy to discover any hope or concern more pleasurable than concern for paidika ...'.

So too when sexual activity is considered in conjunction with expenditure and enjoyment,[7] as in Xen. *Anab.* ii 6.6:

> Klearkhos was as willing to spend money on war as (*sc.* others are willing to spend it) on a paidika or some other pleasure.

Xen. *Mem.* ii 1.21-33 presents a version of a famous allegorical composition in which Prodikos represented Virtue and Vice[8] as offering Herakles a choice between two ways of life. In 1.24 Vice says:

> You will give no thought to war and action, but will pass your time considering what agreeable food or drink you can find, or what sight or sound would give you delight, or what smell or touch, and what paidika's company would make you happy.

All three of these passages might have said 'hetaira' instead of 'paidika'; but they do not. A curiosity may be added from a catalogue (inscribed in the late fourth century B.C.) of miraculous cures experienced by sufferers who slept in the sanctuary of Asklepios at Epidauros, *IG* iv 1².121.104:

> A man (*sc.* had) a stone in his penis. He saw a dream. He thought he

---

6. It is a fair inference from this passage that kissing was not a customary mode of greeting between Greek men in Xenophon's time, except between fathers and sons, brothers or exceptionally close and affectionate friends.

7. Cf. *GPM* 178-80, 210f.

8. *Kakiā*, when predicated of a man, is essentially 'uselessness', the main ingredients of which are cowardice, sloth and failure – through selfishness or incapacity – to meet one's obligations.

was having intercourse with a beautiful boy. Having an ejaculation,[9] he expelled the stone, and took it up and went out with it in his hands [*sic*].

'Boy or woman' (in that order, since the Greeks said 'children and women' in non-sexual contexts also) sometimes occurs as if difference of orientation in the sexual appetite were not important. Thus in Xen. *Anab.* iv 1.14, when the commanders have decided that all captives must be turned loose:

> The soldiers obeyed, except for individual misappropriations through desire for a boy or a woman among the beautiful (*sc.* captives).

In Pl. *Laws* 840a the argument of the context virtually dictates a reversal of order (cf. p. 166), but the presence of 'boy' with 'woman' is still noteworthy:

> Have we not all heard of Ikkos of Taras because of the event he won at Olympia, and his other victories too? Because of his determination to win ..., it is said, he never touched a woman, nor a boy either, in the whole period when he was at the peak of his training.

The readiness of a man to turn in either direction can hardly be more plainly expressed than by Meleagros 18, cited above, and other epigrammatists speak of their own or others' experience as varied, e.g. Kallimakhos 11:

> Kallignotos swore to Ionis that no one, man or woman, would ever be dearer to him than she ... But now he is heated by male fire, and the poor girl ... isn't in the picture any more.

Compare: Asklepiades 37, lamenting that the 'male fires' which now torment him are as much stronger than 'female eros' as men are stronger than women; Meleagros 94, dismissing Theron and Apollodotos now that it is 'female eros' which finds favour with him (the 'squeeze of a hairy arse' he leaves to 'herdsmen who mount their goats'); Anon. *HE* 1, the despair of a man who has had one love-affair with a hetaira, one with a virgin girl, and now one with a youth, from which he has only 'looks and empty hopes'.

---

9. A scholion on Ar. *Clouds* 16, possibly (though not necessarily) originating in the earlier Hellenistic period, says: '*Oneiropolein* is used of those who see a dream, but *oneirōttein* of those who emit semen during the night, as happens to those in a state of desire, when they imagine that they are with their paidika.'

References to 'desire for the beautiful' are necessarily ambiguous, since the genitive plural has the same form for both genders, and in some other circumstances a masculine can do duty for both. We find the masculine nominative plural used even in contexts such as Xen. *Cyr.* v 1.14, '*hoi kaloi* do not compel others to fall in love with them', where the occasion of the statement is heterosexual and its exemplification is:

> Good men desire gold and good horses and beautiful women, but are nevertheless able to restrain themselves and not lay hands on any of these wrongfully.

Since the segregation of women was a feature of most Greek communities, so that women and girls of citizen family would not very often be seen in public by men, and hetairai who knew their business would tend to imitate this discretion in order not to cheapen themselves (cf. p. 88), the publicity associated with modern 'pin-ups' belonged to males rather than females. Anon. *HE* 33, addressing a male whose figure and charm are said (line 5) to 'subdue bachelors' might be interpreted (if we wished, even now, to try to play down the extent of Greek homosexuality) as referring to his effect on *some* bachelors, but Anon. 17, imploring a Persian called Aribazos ('more beautiful than Beauty' in 18) not to 'melt the whole (*sc.* city) of Knidos', takes no account of such limitation. In Asklepiades 20 a girl called Dorkion, who is *philephēbos*, 'fond of young men' (*ephēbos*, strictly speaking, is a male of 18 or 19), is described as exploiting homosexual tastes:

> Dorkion ... knows, like a young boy, how to launch the swift shaft of Aphrodite who welcomes all, flashing desire upon[10] the (*sc.* beholder's) eye; with a hat slung over her shoulder, her (*sc.* young man's) cloak revealed a naked thigh.

A male who has one or more erastai and is accustomed to the attentions and admiration of older males may himself fall in love with a girl, and there is no suggestion in such a connection that he suffers an internal conflict greater than that of someone operating entirely within the heterosexual field or entirely within the homosexual. Compare Meleagros 61:

> The exquisite Diodoros, casting flame into bachelors, has been caught

10. A case could be made for the translation 'flashing desire down from her eye'; in either case, the point is that desire is kindled in the beholder by her glance.

by the coquettish eyes of Timarion, and the bitter-sweet shaft[11] of Eros is in him. This is a miracle that I see: fire is consumed by fire and blazes.

In Theokritos 2.44f. a girl deserted by her young lover casts a spell to bring him back, declaring to Artemis:

Whether a woman lies beside him, or a man, he is as forgetful of me as, they say, Theseus was ... of Ariadne.

She says 'man' (*anēr*), not 'youth' or 'boy', and we are probably meant to understand (cf. however, p. 86 n.44) that he may have passed from an active role in relation to her either to another active role with a woman or to a passive role with a man. Timarkhos, according to Aiskhines (§§42, 75), was in just such a position while supported as an expensive male prostitute by Misgolas; his money went on luxurious food, gambling, hetairai and girl-musicians, and later in life he allegedly displayed a highly-developed heterosexual appetite, pursuing other men's wives during a term of office on Andros (§107) and squandering dishonestly acquired money on a famous hetaira (§115).

All these considerations suggest that Aiskhines' antithesis (§185) between 'according to nature' and 'contrary to nature' cannot rest upon a simple assignation of homosexuality to the category of the unnatural, and a different explanation must be sought. One is ready to hand: the common Greek belief that women lack the moral insight and firmness of purpose which enable men to resist the temptations of safety, comfort and pleasure,[12] coupled with a belief that women enjoy sexual intercourse more intensely than man. Given also the assumption that the passive role in male homosexuality is not physically enjoyable (cf. p. 52), it was deducible that while women have a natural inclination to adultery (indeed, this deduction was an important rationalisation of the sexual segregation which prevented women from coming into contact with potential lovers), males have no such natural inclination to homosexual submission. Equally, the prostitution of women could be seen as conforming with a 'naturally' subordinate and dependent role of women *vis-à-vis* men, whereas the man who chooses a prostitute's role subordinates himself 'unnaturally' to other men. All the evidence which tends to support the hypothesis that the Greeks regarded male homosexual desire as

11. The 'wounding' of mortals by the 'shafts' or 'arrows' of Eros is a commonplace motif in Greek poetry.

12. Cf. *GPM* 98-102 and Hopfner 370-2.

natural concerns the active partner, and we have yet to consider the abundant evidence that for them the differentiation between the active and the passive role in homosexuality was of profound importance.

2. *Male and female physique*

The Athenian Kritias, who was killed in 403 B.C., is quoted by a writer of Roman date as having said (B48) that

> in males, the most beautiful appearance (*eidos*, 'shape', 'form', 'type') is that which is female; but in females, the opposite.

The context of his statement is unknown, and it is by no means certain that he was speaking of human beings rather than of horses or dogs, animals in which Greeks of good family were much interested. If his reference was primarily or exclusively to humans, or if he intended a generalisation which could be extended to humans, he may have meant only that human males were most admired for their beauty before their beards were grown and that tallness was an admired attribute in women.[13] What is perhaps more important is that Kritias, whose standpoint in politics, morals and religion separated him from the majority of his fellow-citizens,[14] cannot be treated as the spokesman for any city, period or class, and his statement cannot be used, unless it is firmly supported by independent evidence, to show that female characteristics in a youth or boy were a stimulus to homosexual desire.

   In modern popular humour, despite much of the evidence furnished by our everyday acquaintance with homosexual men,[15] the homosexual stereotype is extremely persistent: a man of delicate features and slight physique, imitating women in his stance, gestures, movements and voice, and therefore appropriately denoted by such terms as 'fairy' or 'pansy'. Timarkhos is nowhere described in

   13. Xen. *Oec.* 10.2 refers to a woman's wearing high sandals in order to seem taller than she was.
   14. In *Sisyphos*, a play ascribed in antiquity either to Euripides or to Kritias, the theory that religion was an ingenious invention to strengthen law was propounded by the principal character, a legendary king of Corinth (Kritias B25). Sisyphos was in any case impious, and was punished by the gods for his impiety, but the theory put into his mouth is none the less intellectually interesting. Kritias became the moving spirit of the narrow oligarchy which ruled Athens, with Spartan support, after the defeat and surrender of Athens. Having alienated nearly all those whose support he might have had, he was killed in a battle against the returning democrats. Later tradition regarded him as a monster.
   15. Cf. Westwood 83-90, D.J. West 74-6.

Aiskhines' vilification as effeminate in appearance or manner, but as 'excelling others in appearance' (§76), *hōraios* (§42; cf. §126) and *eusarkos* (§41). 'Excelling ...' is a phrase used also of a youth with whom (iii 162) Demosthenes had a homosexual relationship. *Hōraios*, 'at the right stage of growth (for ...)', applicable to any living thing (animal or vegetable), denotes, when applied to humans, the age at which one is most attractive and desirable, and in modern Greek has replaced *kalos* in the sense 'beautiful', 'pretty', 'fine' (*kalos* having become a general word for 'good').[16] *Eusarkos*, analysable as 'having good flesh', is an uncommon word, coupled by Xen. *Lac.* 5.8 with 'of good colour' and 'physically strong', contrasted with 'bloated and ugly and feeble' (cf. the verb *eusōmatein*, lit., 'be in a good state of body', i.e. 'be big and strong'). Later in life (§26) Timarkhos, when he threw back his cloak in the course of a passionate speech in the assembly, revealed a figure 'in bad condition and ugly, through drunkenness and his disgusting way of life'; the latter phrase most naturally refers to his gluttony and heterosexual over-indulgence (cf. §§42, 75). Speaking in general terms, Aiskhines takes it for granted that the boys with whom men fall in love, and over whom they fight in rivalry (even when the boys themselves are disinclined to 'grant favours' to the winner), are those who would be regarded by the public at large, of either sex and any age or 'inclination', as exceptionally good-looking (§§136, 155-7); they include outstanding athletes (§§156f.), and since *erastai* are attracted to the gymnasia (§§135, 138; cf. p. 54) it seems that a sun-tanned skin and good muscular development must have been regarded as attractive attributes. This hypothesis is supported by particular cases at periods earlier and later than Aiskhines: the young Autolykos, whose beauty, 'like a light in the dark', dumbfounded all the guests at the party described in Xen. *Smp.* 1.8-10, had just won the pankration (a ferocious blend of boxing and wrestling) at the Panathenaic Games (*ibid.* 1.2); Alkaios of Messene 9 prays for the Olympic victory of a certain Peithanor, described hyperbolically as 'a second son of Aphrodite', expresses the wish that Zeus may not be tempted to take him up to Olympos in place of Ganymede, and prays also that the poet may be rewarded by 'like-mindedness' on the part of the 'divine boy'; and the author of Anon. *HE* 30 boasts of kissing a boy 'smeared all over with blood' after a victory in boxing.

Suspicion that there may have been a certain shift in taste towards effeminate-looking males during the fourth century (perhaps even somewhat earlier) derives some support from a consideration of the

16. Cf. *GPM* 69-73.

history of human shape, stance and movement in vase-painting. Down to the middle of the fifth century the most striking and consistent ingredients of the 'approved' male figure (cf. p. 6) are: broad shoulders, a deep chest, big pectoral muscles, big muscles above the hips, a slim waist, jutting buttocks and stout thighs and calves. Examples of this general schema are: B76*, B271*, B342*, B502* (courted youths); B486* (youth copulating with erastes); R12 (young athlete); R55* (Theseus); R305* (victorious boy athlete); R313*, R326, R332 (young athletes with javelin or discus); R336*, R458*, R494* (pin-up youths); R340; R701, R783* (Apollo); R348*, R833* (Ganymede); R365 (Herakles); R406* (boy or youth pursued by Poseidon); R716 (youth courting boy); R737 (youth kneeling on one knee). For particular features add: thick thighs in B20 (runner), B526 (youth), R1115 (young athlete); thick thighs and calves in R1067 (running youth); very deep chest in R1047* (boy or youth). Confirmatory negative examples are B80*, satyrs with fat paunches, and R261, in which a fat youth protests against the reproaches and mockery of his fellows. The relative importance of face and body is neatly illustrated by Pl. *Chrm.* 154cd;

> 'What do you think of the young man, Socrates?' said Khairephon. 'Doesn't he have a handsome face?'
> 'Marvellously so!' I said.
> 'Well,' he said, 'if he'll only take his cloak off, you'll forget he has a face at all, he's so overwhelmingly beautiful to look at' (*lit.*, 'all-beautiful as to his form').

The thighs seem to have been a powerful stimulus, to judge from Sophokles fr. 320 (Ganymede's thighs 'set Zeus aflame') and Aiskhylos fr. 228 (Achilles, bereaved, recalls the thighs of Patroklos); cf. pp.197f.

Naked males greatly outnumber naked females in archaic and early classical vase-painting. In depicting the female figure the painter sometimes observes the differences of configuration of hip, abdomen and groin which are determined by the difference between the male and the female pelvis. Examples of good observation are: R8, R321, R571, R671, R805, R809, R917, R930, R1107, RL2, RS26* RS81. On many occasions, however, male and female bodies are distinguishable only by the presence or absence of the breasts and the external genitals; R712*, in which we see men and women together, is a good example (note also the women's massive calves), and very broad shoulders and deep chests are also conspicuous in the women portrayed in R20, R86, R152, R476, R733, R813, R938. In particular, women may be represented as having the characteristically male bulge of muscle above the hip-bone; the girl musician in R309 is the most striking example (note also the steepness of her groin and the aggressiveness of her stance and movement), and compare, in addition to R20 (etc.), cited above, R682* (a girl titillated by a man), R926 and R1135* (this last is only a fragment, but the torso which appears on it combines female breasts with exaggeratedly male hips).

Each painter seems to have adopted a formula for the face and adhered to it consistently so long as he was portraying deities and humans and had no motive for introducing the funny or the fearful. These formulae show remarkably slight variation over a long period and a great number of painters; all approve of a forehead of moderate height and a straight nose, with the lower lip tending to be full but not wide, the chin rather deep and rounded, and the eye commanding but (after the end of the sixth century) of normal size. Satyrs, by contrast, have either a receding hairline or a wrinkled brow under a shaggy mat of hair, bulging eyes, very snub noses and big thick lips (e.g. B80*, R6, R235) while comically ugly men (like comic masks) may have one or more of the features of satyrs (e.g.BB16*, RS163) or, alternatively, heavy hooked noses and bony jaws (e.g. RS159, RS171).

Although some black-figure vase-painters distinguished between female and beardless male faces by giving the latter wider and bolder eyes, it was normal at all periods to give both sexes exactly the same facial contours; see, for example, R659* (Orpheus and maenads), R750* (youth and women), R958* (youths and women). It was also normal practice to make both sexes the same height; R303* is unusual in showing a youth as much taller than the girl whom he embraces (cf.R514). The almost universal absence of hair on the torso of either sex in vase-paintings (exceptions are the youth of R12 and the bearded man of R455*) reflects not so much an assimilation of men to women as a consistent tendency to assimilate adult males to young males; it is apparent also in the virtual absence of pubic hair, understandable enough in pictures of Ganymede (e.g.R348*, R692, R829*) but unrealistic in older youths and youthful heroes (e.g. R55*, R57, R387).

It is arguable that whereas down to the mid-fifth century women were commonly assimilated to men in vase-painting, thereafter men were increasingly assimilated to women. This reversal of assimilation is particularly noticeable in the relaxed stance in which the weight is off one foot and the torso thus not quite vertical. People can sit and stand and walk as they please, or as the conventions of their time require – I do not suggest that physical differences between the sexes determine a difference of posture – but in considering posture in Greek vase-painting it is not practicable to treat the shape of the hips in one context, the overall impression conveyed by the figure in another, and the distribution of subcutaneous fat in a third. (I leave out of account early red-figure cups in which what may seem to us curiously affected poses should be regarded as experiments in composition within a circular frame [e.g. R454*], though the similarity of treatment of a woman and a youth in R471* and R472* is worth noticing.)[17] In R958* a youth, though his feet are planted firmly enough on the ground, thrusts out one hip which is of distinctly female shape, and the painter has shown the line from hip to groin only perfunctorily. Standing or seated male figures, especially youths and youthful deities, become indistinguishable in pose from female: RL4, RL64, RS26* (man and woman), RS56, RS60, RS64 (compare the woman in RS77), RS68 (compare the woman in RS69), RS85 (Dionysos; compare the woman in RS89), RS109. Heroes may stand in 'effeminate' poses and yet have strongly male hips, e.g. RS28, RS32 (Herakles), but the hips of the young heroes Orestes and Pylades in RS101 are female, and so too a man in RS27. The male belly may also be rounded, slightly but yet enough to suggest a sheltered and unathletic life, as in the Orestes of RS31 and the youth of RS73; cf. Dionysos and a satyr in RS52. Dionysos may give us an overall impression of soft plumpness (e.g. RL32), and this is a general characteristic of much Italiote depiction of Eros and similar supernatural beings: RS16, RS113, RS129, RS133, RS137. Some of these Erotes tend to hermaphroditism (e.g. RS12*, RS13), and RS20* is unquestionably hermaphrodite, with breasts and external genitals fully developed.[18] From the early classical period we may collect sporadic examples of youths whose pectoral muscles are portrayed in such a way as to suggest women's breasts, e.g. R219* (youth), R1137, R946 (armed youth), R1119 (youth arming with vigorous movement), but given the great difference of pose and action, these examples can hardly be considered forerunners of the general 'feminisation' to be observed later. It is in fact the general trend of later vase-painting (cf. p. 151), in which even satyrs become tame and respectable and furies no longer frighten, which forbids us to make too much of the effeminacy of its male figures; technical concern with the portrayal of the body in relaxed poses was common to vase-painting and sculpture, and every art-form has a degree of autonomy which turns the artist in the direction of interesting motifs explored by his competitors or immediate predecessors and absolves him from giving faithful

17. Illustrated together in Langlotz pl. 20.
18. Cf. Delcourt (1966) 54-9 on 'Eros androgyne', and (1961) 65 on the homosexual fantasy which finds expression in the portrayal of hermaphrodites.

expression to successive changes of taste in the general public. Nevertheless, even if we rule out as irrelevant to the history of homosexuality the shift of interest from vigour and starkness to repose (or to movement within billowing drapery), we must not ignore the anatomical predilections which culminate in the portrayal of hermaphrodites, and we should take into account the possibility that in the fourth century effeminate boys and youths may have stimulated homosexual desire more often than they would have done a century and a half earlier.

3. *Masculine and feminine styles*

Attic comedy generally assumes that a man who has female bodily characteristics (e.g. sparse facial hair) or behaves in ways categorised by Athenian society as feminine (e.g. wearing pretty clothes) also seeks to play a woman's part sexually in his relation with other men and is sought by them for this purpose. However, the over-simplifications and stark antitheses of comedy require treatment as ingredients of the comic world (Chapter III C) – a world as conventional, in its own way, as the heroic world of tragedy – and in the present section attention will be paid to the implications of other types of evidence.

When Aiskhines describes Misgolas as having 'an extraordinary enthusiasm' for homosexual relationships (§41), he adds, 'and accustomed always to have around him singers' (*kitharōidoi*, 'singers to the accompaniment of the lyre') 'and musicians' (*kitharistai*, 'lyre-players'). Extant citations from fourth-century comedy contain three references to Misgolas. One of them, Timokles fr. 30, tells us only that Misgolas was 'excited by young men in the flower of their youth', but Alexis fr. 3 is more interesting:

> Mother, I beg you, don't threaten me with Misgolas! I'm no *kitharōidos*!

There is also an amusing play on words in Antiphanes fr. 26.12-18:

> And who'll be the first to buy this conger-eel, that's grown a backbone thicker than Sinope's? Misgolas doesn't eat *them* at all. But here's a dab (*kitharos*) – if he sees that, he won't be able to keep his hands off it. People don't realise how extraordinarily stuck he is on *kitharōidoi*.

These comic poets were still alive and active at the time of the prosecution of Timarkhos, but the dates of the three plays from which the citations are drawn are not precisely known; it may be, therefore, that we have to do not with independent confirmation of what Aiskhines says, but with comic exploitation of his allegations. Two generations earlier, Euripides represented in *Antiope* (a famous play in antiquity, but known to us only from fragments and citations) an argument between two legendary brothers, Amphion and Zethos. Amphion (the supreme *kitharōidos* of legend) is devoted to the arts and intellectual pursuits, while Zethos is a hard, tough farmer and warrior. Zethos reproaches Amphion (frr. 184, 185, 187):

> This Muse of yours is disturbing, useless, idle, drunken, spendthrift.
>
> . . .
>
> Nature gave you a stout heart, yet you flaunt an outward appearance that mimics a woman ... Give you a shield, and you would not know what to do with it, nor could you defend others by bold and manly counsel[19]
>
> . . .
>
> If a man possessed of wealth takes no thought for his house but leaves it neglected, and delights in music and pursues that always, he will achieve nothing for his family and city and will be no good to his friends. Inborn qualities are lost when a man is worsted by the delights of pleasure.[20]

Amphion in his reply (frr. 190, 192, 198, 200) praises music and song, decries a philistine absorption in the management of an estate, and declares that brain does more to save a city than brawn.[21] The opposition between toil, combined with athletic and military training, and artistic or intellectual pursuits is a thread that runs through the history of Greek literature; obviously it is always open to people like Zethos to reproach their adversaries for effeminacy, since music and singing do little to develop the muscles of the legs, and their indulgence does not help to accumulate wealth.[22] Phaidros in Pl. *Smp.* 179d is scornful of Orpheus, who according to the legend was not willing to die himself in order to be with his dead wife in the underworld; he was 'faint-hearted, as you'd expect of a *kitharōidos*'. Misgolas's predilection for musicians may imply a distaste on his part for young athletes and warriors of the kind portrayed in earlier vase-painting.

19. The two essential attributes of the warrior were physical valour on the battlefield and a good strategic imagination which heartened his comrades; cf. Odysseus's praise of Neoptolemos to the ghost of Achilles in *Od.* xi 506-16.

20. On the possible alteration or vitiation of an individual's nature cf. *GPM* 90.

21. Xenophanes made this point, forcefully and bitterly, in the late sixth century B.C. (fr. 2).

22. Cf. *GPM* 163f.

The association of the lyre with youthful male beauty is not uncommon in painting. The youth in the wall-painting at Paestum has one, and so has Eros himself in (e.g.) R527, R667, R1143. Compare: R27*, where a boy with a lyre is cuddled by a youth; R603* and R847, where Hyakinthos, holding a lyre, is pursued and grasped by Zephyros; R634, a man in pursuit of a boy with a lyre; R684*, a man putting out his hand to touch the armpit of a youth who brandishes a lyre in self-defence; R716; R875, a man offering a strigil to a youth with a lyre; R912, Tithonos brandishing his lyre to beat off Dawn. It must however be remembered that instruction in playing the lyre and singing to its accompaniment was one of the main ingredients in the secondary education of boys at Athens; that is clear from Ar. *Clouds* 964-72 and Pl. *Prt.* 326a, and in Pl. *Lys.* 209b it is assumed that the young Lysis is asked by his parents to take up his lyre and sing to them (cf. *Clouds* 1354-6). We should therefore expect as a matter of course to find adolescent males often portrayed with lyres, and at the same time to find that men of homosexual propensities would sometimes be specially attracted to musicians because of the strong association between music and adolescence.[23]

One further passage of the Timarkhos speech is relevant. Demosthenes, it appears, laboured under the disadvantage of the nickname 'Batalos', which was interpreted by Hellenistic commentators as 'arse' in a passage of Eupolis (fr. 82; context unknown). He claimed (says Aiskhines i 126) that it was a nickname given him by his nurse when he was a boy ('sit-upon'? 'bumsy'?); if the name was originally 'Battalos', and was distorted maliciously by his enemies, it will have meant 'babbler', 'prattler'. Anyway, Aiskhines attributes it (§131) to Demosthenes' 'unmanliness and *kinaidiā*' as a boy (cf. ii 99, 'certain shameful practices [*aiskhrourgiā*] and *kinaidiā*'). 'Unmanliness' is a charge repeatedly brought against Demosthenes by Aiskhines in later speeches, with particular reference to lack of courage: 'unmanly and womanish in temper' (ii 179), 'unmanly deserter from the ranks' (iii 155); cf. ii 139, iii 160, 209, 247. Vague as *kinaidiā* may be, there is little doubt that Aiskhines means in i 131 and ii 99 to accuse Demosthenes of homosexual submission, and his argument in the former passage is that present facts justify the rumours about Demosthenes' past:

If anyone took those dainty little coats and soft shirts off you ... and

---

23. There are, of course, many representations of adult men, even elderly men, singing to the accompaniment of the lyre, e.g. Napoli 124 with fig. 50 and pl. 2 (and the other side of R336*).

took them round for the jurors to handle, I think they'd be quite unable to say, if they hadn't been told in advance, whether they had hold of a man's clothing or a woman's.

Here 'unmanliness' and feminine clothes are unmistakably linked with passive homosexuality, and indirectly with feminine physique, in so far as one would expect below-average muscular development and abnormal sensitivity to discomfort and privation, expressible in gesture and movement, to characterise a man of the type described by Aiskhines.

The superficial implication of Aiskhines iii 162 (sixteen years after the Timarkhos case) is that an active homosexual role was combined in Demosthenes with effeminate tastes in clothing and with various kinds of 'unmanliness':

There is a certain Aristion, a Plataean ..., who as a youth was outstandingly good-looking and lived for a long time in Demosthenes' house. Allegations about the part he was playing (*lit.*, 'undergoing or doing what') there vary, and it would be most unseemly for me to talk about it.

That Aristion should be a Plataean, not an Athenian, is interesting (cf. Part A Section 3); the alternatives on which Aiskhines incites the jury to prurient speculation (of the kind, 'Who did what to whom?')[24] are first, that Demosthenes himself was sometimes the passive partner, and second, that if Demosthenes was active, he was exploiting the readiness of a shameless youth to prostitute himself as Misgolas exploited Timarkhos. That Demosthenes was actually an erastes of the youth in the sense in which Aiskhines himself claimed to be *erōtikos* (§136) would not have been an allegation by which Aiskhines could expect to damage the reputation of an opponent (cf. §171 and ii 166, discussed on p. 46). Ridicule and vilification in the lawcourts were very close in technique to what we find in comedy, and did not exclude malevolent fictions,[25] but the passages quoted above are significant for popular opinion in their exploitation, for the purposes of practical politics, of an association of effeminacy with passive homosexuality.

Since males and females are not born different colours, the colour of their skin from childhood onwards depends on their exposure to the

---

24. At the same time the speaker presents himself as a man unwilling to soil the jurors' ears with disgusting details.
25. Cf. *GPM* 30-3.

sun, and that in turn is determined by the activities encouraged or discouraged by the society to which they belong. It is noteworthy that in the Tomb of the Diver at Paestum, painted in the early fifth century, the youth whose beauty has proved too much for the man lying on the couch with him is as dark-skinned as the man;[26] and the painter had a freedom to choose his colours which was denied to the maker of decorated pottery. In conformity with the Greek insistence that young males should exercise out of doors and females stay out of the sun (the women in Ar. *Ecclesiazusae*, intending, to disguise themselves as men and pack the assembly, have to do their best to turn brown [62-4]), it was normal practice in archaic black'figure vase-painting to make men and youths black but women white; in red-figure (with few exceptions, notably in the fourth century) males and females alike are reddish-brown. The black-figure contrast is particularly striking in B634*, where ten pairs of copulating men and women exemplify the differentiation of males and females as black and white respectively, but are accompanied by a man and a youth engaged in intercrural copulation, both painted black. Exceptions are sporadic in black-figure, and no doubt variously motivated: an Attic geometric (seventh century) depiction of Odysseus and his companions blinding the Cyclops has the faces of all three light-coloured, the bodies of the companion and the Cyclops black, and the body of Odysseus light within a heavy black outline;[27] a white-painted youth runs with black-painted men in B686.[28] In some cases the figure-painting leaves some room for doubt about the sex of the persons depicted (e.g. B382), and in others (e.g. B518) uncertainties can be created by patchy loss of the white surface. Archaic and early classical vase-painting thus does not offer adequate grounds for supposing that a pale skin, held to be desirable in women, was also desirable in young males. The evidence from the red-figure vase-painting of the fourth century, in which white was freely used for the figures of women, is more equivocal.[29] The boy Eros himself, with whom (as a supreme compliment) a poet may compare a very desirable human boy (e.g. Alkaios of Messene 9, Asklepiades 21, 38, Meleagros 82, 83, 89), is white in RL35 (Thetis too is white, but the other female figures and, of course, Peleus are brown) and RL41 (so too

---

26. Napoli plates 1 and 6; *EG* 104f.

27. Cf. Boardman (1973) fig. 39.

28. Cf. *CVA* Great Britain 13 p. 15 on the use of white for males in Klazomenian vase-painting.

29. In RL14 an apparently livid-white youth is a very special case; he is not only dead; he is also Talos, a creature of metal, drained of its life-blood by Medea.

Pompe, but Dionysos is brown). Dionysos, a bearded god in the earlier period, is later conceived as youthful and beardless,[30] and seems to be painted white in RL52.

Length of hair, like colour of skin, is culturally determined ('short' hair may be short through cutting or through being 'put up'), and since a very early heterosexual courting scene (CE33*) shows us a youth with short hair putting his hands towards the face and genitals of a woman with long hair, we might be tempted to assume that when the same difference between erastes and eromenos is seen in essentially similar homosexual courting scenes it signifies that the artists (and many erastai) admired a positive feminine feature in eromenoi. It is certainly true that this difference in hair-style occurs in many scenes of homosexual courting or pursuit, e.g. B16*, B53*, B102, B130, B250*, B482, B486*, B502*, and in B267 the youth who is the focus of the picture has long hair and the other youths short hair. In red-figure Ganymede is commonly long-haired (R102, R348*, R829*, R833*; cf. a boy with a hoop, R496), and the same is true of gods, heroes and legendary persons, e.g. Apollo (R383), Eros (R527), Orpheus (R659*), Orestes (R546), Phaon (RL2). There is however a considerable measure of arbitrariness, at all periods, in the painters' choices of hair-style; the eromenos has short hair in (e.g.) B65*, shorter than his erastes in B170, and in B598* the boy on one side of the vessel has short hair and the boy on the other long; the styles of Theseus and Korone are identical in R55*. One satyr has short hair, another long hair, in R329*. Wavy hair was perhaps thought more attractive than straight, to judge from the contrast in R847, where Zephyros's hair is straight but that of his eromenos Hyakinthos wavy (there is a similar contrast between Eros wavy and a boy straight in R770). The associations of words for long hair in the classical period are varied. The Spartans, formidable warriors, grew their hair long (cf. e.g. Hdt. i 82.8) and according to Aristotle *Rhetoric* 1367[a] 29-31 thought this a mark of a free man, because it is hard to do servile manual jobs when one's hair keeps getting in the way; Athenian admirers of Sparta, on the other hand, seem (Ar. *Birds* 1282) to have associated refusal to cut the hair with manly indifference to cleanliness, comfort and adornment (cf. Plu. *Lyc.* 22.1). It is evident from Ar. *Knights* 580 (supported by an almost certain emendation in Lys. xvi 18) that long hair characterised young men of the wealthiest class, and in consequence *komān*, 'wear the

---

30. Cf. Delcourt (1961) 24-7. The Dionysos of Euripides' *Bacchae*, mocked by Pentheus for his womanish appearance (453-9), accords with his portrayal in late fifth-century art, e.g. RL13, but it must not be forgotten that he is mocked in similar terms in Aiskhylos's *Edonoi* (fr. 72) – and Aiskhylos died half a century before *Bacchae*.

hair long' is used in comedy in the sense 'give oneself airs', 'think oneself a cut above other people' (e.g. Ar. *Wasps* 1317). The association of long hair with homosexuality is, in the strict sense, accidental; it may go with general hairiness, lust and arrogance in the single-minded pursuer of sex-objects, male or female (cf. p. 38), or with comfortable soft living and thus with effeminacy and readiness to play the passive role (cf. p. 74).

Given the relation between the antithesis male/female and the antithesis dark/light, together with the fact that in the Olympia terracotta which represents Zeus carrying off Ganymede the god's hair and beard are black, while Ganymede's hair is light brown, one might expect that blond hair would be favoured in women (sometimes it is, e.g. R486) and, if favoured in eromenoi, a sign of the assimilation of eromenoi to women; but here again the element of caprice is large: beside a blond Achilles (R748) and a carroty Ganymede (R348*) we must set a mixture of dark and fair hair in the figures[31] of R196*, a pair of Erotes, one blond and one dark-haired, in R705, and a distinction between the infant Herakles and his twin as dark-haired and blond respectively in R351. It appears from an account given by Ion of Chios (F6) of a conversation in which Sophokles participated that the Greeks of the classical period normally thought of Apollo's hair as black. Conversely, giants and gross or barbarous persons may have fair hair in vase-paintings, e.g. R16, R210.

Hellenistic poetry suggests that after the fourth century there was a certain shift of taste towards feminine characteristics in eromenoi. The adolescent Philinos in Theokritos 7.105, with whom Aratos is despairingly in love, is *malthakos*, 'soft', 'unmanly'. Rhianos 3.3 commends the '*pīon akmē* of flesh' of a boy. Although *pīon* is an imprecise word – it can be applied, for instance, to good land – it means 'fat' when applied to people, with a connotation of soft and luxurious living (cf. Ar. *Wealth* 560, Pl. *Rep.* 422d, *Politicus* 309b); *akmē* is 'prime', 'peak', so that it would be hard for a Greek to understand Rhianos's phrase as describing anything but a plump, sleek body rather than the rippling muscles of an athlete. *Hapalos*, 'supple', 'tender', 'soft' (Asklepiades 20, Meleagros 76), distinguishes adolescence from maturity, not simply female from male; there are other words, e.g. *habros* (Polystratos 1) and *trupheros* (Meleagros 61), which convey a suggestion of soft living, delicacy and fastidiousness, and thus indirectly a suggestion of effeminacy, without specifically indicating a female physique.[32] Meleagros 98 evinces equal passion for

---

31. The fair hair of one eromenos in this scene is very clear in *EG* 93.
32. On these words in archaic and classical poetry cf. Treu 176-186. In Pl. *Phdr.*

one boy who is *leukanthēs*, 'white-flowering' (*anthos*, 'flower' is a common term for beauty) and for another who is *melikhrous*, 'honey-skinned', and this shows that a fair skin in a young male was not invariably repugnant to Hellenistic taste. This should hardly surprise us – we do not fall in love only with those whose specifications are in the pattern-book, – and a passage of Plato's *Republic*, in the earlier part of the fourth century, gives us a glimpse of realities. Socrates chaffs Glaukon, who as an *erōtikos* should remember (474de) that

> when a man is a lover of boys and *erōtikos*, all those who are at the right age somehow or other get under his skin and turn him on; he thinks they're all worth looking after and making a fuss of. Isn't that how you behave to beautiful boys? If he's got an upturned nose, you'll call him 'charming' and sing his praises; if he's got a hooked nose, you say he's 'aristocratic' (*lit.*, 'kingly'), and of course, the one in between has exactly the right proportions. If they're dark (*lit.*, 'black'), you say they look manly; if they're fair (*lit.*, 'white'), they're children of the gods.[33] And do you think that the word 'honey-yellow' is anything but the endearment of an erastes who doesn't mind a boy's pallor,[34] if he's the right age?

From the evidence considered in this and the preceding Section it appears that in the visual arts of the late archaic and early classical periods, and also in the majority of literary contexts (at any period) in which homosexual eros is expressed directly or described with approval, unambiguously male bodily features and a specifically masculine life-style constitute a homosexual stimulus. Yet from time to time a gleam of soft white flesh somewhere below the surface indicates that at least by the time we arrive at the second half of the

---

239c it is argued that an ordinary erastes will wish his eromenos to be unmanly; the underlying assumption seems from the context to be that physical toughness means independence of spirit, and that would be fatal to the erastes. The statement that such an eromenos will be 'adorned with alien colour and adornment, through lack of his own' might conceivably refer to cosmetics (to simulate the glow of health?) but more probably refers to dress, as opposed to the 'natural adornment' conferred by health and fitness.

33. Pl. *Laws* 956a treats 'white colours' as the most 'fitting' for artefacts which are to be dedicated to gods. Gods are naturally associated with light and brightness versus dark and dullness, with purity and cleanliness versus dirt, or with costly materials such as gold, silver and ivory.

34. 'Yellow' (*khlōros*) and 'pale' (*ōkhros*) are the colours of sickness and fear, but *khlōros* is also sometimes applied to young, flourishing vegetation and may thus have agreeable associations. In Theokritos 10.26 'honey-yellow' is a lover's word for a woman whom others derogatorily call 'sunburnt', and therefore opposed to 'white', as 'honey-skinned' is in Meleagros 98.

classical period homosexual taste was by no means uniform,[35] and that we may have to reckon with a significant difference between what actually happened and an ideal pattern of sentiment and practice which dominated public utterance and literary convention. We shall see some reason to postulate precisely such a difference in the modes of homosexual courtship and copulation (Section 6).

4. *Pursuit and flight*

In the *Symposium* Plato portrays a dinner-party in the house of the tragic poet Agathon, at which the guests take turns to make a speech in praise of Eros. The exemplifications used by the speakers are for the most part homosexual (cf. Chapter III D), and in that portion of the work which constitutes an exposition of Plato's own doctrine of eros the response of a male to the beauty of another male is treated as the starting-point of a co-operative philosophical effort to understand ideal beauty. One of the speakers, a certain Pausanias, describes the attitude of Athenian society in his own day to homosexual relations, rationalises an apparent contradiction within this attitude and expounds a principle designed to reconcile its implicit scheme of values with more general schemes of moral valuation. In 182a-c he draws a regional distinction:

> The rule (*nomos*)[36] governing eros is easy to understand in other cities, because it is defined in simple terms, but the rule here and at Sparta is complicated (*poikilos*).[37] In Elis and Boiotia, and wherever men are inarticulate, it has been laid down simply that granting favours to erastai is creditable – in order, I suppose, that they may not have the trouble, unskilled in speaking as they are, of trying to persuade young men by words; but in many parts of Ionia and elsewhere, regions which are under non-Greek rule,[38] the established view is that granting favours to erastai is shameful.

35. This is not surprising; on modern homosexual tastes cf. Westwood 88f., 116, 119, 155-65.

36. *Nomos* covers not only explicit legal prescription but also custom and usage.

37. Winckelmann deleted the words 'and at Sparta' as an interpolation, and Bethe 442 n. 10 regards the deletion as necessary; Robin transposes the words to follow 'and Boiotia'. I have argued for preservation of the transmitted text (Dover [1964]37) and I am still of that opinion; the Spartan 'rule', as described (rightly or wrongly) by Xen. *Lac.* 1.12-14, is 'complicated' and is quite explicitly contrasted by Xenophon with the practice of the Eleans and Boiotians.

38. At the time when Plato wrote the *Symposium* (not, however, at its 'dramatic date') Persian sovereignty over the Greek coastal cities of Asia Minor had been formally recognised.

We do not have to take seriously the reason given (from the standpoint of Attic articulateness) for the casualness of homosexual relations in Elis and Boiotia or the reasons which Pausanias goes on to give for disapproval of them in (for example) Ionia, namely the threat posed to tyrants by the love, mutual loyalty and ambition which homosexual relations allegedly engender (inevitably, Pausanias cites [182c] the case of Harmodios and Aristogeiton). The 'complication' of the Athenian attitude (on Sparta, cf. Chapter IV A) is expounded in detail in 182d-184c. Pausanias begins by listing the phenomena which would lead an outside observer to suppose that the Athenians had a very high regard for the relations between erastes and eromenos (182d-183c):

> Being in love openly is said to be more creditable than being in love secretly, and especially being in love with the noblest and best, even if they are not as good-looking as others. And the encouragement given by everyone to him who is in love is quite extraordinary, not at all as if he were doing something shameful. If he wins (*lit.*, 'catches', *sc.* his eromenos), it is regarded as creditable, and if he does not win, as shameful; our custom grants the erastes, in his efforts to win, the possibility of being commended for doing the most extraordinary things, such that if anyone went so far as to do them in pursuit of any other object but this, or through a desire to attain any other end, he would earn the most severe reproach ... making his requests with supplication and entreaty, and swearing oaths, and sleeping in doorways,[39] and being ready to endure a servitude against which any slave would revolt ... When an erastes does all this, people find it attractive ... From this point of view, one would think that being in love and requiting the affection of erastai is held in the highest possible esteem in this city.

Thereupon Pausanias passes to a consideration which, he says, would lead the observer to the opposite conclusion (183cd):

> But when fathers put slaves in charge of boys with whom men are in love, and won't allow them to talk to their erastai, and those are the orders given to the slave in charge, and when the boy's friends of his own age reproach him if they see anything of the kind going on, and their elders don't restrain these reproaches or tell them off for saying the wrong thing – looking at all that, anyone would reverse his opinion and think that eros of this kind is regarded here as absolutely shameful.

So far Pausanias has given us a factual description of overtly

---

39. For this motif in poetry cf. Asklepiades 12, Kallimakhos 8, Meleagros 92.

expressed Athenian attitudes; his description may be true or false, but it is uncontaminated by speculation. That a boy's family tries to shield him from erastai is taken for granted in Xen. *Smp.* 8.19, and Pl. *Phdr.* 255a says that boys discourage one another from listening to erastai. Pl. *Lys.* 208c, 223a give us an idea of the authority of slaves put in charge of boys. Pausanias goes on (183d-184b), to explain the apparent contradiction in the Athenian rule as the product of a wish to discriminate between good and bad eros. The erastes who is 'in love with the body rather than the soul' (183e) loses interest when his eromenos matures, and he breaks his promises of lasting love and gratitude; but the erastes who is in love with the 'good character' of the eromenos 'stays for life', since character, unlike youthful beauty, is lasting. Thus (183e-184a):

> Our rule wishes to test these (*sc.* good and bad erastai) well and truly, and (*sc.* wishes eromenoi) to grant favours to the good but keep clear of the bad. Therefore it encourages erastai to pursue, but eromenoi to flee; it organises a contest, and puts erastes and eromenoi to the test to see to which category each belongs.

At this point another item of information about the Athenian attitude is introduced (184ab):

> So for this reason it is regarded as disgraceful, first of all, (*sc.* for an eromenos) to be caught quickly – the idea is that time, which is held to be a good test of most things, should intervene – and secondly, disgraceful to be caught by (*sc.* the offer of) money or (*sc.* the exercise of) political influence, whether he (*sc.* the eromenos) has been intimidated by maltreatment and fails to hold out, or whether, offered advantage in material terms or attainment of political ends,[40] he has failed to reject this with contempt.

The circumspect language is precisely that which we have observed and have learned to interpret in contexts of a more down-to-earth nature (pp. 44f.): *kharizesthai* (182a-c, 183d, 184ab, 184de, 185ab), *hupourgein* (184d), 'pursue' (184a, cf. 182e), 'flee' (184a), 'catch' (182d, 184a), 'entreat' (183a), 'accomplish' (183ab, 184b). It would be a mistake to imagine that when Pausanias distinguishes (183e) 'the man who is in love with the body rather than with the soul' from 'the man who is love with the good character (*sc.* of the eromenos)' he

---

40. An adolescent youth could not actively engage in politics, but all kinds of changes in the balance of power and influence within the citizen-body can be covered by the Greek expression '*politikos* achievements'. (or '... accomplishings').

denies the latter any desire for bodily consummation or any inclination to refuse it if it is eventually offered.

Pausanias himself is represented by Plato (*Prt.* 315de) as erastes of Agathon when the latter was about eighteen, and as remaining so more than a dozen years later (the dramatic date of *Smp.* is 416), when Agathon had become an established dramatist (*Smp.* 193b; cf. Xen. *Smp.* 8.32); when Agathon emigrated to Macedonia, at some time between 411 and 405, Pausanias seems to have followed him there.[41] He therefore has a strong personal reason for treating erastai who turn their eros into an enduring relationship as superior to those whose interest in a given eromenos is more transient, and for treating the endurance itself as a justification of the original homosexual relationship.

It is not necessary to accept as true his explanation of Athenian motives as essentially rational. The situation which he describes – sympathy for the erastes, but at the same time protection of the eromenos and criticism of an eromenos who is 'quickly caught' – resembles to a striking degree the situation which can be observed in many societies which are strongly heterosexual in their orientation but at the same time allow women a certain freedom of movement.[42]

In the first place, we notice that heterosexual relationships in such a society and homosexual relationships in Greek society are regarded as the product not of the reciprocated sentiment of equals but of the pursuit of those of lower status by those of higher status. The virtues admired in an eromenos are the virtues which the ruling element in a society (in the case of Greek society, adult male citizens) approves in the ruled (women and children). Anakreon fr. 360 addresses one of his eromenoi thus:

> O boy with the virginal eyes, I seek you, but you do not listen, not knowing that you are the charioteer of my soul!

The 'virginal eyes' go with readiness to blush (e.g. Pl. *Chrm.* 158c), shyness (e.g. Pl. *Lys.* 207a, 222b) and unobtrusiveness. Kharmides, asked by Socrates to define *sōphrosunē* (Pl. *Chrm.* 159b), hesitates becomingly, and in the end says it is 'doing everything in a quiet and orderly way, including walking and talking in the streets'. Right in Ar. *Clouds* 963f. puts these virtues at the head of his praise of boys as they were in the good old days:

41. Cf. Dover (1965) 13f.

42. The artful attempts of an erastes to create a situation from which he may profit, as described in Pl. *Smp.* 217c, have an exceedingly familiar ring if transposed into modern heterosexual terms.

In the first place, the rule was that no one should hear so much as a murmur from a boy. Secondly, they had to walk in an orderly way through the streets to the music-master's ...

A boy who speaks seductively to his erastes, 'acting as his own procurer with his eyes', or is the first to snatch delicacies at a meal, or 'giggles or crosses his legs', is the product of these degenerate days, according to the complaint of Right (979-83). When an eromenos reminds an erastes, by 'putting on airs', which of them is the beggar and which the potential giver, it is disconcerting to an erastes, and in Xen. *Smp.* 8.4 Socrates puts on a delightful act as a conceited and coquettish boy:

> 'Are you the only one, Antisthenes, who isn't in love with anyone?'
> 'By God I am!' said Antisthenes, 'I'm in love with you!'
> Socrates, making fun of him, as if putting on airs, said 'Now, don't bother me now! Can't you see I'm busy?'
> Antisthenes replied 'You – your own pimp! – always behave like that. Sometimes you make your "sign from a god" the excuse and don't talk to me, and sometimes you're after something else'.
> 'O, I beg you, Antisthenes,' said Socrates, 'please don't beat me up! Any other bad temper I put up with from you, and I'll go on putting up with it, because I'm fond of you. But look, let's keep our eros quiet, because it isn't my soul you're in love with, but my good looks.'

The junior partner in homosexual eros is called *pais* (or, of course, paidika) even when he has reached adult height and hair has begun to grow on his face, so that he might more appropriately be called *neāniskos, meirakion* or *ephēbos*.[43] There is a clear distinction between *paides* and *neāniskoi* in (e.g.) Pl. *Lys.* 206de, and in *Chrm.* 154a Socrates says of Kharmides:

> He wasn't unremarkable even then, when he was still a *pais*, but by now, I imagine, he must be quite a *meirakion*.

When Kharmides appears, Khairephon asks Socrates 'What do you think of the *neāniskos*?' (154d). In Plato's *Euthydemos* Kleinias is repeatedly called *neāniskos* (271a, 275a) or *meirakion* (273ab, 275a, 275de), but when Ktesippos, one of his erastai, shifts position he does so in order to 'get a better view of his paidika' (274c), and in *Lys.* 205bc *pais* and *neāniskos* have the same reference, the adolescent Lysis.

---

43. Cf. Hopfner 233-6. *Neos*, 'young', can be applied to an infant, a youngish man, or anything in between, according to context.

Meleagros 117 describes a blissful erotic dream in which he embraced an 'eighteen-year-old *pais*', and the young man whose beauty so moved the *paiderastēs* Episthenes in Xen. *Anab.* vii 4.7 is described by Xenophon as 'a *pais* who had just reached maturity'. Once the beard was grown, a young male was supposed to be passing out of the eromenos stage; that is why Socrates' friend says to him in Pl. *Prt.* 309a:

> I thought he (*sc.* Alkibiades) was a handsome man – but a *man*, Socrates, between ourselves, and getting quite a beard by now.

Cf. the witticism of Bion, recorded in Plu. *Dial.* 770bc: the beard, appearing on the eromenos, 'liberates the erastes from the tyranny of eros'. The sordidness of the Sausage-seller's way of life in Ar. *Knights* 1242 lies not merely in his having been 'fucked a bit', but in his earning money that way when he was grown-up.

The very numerous painted inscriptions on vases which comment on the beauty of a young male always, when they do not name the individual instead, speak of *pais*, never using a word for 'youth'. The same word, with the feminine definite article *hē*, is used in the comparatively small number of vase-inscriptions which refer to female beauty; similarly in Ar. *Peace* 869f., where preparations are being made for the wedding of Trygaios with the supernatural being Opora, we are told 'the *pais*' – i.e. the bride – 'has had a bath'.

Ktesippos, like his paidika Kleinias, is *neāniskos* (*Euthd.* 273a), and some, at least, of the erastai of Kharmides are *neāniskoi* (*Chrm.* 154a). This suggests the possibility of homosexual relationships between coevals,[44] perhaps conventionally disguised by the acceptance, on the part of one partner, of the designation *pais*; but the vase-paintings do not make much use of such a relationship.[45] Instances known to me are: B696, two youths wrapped in one cloak; R200*, one youth caressing another, who reclines beside him, and swinging a leg over him, much as in the heterosexual scene R82*. Other instances are each in some way peripheral, special or ambiguous: C74, abandoned behaviour on the part of comasts (cf. p. 7); CW16, where it is hard to be sure that both participants are male, and even harder to decide on their age[46]; R223*, in which a squatting youth, becoming impatient

44. Asklepiades 24 and Meleagros 80 *may* be examples. In Xen. *Mem.* ii 1. 30, 'using men (*andres*) as women', the word 'men' as representation of the male sex, rather than 'youths', is probably chosen in order to make a disagreeable impression on the reader. The same phenomenon may occur in Theokr. 2.44f. (cf. p. 67), on the lips of a girl discarded by her lover.

45. Cf. Schauenburg (1975) 119.

46. Cf. Schauenburg (1971) 73-5.

while some of his friends are engaged in heterosexual activity, tries to pull another youth down on to his erect penis;[47] R243*, an unusual scene of 'group activity', in which two youths, bending over, have backed towards each other while a third prepares to thrust his penis between their buttocks;[48] R954*, in which a boy with a small but no doubt imperious erection lolls seductively on a chair while another boy mounts the chair to oblige him (perhaps they will change places afterwards);[49] R1127*, satyrs; R1167, a boy or youth holding a ladle under the half-erect penis of another youth. It was shocking if an erastes was younger than his eromenos; Xen. *Anab.* ii 6.28, in the course of portraying Menon as a man almost too bad to be credible, alleges that he treated as his paidika Tharypas, whose beard was well advanced, though Menon was still beardless. The boys in Pl. *Chrm.* 154c are enchanted by Kharmides' beauty, but hero-worship of that kind is nothing out of the ordinary. One could be erastes and eromenos at the same stage of one's life, but not both in relation to the same person; cf. Xen. *Smp.* 8.2 on Kritoboulos.

Aiskhines i 195 refers to 'hunters of such young men as are easily caught', and hunting is not an uncommon metaphor of homosexual pursuit; cf. Pl. *Prt.* 309a, Socrates 'out with the hounds' after Alkibiades' beauty; Pl. *Phdr.* 241d, comparing the fondness of an erastes for his eromenos to the fondness of wolves for lambs;[50] Pl. *Lys.* 206a, a simile from hunting, Meleagros 116, 'boy-hounds'; Rhianos 5.1, 'I caught a fawn and lost it'. This usage and the very frequent use of words for pursuit, flight and capture sustain the notion that the eromenos is the quarry or victim of the erastes. Hunting is a sport, and one of the favourite sports of the Greeks; although the object of pursuit is capture, a quarry which sits waiting to be picked up spoils the fun of the chase, and conversely a quarry which gives the huntsmen a good run for their money earns their respect and affection (the more difficult the chase, the greater the happiness at completing it

---

47. Vermeule 12 describes the second youth as a woman, but the figure has an unmistakably male torso (contrast the woman's breasts on a figure to the right); the position of the legs hides the genital region.

48. The scene makes me think of the young men, a hundred and fifty years later, at whose behaviour the speaker of Dem. liv 16f. is so shocked (cf. p. 38). Closer in time is Theopompos Comicus fr. 29, where (lit.) 'the excessively youths (*meirakia*)' – i.e. those who overplay their role as *young*? – 'grant favours to their fellows of their own age' on the slopes of Lykabettos. (I withdraw the interpretation I offered in Dover [1964]41 n 7).

49. Cf. von Blanckenhagen, who compares R970*.

50. In prisons the 'wolf' is the active homosexual, and does not reverse roles with his partners (D.J. West 233f.).

successfully). If the quarry is human and the object copulation, the difficulty of the chase enhances the value of the object, and eventual capture, after fierce competition with rival hunters, is incalculably reassuring to the hunter himself. No great knowledge of the world is needed to perceive the analogy between homosexual pursuit in classical Athens and heterosexual pursuit in (say) British society in the nineteen-thirties. So long as there were female slaves who had no say in how they were used and female prostitutes who needed to earn money for themselves or for their owners, a young Athenian male, especially if he was well-off, was not short of sexual outlets. Purchased sex, however, could never give him what he needed emotionally, the experience of being valued and welcomed for his own sake. Since girls of citizen family were protected by their families against contact with men, the seducer was necessarily directed towards his own sex. In a heterosexual society a young man is not merely excused by his peers and elders if he pursues women with intent to seduce; if it is believed that he has been successful, he is envied by most of his peers and elders and openly admired by many; he may even be treated with ridicule, contempt or mistrust if he shows no inclination for the pursuit. The women whom he seduces, on the other hand, win no respect or sympathy for their co-operation in his attainment of an apparently praiseworthy end, but very much the reverse; pursuit is the role prescribed for the male, flight for the female, and both are judged and valued in accordance with their success in carrying out their respective roles.[51] Parents are therefore apt to issue different commands (explicit or implicit) to their sons and to their daughters. Social competition is among the factors affecting what we say to our children; there can be no winners without losers or losers without winners, and it matters to us very much that we should be the winners and others the losers.[52] If my son seduces my neighbours' daughters, but their sons do not succeed in seducing my daughter, I have demonstrated both that I am a more conscientious and efficient guardian of what I am supposed to guard and also that the member of my family of whom enterprise and virility are expected possesses it in greater measure. An Athenian father, similarly, who sternly told his fourteen-year-old son never to speak to strange men on the way home from the gymnasium, yet betrayed by a glint in the eye and a curl of the lip that he was not wholly displeased by a rumour that his twenty-

51. Cf. Dover (1964) 31; Mead 290f.
52. Cf. Slater 36-8 on the Greek passion for competition and its relation to what he calls Greek 'narcissism'. I do not think the Greeks were as different from us as he seems to imply, but that is because I define 'us' differently; cf. *GPM* 228-42.

year-old son had 'caught' the fourteen-year-old boy next door, was acting as humans act.

The prescription of heterosexual roles today (or rather, until recently) and the prescription of homosexual roles in ancient Athens differ in two important respects which have the effect of cancelling each other out. On the one hand, the Athenian father of a handsome boy did not have to worry about the financial and organisational problems which are created by the birth of an illegitimate baby, and to that extent we might have expected him to take a less repressive attitude towards the boy's homosexual affairs. On the other hand, whereas a woman insulated from contact with men throughout her youth and encouraged to treat all men alike with mistrust may find it hard to make the transition from the approved role of virgin daughter to the approved roles of bride, housewife and mother, a boy who rejects the advances of erastai will nevertheless turn into an adult male citizen, and his performance of that role will not be impaired by his past chastity. From that point of view it is not easy to see any reason why a boy (or his father) should have tolerated erastai at all, no matter how decorously they behaved.

Yet some reasons emerge on reflection. Anyone would rather be good-looking than ugly; the attentions of an erastes, assuring a boy that he is not ugly, are welcome to him for that reason alone (the young Alkibiades felt 'dishonoured' [Pl. *Smp.* 219b] when Socrates did not try to seduce him),[53] and the boy's glory is reflected on the father. A generous erastes earns gratitude, and generosity has many forms, from a giving that can be crudely assessed in monetary terms to an unobtrusive sacrifice of one's time, convenience or advantage. A patient erastes can earn his reward by working upon a boy's sense of justice (we tend to think that patience deserves reward); an unhappy and desperate erastes earns compassion; an erastes who has demonstrated military, athletic or artistic prowess earns a boy's admiration and is taken by him as a model; and a lovable erastes earns love. One can see in all such cases how, if the boy is at all inclined to yield, his father's opposition may weaken too, especially if the erastes belongs to a powerful and influential family or is in truth an excellent model for the boy to imitate. Of course, if homosexual desire were in itself regarded as a moral defect, so that one might hear 'I *thought* X was a real friend' (or 'I *thought* X was a good influence on my son') '*but* it turned out that he wanted ...', none of the ways in which an erastes might hope to earn consummation of his desire would avail him much; but as we have seen, neither an Athenian boy

53. Cf. Slater 33f., Devereux (1967) 75, 90.

nor his father is in the least likely to have regarded the existence of the desire in the erastes as a defect, and criticism could only take the form '... but he *only* wanted ...'.

The analogy between an ancient homosexual and a modern heterosexual society can be pursued further if we extend the category 'modern' to include the presentation of respectable British society in the literature of the nineteenth century. The good woman, in this literature, does not desire or seek sexual intercourse.[54] She does not even desire marriage; but if a man of good character and ability asks her to marry him, obtains her father's consent, displays patience, tact and modesty in all his dealings with her, and participates with her in a prolonged and complicated ritual of which the essential element is the utterance of formulae and responses in a church, thereafter she has sexual intercourse with him whenever he wishes. He has not at any time alluded directly to this aspect of marriage. She does not enjoy it or take the initiative in it; she accepts it because she loves him and because it is her duty. She does not speak to her friends of what she and her husband do in bed; nor does he, if he is a gentleman, speak of it to his. A woman who seeks sexual intercourse outside the sequence of courtship and marriage as just described, whether because she likes it or because she needs to earn money, is excluded from association with those who have obeyed the rules, and it is difficult for her ever to resume association once she has demonstrated, however briefly, her possession of a disposition and moral character which has made deviation from the rules possible. Elements of this moral schema persist to this day, varying from country to country and from class to class. The analogy with Greek homosexual eros is not complete – heterosexual relationships, after all, produce and rear children, and the utterance of the crucial words of the marriage ceremony, whether in church or in registry, is an event distinct in kind from the partners' enunciation of their wishes and society's acceptance of their relationship – but the common ingredients are not negligible.

Just as a great deal can be said about marriage, and indeed has been said, without any direct reference to sexual intercourse, and at the same time without going so far as to suggest that respectable married people abstain from intercourse, so Aiskhines finds it possible to omit all mention of favours granted by an eromenos to a good erastes, without ever committing himself to the opinion that it is wrong in all circumstances to grant such favours. Clearly, in his view, the eromenos must be exceedingly modest and circumspect if he is to escape censure, and if the deep emotions of the erastes find expression

54. Cf. Trudgill 56-64, 123-5.

in poetry it must be poetry which admits of 'innocent' interpretation; whatever reward the erastes receives in the end, it must be the reward of long restraint. With these provisos, however, what eventually happens is shielded from comment or description by conventional reticence. Plato's Pausanias is a little less reticent. The eros of which he approves is a protracted relationship, in which the resistance of the eromenos makes great demands on the erastes, but there are circumstances in which resistance should cease. Pausanias makes the point (*Smp.* 184c) that total subordination of oneself to the wishes and commands of another is exempt, in the eyes of Athenian society, from blame and dishonour if its purpose is self-improvement in skill, knowledge or any other form of excellence; no doubt he has in mind apprentices, trainees, pupils and disciples. If this principle is applied to homosexual eros, then (184de):

> When erastes and eromenos meet, each observing a rule, the erastes (*sc.* the rule) that it would be right for him to subordinate himself in any way to an eromenos who has granted him favours, and the eromenos (*sc.* the rule) that it would be right for him to perform any service for one who improves him in mind and character (*lit.*, 'who makes him *sophos* and *agathos*'). ... then ... in these circumstances alone, and in no others, it is creditable for an eromenos to grant favours to an erastes.

In short (185b):

> It is creditable to grant *any* favour in *any* circumstances for the sake of becoming a better person (*lit.*, 'for the sake of goodness').

To translate from euphemism into plain English: acceptance of the teacher's thrusting penis between his thighs or in his anus is the fee which the pupil pays for good teaching, or alternatively, a gift from a younger person to an older person whom he has come to love and admire. In any individual case, each of these alternatives may contribute half of the truth; if one is nearer the truth than the other, it is not easy for anyone but the eromenos himself to know which. That the eromenos should initiate a homosexual act for its own sake is not a possibility admitted by Pausanias or by any other Greek enthusiast or apologist for homosexual eros.

5. *Courtship and copulation*

As references to the erastes' 'requests' in literature would have led us to expect, the erastes in vase-painting is sometimes depicted as expostulating with the eromenos or imploring him: B142; B146;

R196*; R789; R791* (a man with a gift, the boy heavily swathed); R851*; R853 (the youth is naked, the boy clothed). In R867* men and youths expostulate in the same way with women. B266, with which Beazley[55] compares the man and boy of B622, shows an unhappy man sagging at the knees and looking up piteously into a woman's face. The eromenos is sometimes apprehensive (R529), sometimes plainly angry; in R322 a boy, speaking to a youth, holds finger and thumb together in an argumentative gesture (cf. the man and woman of R589) which is clearly not accommodating, for the corners of his mouth are drawn down, scowling in the same way as a woman in R361 when a man seated on the ground, with penis erect, lifts her skirt and peers under it. In R547* a boy hastening away from a youth indignantly thrusts his hand downwards and outwards in a gesture of denial; the outstretched arm and outspread fingers of the youth in R638, as he turns away, reject a gift offered by a man. In R863 a boy seems to be closing his eyes shyly when a seated youth steals a glance at him.

Certain gifts are conventional, notably a cockerel (e.g. B76*, B190, B254, B262, B267, B614, B622, R348*, R405, R758*, R791*, R833*; cf. a terracotta from Olympia[56] depicting Zeus carrying off Ganymede), a hare (e.g. R418, R502*, R637*, R638) and a fox (e.g. B107);[57] a stag, not easy to carry, appears as a gift in B250* and B262. Ar. *Birds* 707 names quail, coot, goose and cockerel as gifts to paidika, *Wealth* 157 horses and dogs (cf. Pl. *Lys.* 211e, 'a good friend is better than quail, cock, horse or dog'); in B16* a kneeling youth affectionately embraced by a man holds a bird of uncertain species. A dog accompanying the erastes in some paintings may or may not be intended as a gift: B76* (where it sniffs at the genitals of the eromenos), B262, B592. In R720 a lyre and a ball are offered to a boy, and in R875 (as it seems) a strigil.[58] Women are more often offered money;[59] as in R589, R627, R632, R728, R817, though a cockerel is not unknown (B84) as a gift to a woman. Since copulation is naturally associated with festivity and the brighter side of life, both partners in a sexual approach or embrace may be shown holding garlands: B250*, youths *vis-à-vis* men; B254, a boy holding a garland and a man holding a cockerel; B450, women holding garlands during copulation; B502*, a

55. Beazley (1947) 213.
56. Lullies and Hirmer 20, 72 and pl. V; Kunze.
57. Cf. Schauenburg (1965) 863-7, Lullies (1957) 378f.
58. Cf. the complaint of Glaukos 1 about boys who put their prices up.
59. Cf. Rodenwaldt 14-21. In R638 the youth making off has not accepted a purseful of money; he is carrying nuts, figs, etc., like the boy in R520*.

man bringing a garland and a dog to a youth; B610, a naked woman holding a garland and a flower while she converses with a youth; CE34*, two women in an affectionate relationship (cf. p. 173); CW16, a male(?) holding a garland[60], and penetrated anally by another male; R627, a seated woman holding out a garland to a youth whose hand gropes towards her vulva.

Whereas men and youths are often depicted as mauling and hauling women (e.g. B299, B334, R144, R519, R843) – not, of course, women of citizen status[61] – the protection afforded to freeborn boys by the law on hubris is reflected in the rarity of homosexual assault in the visual arts. Rarity, that is, when the aggressor is human, for gods could not be indicted for hubris. Zeus in B186 and R348* commands Ganymede in a manner that will not accept refusal (so too Poseidon in pursuit of Pelops, who looks back apprehensively on the point of flight [R406*]), and in R405, R829*, R833* he simply grasps Ganymede, who struggles violently; in the Olympia terracotta he has tucked Ganymede (no longer struggling) under his arm and is striding off to Olympos. Eros in R770 simply launches himself on a boy; Pan, penis erect, runs full-tilt after a young herdsman (R693; cf. his onslaught on a woman in RL60). Zephyros seizes Hyakinthos by the arm (R847) and wafts him through the air (R574). Dawn, a female deity, rushes at Tithonos, who tries to beat her off with his lyre (R912; cf. R391, R801). Such treatment of eromenoi by human erastai, when it occurs in art, is perhaps wishful thinking, playing god;[62] indeed, one such scene is on the other side of B186. Cf. B194 (a man and a youth); R663 (a man and a boy); R1095 (a man, penis swollen, and a – slave? – boy); a man's seizure of a youth by the wrist (R279) should perhaps be classed as an arresting gesture rather than as an assault.

This classification certainly applies to R934*, where a man at a sacrifice puts his hand on the shoulder of a passing naked youth, who does not look disposed to stay; in R692, on the other hand, where Hermes puts a hand on the shoulder of Ganymede, Hermes is acting on behalf of Zeus. Extending a hand to the armpit of the eromenos is a more tentative approach, as in R684*, though the boy there takes it badly and brandishes his lyre in self-defence, like Tithonos in R912. The same approach is used to a woman in R35, R628, R682*; in the third of those the woman is naked and the man is perhaps aiming at one of her breasts rather than her armpit. The erastes commits himself less directly by affectionately putting his hand to the head

60. Vorberg (1932) 463 mistakes the garland for a discus.
61. Some scenes are mythological, e.g. R112 (Peleus and Atalante); R928, in which a youth carrying two spears grasps an apprehensive woman, is mysterious.

(B262) or face (B166) of the eromenos, as a mother does to her child's (R741), a master to a good young slave's (R480),[63] a man to a woman's (R623, where both are seated on a bed; cf. the excited satyr and woman in B566),[64] one woman to another's (CE34*), a youth to his father's as the latter departs on military service (B79), or the god Dionysos to his mother Semele's (B152). The beds on which guests lay at a symposium, commonly two to a bed, were equally adapted for homosexual and heterosexual approaches, with the difference that the eromenos was the fellow-guest of the erastes, whereas the hetaira or female dancer or musician must be got on to the bed before serious embracing and titillating (e.g. B338) could begin. The man's arm round the youth in C42 (late seventh century B.C.) would be interpreted by any reasonable person as comradely if the erotic pictures of the following two hundred years were not there to influence our interpretation. In R795 and R797 (men and youths at symposia) the apparent touching may be no more than the gestures of intimate conversation, but there is no doubt about the wall-paintings at Paestum:[64] overcome with desire for the youth who lies on the same bed, the man puts his hand round the back of the youth's head and tries to bring their faces together for a kiss, while the youth, whose expression gives nothing away as he gazes at the wide eyes and parted lips of the man (the man on the next bed looks more startled), puts out his hand in a gesture of dissuasion. R283* shows a youth at a symposium embraced by a man from behind in an ardent stranglehold while he is handing wine to another man and cannot wriggle free without spilling the wine. In R200* a youth has thrown one leg over the waist of the youth who lies below him, and lays a hand affectionately on his head; as so often, there is a heterosexual analogue (R82*) in which a youth has thrown one leg over a woman piper, one arm embracing her round the neck and the other hand fingering her left breast.

The most characteristic configuration of homosexual courtship in vase-painting is what Beazley calls the 'up and down' position;[65] one of the erastes' hands touches the eromenos's face, the other moves towards the eromenos's genitals (e.g. B426, B578). It is interesting to note that the earliest example of this approach, CE33* (seventh century B.C.), is heterosexual; the woman is fully clothed, and she grasps the wrists of the youth to push his hands away. The eromenos

---

62. Cf. Sichtermann (1959) 12-14. Scenes (some patently erotic) in which blows are threatened are listed by Boardman (1976) 286f.

63. Cf. G. Neumann 71-5.

64. Cf. n. 26 above.

65. Cf. Beazley (1947) 199.

in the 'up and down' scenes is usually naked, or at least has allowed his cloak to fall aside and expose the front of his body. In B102 one youth offers no resistance to being touched (he holds a spear, butt on ground, in one hand, and a garland in the other), while the youth in the scene on the other side of the vessel grasps the man's wrist in restraint. Both resistance and non-resistance are attested in the long series of scenes which runs from the second quarter of the sixth century to the second quarter of the fifth.[66] Non-resistance seems to predominate among the pairs in B510, and the erastes of R651* (the upper part of the picture is lost) has clearly gained one important objective, for he is handling the penis of the eromenos as if shaking hands with it. One youth in B250* expostulates, but does not protect his genitals from the touch of the man's fingers or from the man's (horizontal) erection hovering an inch away; a youth in B271* grasps the man's left wrist – that is to say, the hand that approaches his face – while permitting his genitals to be touched. The youth in B65* puts his hand over his genitals as a shield, but the normal defence is to hold the erastes by the wrists: B64, B342*, B458, B558. R463 has the inscribed dialogue, 'Let me!' – 'Stop it!' (cf. p. 6). The pairs of youths and boys in R196* illustrate different stages of seduction admirably. In one pair, the boy tries to restrain the arm of the youth which has stolen tentatively to the back of his head. In another, the boy is close to surrender; he gazes up into the face of the youth and satisfies honour by taking hold of the youth's right arm above the elbow, which does nothing to interrupt the dandling of his penis by the youth's fingers. The most dramatic pair stands between those other two; here the youth sags at the knees, looking up in abject entreaty, his penis swollen and the fingers of his right hand spread despairingly, while the boy, chin high in a defiant pose, grips the arm of the youth hard and keeps it from its goal. What gives this picture its peculiar interest is that it is matched on the other side of the vessel by heterosexual pairs, where the atmosphere is quite different, though in an unexpected way: the youths and women do not touch each other at all, but seem immersed in a patient, wary conversation, in which a slight gesture or an inflexion of the voice conveys as much as the straining of an arm in the other scene.[67] Compared with its

66. The great majority belong to the black-figure period; cf. Beazley (1947) 219-23. Decrease in numbers in the red-figure period, however, is not accompanied by increase in reticence; cf. (e.g.) R520*. The configuration is not peculiarly Attic, but appears also on a Klazomenian sarcophagus (Friis Johansen 186).

67. Robinson and Fluck 13 cite without comment Furtwängler's judgment (iii 21) that the heterosexual scene is comparatively insipid.

homosexual counterpart, representation of a male hand moving towards the female genitals is not so common: R62; R627, youths groping; R619, R1079, satyrs crudely molesting women; B610, an 'up and down' approach by a man to a naked woman who, like the women in R196*, has a flower and a garland. R295* shows a man at a symposium, on whose head a naked boy is putting a garland, seizing the opportunity to finger the boy's penis; the boy may be a slave, and in any case the tone of the picture seems to be roguish humour. The word *orkhipedizein* is used in Ar. *Birds* 142 of a man's attempt to seduce a neighbour's young son; coupled there with 'speak to ...' and 'kiss', it presumably means 'take by the testicles' (*orkhipeda*) and therefore denotes an action very similar to, but not identical with, the penis-tickling of the vase-paintings.

As we saw in R196*, the response of the eromenos may be positively affectionate, and several other vases depict such a response. When a youth touches a man's beard (B12, B594) he might possibly be making a gesture of supplication,[68] 'Leave me alone!'. But touching any part of the face is also affectionate (naturally enough; cf. p. 94), and in B598*, where one side of the vessel shows a boy touching a man's beard, the other side shows him jumping up to throw his arms round the man's neck (not a gesture of supplication). In the very early B16* a man and a youth kneel facing each other, the youth holding a bird and the man having one hand round the back of the youth's neck; the circular interior surface on which the picture is painted encourages the artist to depict kneeling or loping figures, but it hardly compels him to do so, and this artist cannot have been unaware of the impression of affectionate acceptance which the picture conveys. A boy accepts the loving embrace of his erastes in R27*, R59*, R539; in the third of these the boy responds positively by putting his hand round the man's head, as does the boy in R520*, while the man's penis approaches his thighs. This affectionate gesture naturally occurs in heterosexual scenes: B302; R569; R630, in which the woman nevertheless coyly pushes the man's hand away from her lap. We should hardly expect to find a homosexual analogue to RL68, where a naked woman pulls a man down towards her by the arm.

The penis of the erastes is sometimes erect even before any bodily contact is established (e.g. B107, B250*), but that of the eromenos remains flaccid even in circumstances (e.g. R573) to which one would expect the penis of any healthy adolescent to respond willy-nilly. One youth in B250* looks like an exception to this generalisation, but his

68. Cf. J. Gould (1973) 6f.

penis is perhaps pushed up by the man's belly;[69] in BB20 the crudity of the figure-painting makes interpretation difficult, but it is just possible that the penis of the eromenos in some of the courting pairs has been erected through titillation by the erastes. The rule is (as we have observed from the literary evidence, pp. 52f.) that the eromenos may in the end decide to grant his erastes a favour, but he himself has no sensual incentive to do so. This *sōphrosunē* on the part of the eromenos can be contrasted with its outrageous absence in ugly, earthy, drunken satyrs, amoral creatures who obey their impulses. They masturbate constantly (e.g. B31, B118, B126, B138, B178) if no living being with a suitable orifice is available, but prefer horses, mules or deer (B154, B336, B362, B554, CE20; cf. their purposeful approaches in B24, B122, B158, B287, B366, B378, R762); even the neck of a jar may be pressed into service (R148). By contrast, a youth masturbating (R173)[70] or penetrating an animal (B354)[71] is a rare subject. There is a certain tendency in comedy to treat masturbation as behaviour characteristic of slaves, who could not expect sexual outlets comparable in number or quality with those of free men. In Ar. *Frogs* 542-8 Dionysos imagines himself, in the role of a slave, as 'clutching my chick-pea' while watching his master 'on Milesian blankets ... kissing a dancing-girl', and then being struck in the face by the master. R18, in which a seated youth strikes a slave-boy whose penis is swollen, though not erect, may indicate that the painter (a hundred years earlier) had in mind such an incident.[72] The two slaves in *Knights* 21-9 speak as connoisseurs of masturbation, and in *Peace* 289-91 the Persian general Datis, immortalised in popular song, is humorously assimilated to barbarian slaves by being depicted as enjoying masturbation in the afternoon siesta. *Clouds* 734 affords the only example of masturbation by a male citizen, and the performer there is the grossly rustic Strepsiades.[73]

69. In this picture the penises of the other youths are drawn as horizontal, but certainly not erect; cf. p.125.

70. I would restrict the term 'masturbation' to scenes in which the figure is alone or in which (as in B118 [satyr]) semen is emitted; it is not appropriate to scenes in which a man clutches his erect penis while importuning a potential partner or waiting his turn. It is possible that a boy shown in a crouching position below the handle of B522 is masturbating.

71. In a drawing from the agora (Lang no. 30) the sex of the person penetrated from behind by a shaggy dog is uncertain.

72. In the *Frogs* passage the master strikes the slave, presumably, because he has called for a chamber-pot (544) and the slave was inattentive; but we have a certain tendency, impelled by a perverted jealousy or insecurity, to react angrily to the sexual activity of those over whom we have authority.

73. In my note on this passage I drew attention to a 'common assumption of vulgar

When courtship has been successful, the erastes and eromenos stand facing one another; the erastes grasps the eromenos round the torso, bows his head on to or even below the shoulder of the eromenos, bends his knees and thrusts his penis between the eromenos's thighs just below the scrotum. Examples are: B114*, B130, B250*, B482, B486*, B534, R502*, R573*, in all of which the erastes is a man and the eromenos a youth.[74] B458 is unusual in that the man looks up into the face of the youth, but perhaps the youth has not yet wholly surrendered (the vessel is damaged at a vital place) and the man is still at the stage of entreaty. In R520* the eromenos is a boy, and the man's gaze is fixed on his throat, but the final position is not yet reached; the difference of stature is considerable, and the man has to put his half-crouching legs outside the boy's. Gods favour the same method as men; in R603*, where Zephyros is flying off with Hyakinthos, both figures are clothed, but the painter has superimposed the god's penis somehow thrusting its way between the thighs of Hyakinthos. The original specific word for this type of copulation was almost certainly *diamērizein*, i.e. 'do ... between the thighs (*mēroi*)'. When we first encounter the word in Aristophanes' *Birds* it takes an object of either sex (male in 706, female in 669), and in 1254, where Peisetairos threatens Iris that he will 'stick [her] legs in the air' and *diamērizein* her, the reference is most naturally to any one of several modes of vaginal copulation from the front (cf. p. 101). The inscription on the bottom of B406, from the richest period of homosexual iconography, says *apodos to diamērion*, which is to be interpreted as 'grant me' (or 'pay me back') 'the act of *diamērizein*' (or 'payment for *diamerizein*') 'which you promised' (or 'which is my due').[75]

In B538* a man and a youth, facing each other, are wrapped in a single cloak, and it may have been customary to veil homosexual copulation, standing or lying, in this way; cf. Asklepiades 1.3f., 'when lovers are hidden by one cloak', and Alkibiades' desperate attempt (cf. p. 158) to seduce Socrates by creeping under his cloak. Action concealed is a dull subject for vase-painters, who prefer to show the

---

humour, than an adult male cannot be in bed alone and awake for long without masturbating'. Henderson 220 n. 45 thinks I derived this assumption from 'the English public schools'; actually, I first encountered it in a reveille-call used among American GIs in Italy in 1943, and heard it again in the film *Kes*, where the speaker is a Barnsley miner. I do not, however, disagree with Henderson that Strepsiades' behaviour is intended to strike the audience as gross and earthy.

74. On B482 cf. p. 78.

75. Kretschmer's interpretation (89) is slightly, not essentially, different.

erastes as inviting the eromenos into a cloak (e.g. B592) or to treat the cloak as a backcloth.[76]

Homosexual anal copulation, by contrast with the intercrural mode, is portrayed by vase-painters only when it involves people of the same age-group (CW16, R223*, R954*; cf. p. 86), comasts (C74) or satyrs (R1127*). It is commonly believed at the present time to be the characteristic mode of homosexual consummation;[77] in Greek comedy it is assumed, save ir *Birds* 706 (see above), to be the only mode (cf. p. 145); and when Hellenistic poetry makes a sufficiently unambiguous reference to what actually happens on the bodily plane, we encounter only anal, never intercrural, copulation. So Dioskorides 7 recommends a friend to 'delight in the rosy bum' of his wife when she is pregnant, 'treating her as male Aphrodite', and Rhianos 1 rapturously apostrophises the 'glorious bum' of a boy, so beautiful that even old men itch for it. Meleagros 90 is addressed to a boy whose beauty has faded with maturity; a 'hairy pelt' now 'declares war on those who mount from behind', and Meleagros 94, expressing love for a woman, abjures his former eromenoi and 'the squeeze of a hairy arse'. Homosexual fellation seems, so far as vase-painting is concerned, peculiar to satyrs (B271*, R1127*), though it appears from Polybios xii 13 that at the end of the fourth century Demokhares, a prominent figure in Athenian politics, was accused by a comic poet[78] of 'being *hētairēkōs* with the upper parts of his body, so that he was not a fit person to blow the sacred flame'. Aiskhines ii 88 imputes to Demosthenes 'bodily impurity – even of the organs of speech', and Krates of Thebes 1 is a learned joke about activity of this type. Masturbation of one male by another, envisaged by Meleagros 77, a fantasy in which eight eromenoi are simultaneously engaged with one erastes, is suggested – but not very clearly – by a black-figure fragment, B702.

As we have seen, homosexual and heterosexual courting sequences, as portrayed by the vase-painters, are virtually identical; consummation, however, is radically different in so far as the intercrural mode is normal when the sexual object is male but unknown when it is female.[79] Consideration of the modes of

---

76. Cf. Schauenburg (1965) and Beazley (1947) 203, 221f.

77. Corrected by Westwood 129-31.

78. Arkhedikos fr. 4, taken seriously by Timaios F35(b).

79. The giraffe has developed a courtship technique, exploiting the aesthetic potentialities of his long neck, which he uses in homosexual relations but not in heterosexual mating; the technique culminates in erection, mounting and occasionally spontaneous ejaculation or attempts to induce ejaculation by friction, though not (so far) in anal penetration; cf. Innis 258-60, Moss 45f. Observation in recent years has provided similar evidence for other species. I see no reason to refrain

heterosexual copulation, and of the circumstances in which homosexual anal copulation is practised, threatened or symbolised, may throw some light on the terms in which the important distinction between prostitution and 'legitimate eros' was conventionally drawn.

6. *Dominant and subordinate roles*

When heterosexual intercourse is portrayed in vase-painting, we very commonly see the woman bending over (sometimes with her hands on the ground) while the man stands and penetrates her from behind and below: B134; B450; B518 (the man kneels); B666; B676; C78; CE36; CE37; R361; R434; R545* (the woman almost standing on her head); cf. B60 and B586, in which the man is closing up but has not yet penetrated. In some cases there can be no room for doubt that it is the woman's anus, not her vagina, which is being penetrated;[80] the clearest case is B51*, where the vulva, carefully depicted, is nowhere near the point of penetration, and in R543* the painter cannot have been unaware of the distance he has put between the woman's pubic hair and the point of entry of the penis. In many other cases (e.g. B670, CP16, R577*) the point of entry is so high that is is reasonable to suppose that the painter had anal penetration in mind; unambiguous portrayal of vaginal penetration from the rear (e.g. B516, R490) is less common.[81] The characteristic configuration – the woman bent over, the man standing behind her – is described in the late fifth century by a passage of Aristophanes (*Thesm.* 479-89), where the speaker is a man disguised as a woman and 'confessing' to a woman's tricks:

> My husband was asleep beside me. I had a friend who'd popped me when I was seven, and he missed me so much he came and scratched on the door. I knew at once who it was, so I tiptoed down. My husband asks me, 'Where are you going?' 'Why, I've got an awful pain in my stomach, so I'm going to the loo'. So he mixed me juniper and dill and sage, and I put a bit of water on the hinge (*sc.* of the outer door) and

---

from using the term 'homosexual' with reference to wild animals if the definition given at the start of I A 1 is satisfied. A Peruvian community mentioned by Tripp 70f. seems to divert almost all its sexually motivated behaviour into homosexual relationships; if so, it invalidates the generalisation of Karlen 476.

80. Correctly observed by Pomeroy 144. Peisistratos fell out with Megakles because, married to Megakles' daughter, he 'had intercourse with her not in the normal way' (Hdt. i 61.1f.), but he had strong reasons for not wishing her to conceive.

81. Devereux (1970) 21 n. 1 regards the urge towards the portrayal of heterosexual anal intercourse as a manifestation of homosexuality (cf. Pomeroy loc. cit.), and we may well suspect a divergence between homosexual copulation in vase-paintings and what an erastes actually hoped to achieve.

went out to my lover, and I was screwed bending over next to the statue, holding on to the bay-tree.

In Ar. *Wealth* 149-52 it is said of hetairai at Corinth that when a rich customer arrives, they 'turn their anus (*prōktos*) to him straight away', which suggests that hetairai may commonly have insisted on anal intercourse as a simple contraceptive measure. This explanation will hardly do for the wedding preparations in Ar. *Peace* 869, where a slave announces, 'The bride (*lit.*, 'girl') has had a bath, and her bum (*pūgē*) is lovely!' The passage seems rather to show an indifference to the actual point at which the 'bottom end' of Trygaios's bride will be penetrated; and *ibid.* 876 the anus of Theoria seems to be the focus of admiration.

Vaginal penetration from the front, the woman lying supine, is shown in R247 (a youth and a woman under one blanket). The woman may put her legs in the air and rest them on the man's shoulders, as in B662, R192, R506, R507 (in R490 a youth is forcing a woman's legs up); Ar. *Birds* 1254, 'I'll stick your legs in the air!' and *Lys.* 229, 'I won't stick my slippers up towards the ceiling!' refer to this mode. Sometimes the man stands, and the woman locks her legs round him; this is essentially the position shown in B694, where, however, the women are provided with mushroom-like stools for their support. In R970* a youth sits on a chair and the woman mounts the chair so that she may lower herself on to his penis by squatting. The 'political victory' of a woman prone or seated on a supine man seems to be unexampled in vase-painting, though perhaps imminent in one part of the complicated orgy of R1151; Ar. *Wasps* 501 and *Thesm.* 153 refer nevertheless to the 'racehorse' position, in which the woman sat like a jockey astride the man.

An interesting contrast between heterosexual intercourse and the intercrural activity ascribed to erastes and eromenos by the vase-painters suggests itself. The woman is almost invariably in a 'subordinate' position, the man 'dominant'; the woman bent over or lying back or supported, the man upright or on top. In intercrural copulation, on the other hand, the eromenos stands bolt upright, and it is the erastes who bows his head and shoulders. The contrast exists also in respect of what one might call 'general penetrability'; against the absence of scenes of human homosexual fellation, we must set scenes in which a youth is cramming his penis into a woman's mouth (R156, R223*) or a man threatening a woman with a stick and forcing her to 'go down on' him (R518). The compliment is not returned; R192, a naked woman cavorting over a collapsing youth so that his face is within a few inches of her vulva, hardly qualifies as cunnilinctus, and a certain Ariphrades, reputed to enjoy it, is attacked in Ar. *Knights* 1280-9 and *Wasps* 1280-3 in terms of hatred and disgust developed so explicitly as to suggest that the topic put Aristophanes' sense of humour under strain (a year after *Wasps*, in *Peace* 883-5, the tone of reference to Ariphrades is more urbane).[82] Double penetration is the game in R156 and R223*; in the former, a man parts the legs of a woman who is taking the penis of a youth in her mouth, and in the latter a woman similarly occupied is about to have an olisbos (artificial penis) pushed into her by a youth. It is possible that the threesome in R898 is meant to end in the simultaneous penetration of the woman's vagina by one man and of her anus by another.[83]

There can be no doubt of the woman's enjoyment of intercourse in (e.g.) B49 and R506, and when a frontal position is adopted the two partners look at each other affectionately; this contrasts with the eromenos who stares ahead while the face of the erastes is hidden from him. It is not therefore surprising that women are shown by the painters as satisfying their sexual cravings artificially by means of olisboi: R132 and R212 both show a woman with two olisboi, the second one for her anus in R132 and her mouth in R212; in R152 an olisbos hangs up in the background while women wash; R227, a woman brandishing an olisbos while penetrated by a satyr; R1163, women lowering themselves on to fixed olisboi; R114, a woman lowering herself on to the pointed base of a jar; R593, a woman drinking from a vessel with a penis-shaped spout; cf. R414*, R1071*, a potful of olisboi (but their significance may be religious).[84] Comedy refers to women's use of olisboi (as it does, often, to their greed and drunkenness), notably in Ar. *Lys.* 107-9 (which indicates that an olisbos was made of leather) and *CGF* 62.16-28 ('as like the real thing ... as the moon is like the sun'). In the Hellenistic period Herodas 6 and 7 are concerned with the purchase of an olisbos from a discreet and skilful shoemaker recommended by one woman to another. Like women, but unlike the upstanding eromenoi of the vase-painters' world, a satyr positively enjoys having his anus penetrated; in BB24* a wild and hairy satyr rams a stick up his own anus while masturbating, and in CW12 a satyr lowers himself on to a fixed olisbos. The vase-painters sometimes amuse themselves by giving satyrs names in which

82. A lamp in the museum at Herakleion (Marcadé 59) portrays fellation of a supine man by a woman, but her vulva is hoisted well out of reach of his face. Galen xii 249 (Kühn) states as a matter of fact that 'we are more revolted' by cunnilinctus than by fellation.

83. A common fantasy in ancient and modern pornography; how practicable, I confess I do not know.

elements denoting 'penis', 'glans', 'erection' and the like play a prominent part,[85] and a satyr in R44 is called *Phlebodokos*, lit., 'vein-accepter'; *phleps*, 'vein', is known as a jocular term for the penis.[86]

If an honourable eromenos does not seek or expect sensual pleasure from contact with an erastes,[87] begrudges any contact until the erastes has proved himself worthy of concession, never permits penetration of any orifice in his body,[88] and never assimilates himself to a woman by playing a subordinate role in a position of contact, and if at the same time the erastes would like him to break rules (iii) and (iv), observe a certain elasticity in his obedience to rule (ii), and even perhaps bend rule (i) a little on occasion, in what circumstances does a male in fact submit to anal penetration by another male, and how does society regard his submission? There seems little doubt that in Greek eyes the male who breaks the 'rules' of legitimate eros detaches himself from the ranks of male citizenry and classifies himself with women and foreigners; the prostitute is assumed to have broken the rules simply because his economic dependence on clients forces him to do what they want him to do; and conversely, any male believed to have done whatever his senior homosexual partner(s) wanted him to do is assumed to have prostituted himself. Timaios (F124b), according to Polybios xii 15.1f., alleged that:

Agathokles, in his first youth, was a common prostitute (*pornos*) available to the most dissolute (*lit.*, 'the most lacking in self-control'), a jackdaw, a buzzard, putting his rear parts in front of anyone who wanted.

The jackdaw here probably symbolises impudence and shamelessness; the buzzard, in Greek *triorkhēs*, 'having three testicles', presumably symbolises insatiable lust, which is assumed to characterise the true *pornos*.

It is not only by assimilating himself to a woman in the sexual act that the submissive male rejects his role as a male citizen, but also by

---

84. Cf. Deubner 65-7; and cf. p.132 below on phalloi.

85. Cf. Charlotte Fränkel 24f., 74, and for other examples B31 (*Dophios*, cognate with *dephesthai*, 'masturbate', and *Psōlās*, derived from *psōlos*, 'with foreskin retracted').

86. Cf. Henderson 124.

87. From the Roman period, we have a striking expression of opinion in Plu. *Dial.* 768a: 'Those who enjoy playing the passive role we treat as the lowest of the low, and we have not the slightest degree of respect or affection for them.'

88. Westwood 133f. notes that those homosexuals who practise intercrural copulation or mutual masturbation and reject anal penetration tend to 'take a spiritual view of homosexuality'. See n. 77 above.

deliberately choosing to be the victim of what would be, if the victim were unwilling, hubris. The point of the fierce sanctions imposed by Attic law on hubris was that the perpetrator 'dishonoured' (*atīmazein*) his victim,[89] depriving him of his standing as a citizen under the law, and standing could be recovered only by indictment which in effect called upon the community to reverse the situation and put down the perpetrator. To choose to be treated as an object at the disposal of another citizen was to resign one's own standing as a citizen. If it is not yet sufficiently obvious why the male prostitute's choice was regarded in this way, it should become so when we recall circumstances in which homosexual anal penetration is treated neither as an expression of love nor as a response to the stimulus of beauty, but as an aggressive act demonstrating the superiority of the active to the passive partner. In Theokritos 5, where Lakon the shepherd and Komatas the goatherd are engaged in a contest of song, a contest in which brutality and mockery play a considerable part, we hear in 39-43:

> LAKON: When can I remember learning or hearing anything good from you ...? KOMATAS: When I went up your arse (*pūgizein*), and it hurt you; and the she-goats bleated away, and the billy-goat tupped them. LAKON: I hope your grave's no deeper than you got up my arse!

That herdsmen should console their loneliness by making do with animals or with one another is a commonplace enough joke; but here Komatas is triumphing over Lakon by recalling an occasion on which he played the part of a male animal and Lakon the part of a female. That the act hurt Lakon, who nevertheless put up with it, is part of Komatas's triumph, and Lakon's riposte is a malevolent slur on the virility of Komatas. A similar note is struck *ibid.* 116-9:

> KOMATAS: Don't you remember when I got stuck into you and you grinned and moved your tail to and fro very nicely and held on to that oak-tree? LAKON: No, I don't remember – but I know very well about the time when Eumaras tied you up and gave you a dusting!

The insulting element here is that Lakon enjoyed playing the woman's role (holding on to a tree, like the young wife in Aristophanes); this time, Lakon denies that it ever happened, and the nature of his reply shows the light in which he sees Komatas's insult.

---

89. Aristotle *Rhet.* 1378[b]29f., Dem. xxi 74. The verb which denotes formal deprivation of citizen rights is *atīmoun*, but the abstract noun *atīmiā* corresponds both to *atīmazein* and to *atīmoun*.

In the old Norse epics the allegation 'X uses Y as his wife' is an intolerable insult to Y but casts no adverse reflection on the morals of X.[90]

Anthropological data indicate that human societies at many times and in many regions have subjected strangers, newcomers and trespassers to homosexual anal violation as a way of reminding them of their subordinate status.[91] The Greek god Priapos, as guardian of orchards and gardens, was represented as having a massive penis in a state of readiness to penetrate a thief of either sex.[92] In some primate species watchful males react by penile erection to a threatened encroachment on the boundaries of their community;[93] and some types of boundary-marker – with which we should include the ithyphallic herm which normally stood at an Athenian front door – suggest that this behavioural trait extends to the human species also.[94] Among some animal species, again, rank among the males of a community is regularly expressed by a subordinate's presentation of his buttocks to a dominant male (whose mounting, however, is perfunctory and formalised).[95] Vulgar idiom in many languages uses 'buggered' or 'fucked' in the sense 'defeated', 'worsted',[96] and one Attic red-figure vase (R1155) is a pictorial treatment of this notion.[97] A man in Persian costume, informing us, 'I am Eurymedon. I stand bent over', suits his posture to his words, while a Greek, half-erect penis in hand, strides towards him with an arresting gesture. This expresses the exultation of the 'manly' Athenians at their victory over the 'womanish' Persians at the river Eurymedon in the early 460s; it proclaims, 'We've buggered the Persians!'

The imposition of a woman's role on a subordinate by a dominant male underlies a curious Athenian treatment of adulterers. An adulterer caught in the act could be killed by the offended husband or guardian of the woman, but as an alternative he could be subjected to

90. Cf. Vanggaard 76-81.

91. Cf. Fehling 18-27, Vanggaard 101-12. Karlen 414 observes that humans, unlike many animal species which have ritualised homosexual 'submission', can *complete* a genital act 'in expressing a power relationship'. John Boorman's film *Deliverance* makes striking use of this theme in depicting the maltreatment of urban 'trespassers' by rustic hunters.

92. Cf. Herter (1932) 209-221, Fehling 7-14, 18-20.

93. Cf. Fehling 8-11. I have myself seen this reaction in angry or apprehensive captive apes.

94. Cf. Fehling 7f.

95. Cf. D.J. West 116, Vanggaard 71-5. The eland, however, reverses the usual process; the subordinate male mounts the dominant at the end of a tussle (Moss 188).

96. E.g. Italian *inculato* (~ *culo*, 'arse'), 'defeated', is applied to a football team.

97. Cf. Schauenburg (1975) 97-122; Fehling 103f.

painful indignities, his pubic hair being burnt off and a large radish being forced up his anus (Ar. *Clouds* 1083f.; cf. Lucian *Peregrinus* 9). Since women commonly reduced their pubic hair by singeing,[98] the punishment of an adulterer symbolised his transformation into a woman and subordinated him lastingly, in the eyes of society, to the man whom he had wronged, for whose penis the radish was a substitute.[99] A similar notion, transformed into more decorous terms, underlies a Corinthian vase-painting (C62) in which Tydeus has caught his wife Ismene in bed with Periklymenos; he stabs her to death, while Periklymenos flees; in accordance with normal convention, Tydeus is painted black and Ismene white, but in this instance Periklymenos, the worsted adulterer running naked from the fierce armed husband, is also painted white.

A long and discursive exploration of the issues raised by Aiskhines' prosecution of Timarkhos has revealed an antithesis between two groups of motifs: on the one hand, acceptance of payment, readiness – even appetite – for homosexual submission, adoption of a bent or lowered position, reception of another man's penis in the anus or mouth; on the other hand, refusal of payment, obdurate postponement of any bodily contact until the potential partner has proved his worth, abstention from any sensual enjoyment of such contact, insistence on an upright position, avoidance of meeting the partner's eye during consummation, denial of true penetration. In Greek eyes (and whether they saw straight or crooked, each of us must decide for himself) this was the antithesis between the abandonment or the maintenance of masculinity; it is not without significance that the erastes, in the importunity of courtship, touches the genitals of the eromenos, not the buttocks or anus.[100] Since the role of a prostitute entailed permanent debarment from the exercise of a citizen's rights, and the role of an eromenos observing the ritual and convention of legitimate homosexual eros entailed no such debarment, one might have expected not only that the difference between these roles would be precisely defined by law but also that any allegation of prostitution should be demonstrable or refutable in a court of law no less clearly than an allegation of embezzlement or fraud. Yet a homosexual

---

98. Depicted in R476; cf. Ar. *Eccl.* 12f. and Ussher's note ad loc.

99. Cf. Devereux (1970) 20, (1973) esp. 181, 193.

100. B60 is an exception, but the youth there is about to penetrate a woman, and his genitals are not accessible to the man who touches him. In B258 the youth touching his own buttocks (invitingly, insultingly, or accidentally?) has been rejected in favour of a conventional eromenos. In R189* and R255 we see the crude horseplay of drunken and high-spirited youths; the humorous character of the latter is quite obvious.

relationship between a given pair of males, whatever they did together and however squalidly commercial the basis of the relationship, was protected against hostile allegation by privacy, discretion and reticence,[101] while at the same time, however ritualised and restrained and sentimental, it was exceedingly vulnerable to malicious gossip. What, after all, is prostitution? When monetary payment is made and the conditions stipulated, there is no doubt about it; but what about a handsome present which one could not otherwise afford (cf. p. 92),[102] or free coaching in throwing the javelin, or a word in the ear of an influential person – or any gift or service which we habitually render to those whom we love, like, admire, pity or wish to encourage, without thought of sexual pleasure? It is not for nothing that Aiskhines attaches such importance, in building up his case against Timarkhos, to the power of rumour and gossip. If an Athenian youth became aware that he was commonly regarded as 'available' for payment, prudence would dissuade him from any persistent attempt to exercise the rights for which public opinion considered him ineligible. A very fat youth might equally seek to avoid situations in which he could be publicly ridiculed and vilified as unworthy to address citizens whose bodily condition made them more admirable objects and more efficient defenders of the community on the battlefield. A youth of 'easy virtue', ready to live off men who were attracted by his good looks, would have less hesitation over embarking on a political career if he had plenty of friends who laughed off or brushed aside the allegations made by his enemies. Such a youth took a calculated risk; how it turned out depended on the balance of forces on political issues which he could not in his youth foresee, and in the case of Timarkhos it turned out badly.

People turn to prostitution for many reasons, but sometimes they turn to it because otherwise they, or others dependent on them, would starve. An aristocratic boy who yielded coyly to the flattery of an erastes was under no such compulsion. Why then did public opinion deal so harshly with the one and so tolerantly with the other? Partly, perhaps, because public opinion was the opinion of adult males who in their younger days had yielded to erastai and would have been very

---

101. Plu. *Dial.* 768f tells a story about a sixth-century tyrant, Periandros of Ambrakia: Periandros asked his eromenos, 'Aren't you pregnant yet?', and paid a heavy penalty for this gaffe, for the eromenos killed him. We do not know where this story came from, nor whether it represented the jocular question as put in private or in front of other people (cf. p. 159 on Xen. *Mem* i 2. 29ff.), but it implies that the eromenos was prepared to play a female role so long as no one called it female.

102. Kallimakhos 7 and Dioskorides 13 lament the rapacity of their eromenoi.

indignant indeed if anyone had likened them to prostitutes. The principal reason, however, is that the evaluative judgments implicit in Greek law and openly expressed by individual writers and speakers often took little note of the extent to which a morally good disposition or intention is warped or frustrated by circumstances outside one's own control; they were more concerned with the human being as a good or bad object, an efficient or defective working part of the communal mechanism.[103] Conservative sentiment treated a poor man as a bad man because he is prevented by poverty from serving the community as cavalryman or heavy infantryman and from enriching the public festivals (and so conciliating the gods) by lavish expenditure on a chorus's costumes, handsome dedications in sanctuaries, and the like. Equally, he is prevented from acquiring athletic and musical skills; prevented, that is to say, from being and doing what he, and anyone else, would like to be and do.[104] This evaluation, of much the same kind as we apply to horses, dogs, tools or bushes, cannot be affected by any statement whatsoever about the reasons for poverty. Refusal to admit the validity of such evaluation is a cause of infinite confusion in our own moral thinking, and refusal to admit the simultaneous validity of quite different kinds of evaluation was a sorry weakness in the moral thinking of the Greeks. Plato represents Kritias (a man untouched by democratic sentiment) as enlarging on the difference between *ergazesthai*, 'make (by working at...)' and *poiein*, 'make', 'create' (*Chrm.* 163b):

> I understood (*sc.* the difference) from Hesiod, who said that no work (*ergon*) was (*sc.* a matter for) reproach. Do you imagine that if he meant by 'works' the sort of thing you were talking about just now (*sc.* the work of craftsmen and tradesmen) ... he would have said that there was no reproach in being a shoemaker or selling salt fish or sitting in a room?

'Sitting in a room' (*oikēma*)' means 'plying one's trade as a prostitute in a brothel', as is clear from Aiskhines i 74, 'consider those who sit in the *oikēmata*, openly carrying on this practice', and from several other passages referring to heterosexual or homosexual prostitutes. No speaker in court, addressing a democratic jury, would have ventured to put shoemakers in the same category as male prostitutes,[105] but the

103. Cf. *GPM* 144-60, 296-8.

104. Cf. *GPM* 109-12, 114-16.

105. In Ar. *Eccl.* 432 that element in the assembly which was constituted by the urban poor is called (*lit.*) 'the shoemakerish majority', i.e. 'all those shoemakers and the like'.

embarrassment of a certain Euxitheos (Dem. lvii 31-5) in dealing with the 'charge' that he and his mother had been ribbon-sellers is an index of the extent to which the Athenian citizen-body as a whole, accustomed to considering themselves an élite *vis-à-vis* slaves and resident or visiting foreigners, tended to adopt the values of those whose wealth and leisure were well above the average.[106] Compare Anakreon fr. 388.4f. on association with 'bread-women and people who're ready to prostitute themselves', and Theophrastos *Characters* 6.5, 'ready to keep an inn, or run a brothel, or collect taxes ...'.

Exclusion of the once-prostituted male from the full exercise of a citizen's rights could be rationalised in either of two ways: on the one hand, he had revealed by his actions his true nature, accepting a position of inferiority; and on the other hand, whatever his original nature, his moral capacity and orientation were determined thereafter by his prostitution. On the whole the Greeks attached more importance to the effect of practice and habituation than to genetically determined qualities and dispositions,[107] and were not disposed to vacillate in their beliefs about the causal relation between habituation and character in the light of evidence bearing upon the antecedent causes of the habituation itself. Hence, as we have seen (p. 29), an Athenian boy who was forced into prostitution by fraud or abuse of authority on the part of his father was deprived of rights in just the same way as an Athenian youth who had chosen, perhaps in defiance of his father, to submit to another man in return for a stipulated sum.

106. Cf. *GPM* 34-45.
107. Cf. *GPM* 88-95.

III

Special Aspects and
Developments

A. Publicity

Two passages of Aristophanes introduce us to a phenomenon of Greek life which expressed and sustained the homosexual ethos. In the first (*Ach.* 142-4) an Athenian envoy who has returned from a visit to Sitalkes, a Thracian king, says:

> And he was quite extraordinarily pro-Athenian (*philathēnaios*), and a true erastes of you (*sc.* the Athenian people), to such an extent that he actually wrote on the walls, '*Athēnaioi kaloi*'.

In the second passage (*Wasps* 97-9) a slave from the household of Philokleon describes the old man's mania for serving on juries:

> And if he's seen Demos anywhere, the son of Pyrilampes, written on a door (*sc.* as being) *kalos* (*i.e.* ' ... "*Dēmos kalos*" written on a door') he goes and writes beside it '*kēmos kalos*'.

Demos, son of Pyrilampes, was outstandingly good-looking (Pl. *Grg.* 481de, where Kallikles is treated as being in love with him), and it would seem from the passage of *Wasps* that in the late 420s anonymous graffiti acclaimed him for his looks (Philokleon's *kēmos* is the funnel of the voting-urn used in a lawcourt). The passage of *Acharnians* expresses the passion of Sitalkes for the Athenians by imagining the king as playing the part of an erastes who writes on walls the name of his eromenos followed by '(*sc.* is) beautiful'.

Several references to this practice are made in Hellenistic epigrams, notably Aratos 1:

> Philokles the Argive is beautiful at Argos, and the stelai[1] of Corinth and

1. Stone slabs, which were used for tombstones or commemorative or informative documents of any kind, national, local or private.

the tombs of the Megarians cry the same things; and he is written as far as the Baths of Amphiaraos as (*sc.* being) beautiful.

Anon. *HE* 27.1-4:

> I said, and I said again, 'Beautiful, beautiful!' Yes, I will go on saying how beautiful Dositheos is, how lovely to look at. I did not engrave this utterance on oak or pine or wall, but my eros is contained within my heart.

Cf. Meleagros 94.1, 'No longer is Theron written by me (*sc.* as being) beautiful', i.e. 'No longer do I write "Theron is beautiful"'. Anon. 27 suggests that a graffito[2] of this type is simply the transformation into written form of an admiring exclamation, such as Pindar reproduces in *Pythian Odes* 2.72, 'Beautiful is a monkey among children, always beautiful'; we can almost hear them gooing over a furry animal and saying, 'Aaaah! Isn't he *lovely?*' A clear example in a sexual context is [Theokritos] 8.73f.:

> Yesterday a girl with brows that meet saw me from her cave as I drove my heifers past and said that I was beautiful, beautiful; but I did not say a word, not even a push-off...[3]

The despairing erastes seems to have used 'X is beautiful' as a means of declaring 'I am in love with X'; cf. Kallimakhos 2.5f.:

> Lysanias, you are – yes! – beautiful, beautiful! But before it's properly out of my mouth, an echo says, 'He's someone else's'.[4]

Cf. id. 5.3, 'The boy's beautiful, marvellously beautiful!' (addressed, it seems, to the water which the poet is not putting into the wine in which he drinks the boy's health); Anon. *HE* 18.1, 'You mothers of Persians have borne beautiful, beautiful children'.

The earliest of these epigrams is a century and a half later than Aristophanes' *Acharnians* and *Wasps*; there is no better illustration of the continuity of Greek culture than the fact that actual examples of *kalos*-graffiti take us back to a starting-point a century before

---

2. Most surviving Greek graffiti are incised, not painted (cf. p. 9, n. 13), though there are sometimes traces of paint in the incision.

3. *Lit.*, 'I did not answer even the bitter utterance', i.e. not even that one of the two alternative answers, favourable or unfavourable, which is unfavourable.

4. *Allos ekhei*, 'another has (*sc.* him)' echoes (after a fashion) *naikhi kalos kalos naikhi* (etc.)

Aristophanes and lead us down towards and into his time: *IG* i² 925 'Lysias is beautiful' and 926 'Beautiful is Arkhias', both from the Acropolis at Athens; 923 '...]oos is beautiful to look at and delightful to speak to' (the inscriber was barely literate, to judge from his spelling, but capable of composing a respectable verse); *IG* xii.2.268 (Mytilene) 'Phaestas (*sic*) is beautiful, says Ogesthenes, who wrote (*sc.* this)', an interesting indication that the admirer was not always anonymous; *IG* xii.5.567 (Keos) 'Boethos the Athenian is beautiful'.

A fragment of Kallimakhos (*HE* 64) would suffice to show, even if we had no inscribed examples, that the expression of sentiment in graffiti was not always erotic:

> Momos ('Criticism') himself wrote on walls:
>   'Kronos is *sophos*' (i.e. ' ... knows all the answers').[5]

Archaic graffiti on rocks on the island of Thera, some of which may well be the best part of four centuries earlier than Kallimakhos, include the following: *IG* xii. 3.540(I) 'Lakydidas is good (*agathos*)'; 545 (1415) 'Korax (?) is good, the (*sc.* son) of]ronos'; 541 (and p. 308) '...]x is best (*aristos*)'; 547 'Pykimedes is best of the family of Skamotas'; 1414 'Kudros is best'; 540 (III) 'Krimon is foremost ...' (the words which follow are not intelligible); 581 (1437) 'Ainesis is sturdy (*thaleros*), Meniadas is first'; 540 (II) 'Eumelos is the best dancer'; 543 (and p. 308) 'Barbax is a good dancer and [...'; 546 'Helekrates is a good [dancer (?)'. It would be surprising if all surviving graffiti were complimentary, and some of them are not, e.g. *IG* i² 921 (Athens) 'Arisemos is beautiful, Polytime is a whore (*laikastria*)'.[6] Favoured derogatory words at Athens are *katapūgōn* and its feminine *katapūgaina*; the original denotation of. *katapūgōn* was probably 'male who submits to anal penetration', and the feminine was formed on the analogy of such pairs as *therapōn/therapaina*, 'servant' and *leōn/leaina*, 'lion'/'lioness', but at least by Aristophanes' time and perhaps by a much earlier date the words had no more specific a denotation than colloquial English 'bugger', 'Louse' and 'bitch' are perhaps the best current equivalents.[7] Words incised on

---

5. Gow and Page and Pfeiffer (fr. 393) *ad loc.* seem to regard 'Kronos *sophos*' as a conceit modelled on '... *kalos*', as if the erotic graffito were the only type in actual use. For acclamatory *sophos* cf. the cries of encouragement to hounds, '*kalōs, sophōs*', i.e. 'Nice work!' in [Xen.] *Cynegeticus* 6.17.

6. The word occurs also in Attic comedy; it is the feminine agent-noun of *laikazein*, a vulgar word for sexual intercourse.

7. Cf. p.142 on attitudes in comedy. The earliest use of *katapūgōn* so far known is on an eighth-century sherd (Blagen 10 f.; cf. Jeffery 69). I am not sure that Fraenkel 44f.

broken fragments of pots at Athens inform us: *SEG* xiii 32 'Anthyle is a bitch'; *ibid.* 'Sikela is a bitch'; R994 'Pythodoros is beautiful. Alkaios is a louse in the opinion of Melis(?)'; *SEG* xxi 215 'Sosias is a louse, says Euphronios, who wrote (*sc.* this)'.[8] From the island of Tenos comes *SEG* xv 523 'Pyrrhies (*sc.* son) of Akestor is *oipholēs*' (probably 'sex-mad'),[9] 'Thressa is a louse'.[10]

It is against this background that we must consider a phenomenon which has naturally played an important part in the study of the Greek homosexual ethos by modern scholars, although (like vase-painting in general) not mentioned by ancient writers: the many hundreds of vase-inscriptions which acclaim the beauty either of a named person or of an unnamed boy. These inscriptions are not graffiti, but were painted on the vessel before firing;[11] they were therefore conceived by the painter as an ingredient of his design, and one would suppose *prima facie* that any given inscription of this genre expressed the sentiment of the artist, or of the customer (who could, of course, commission a painted vase just as easily as a dead man's family could commission an epitaph),[12] or of the public in general at the time when the vessel was made.

When a person is named in the inscription, his name is preceded or followed by *kalos*, '(*sc.* is) beautiful', e.g. 'Nikon is beautiful', 'Beautiful is Nikosthenes'. The bare statement may be extended in various ways, e.g.: R78 'the boy Leagros is beautiful'; R204 'Epidromos is beautiful, yes!' (cf. R50, R1015); B94 'Theognis is beautiful, by Zeus!'; B422 'Sostratos is extremely beautiful'; B410 'Andrias is most beautiful (*sc.* of all)'; R299 'Khairas (*sic*) is beautiful, beautiful' (cf. p. 112).[13] More rarely the person praised is a woman, e.g.

---

is right in regarding *-aina* as having a strongly derogatory colouring; in Ar. *Clouds* 660-9 Socrates tells Strepsiades that he ought to say *alektruaina* for 'hen', reserving *alektruōn* for 'cock'.

8. Cf. *ARV* 1601, Lang nos. 6, 20.

9. On *oiphein*, 'copulate (with ...)', cf. p. 123; *oipholēs* occurs also in *IG* xii 5.97 (Naxos). *Mainolēs*, 'crazy', may have served as a model.

10. The inscription has THRESA; 'Threissa' in Attic is a common female slave-name ('Thracian woman'). The form *katapūgōn* is unobjectionable here, since *katapugaina* was probably an Attic invention which had a limited life.

11. It was also possible to incise an inscription on a vase after firing (or after many years of use in different hands and different places), as on anything. 'Neokleides is beautiful' (B418) is an example. Immerwahr describes a terracotta ball on which 'I belong to Myrrhine' was painted ('Myrrhine' is a woman's name) and 'the boy is beautiful' subsequently added.

12. Webster 42-62 explores the hypothesis of special commissions.

13. Talcott 350 cites a complicated graffito written on a grid-pattern on the foot of a vessel (Agora P5164; cf. *ARV* 1611): 'Gods. Therikles is beautiful. Gods. P[ ]xonos

B222 'Sime is beautiful'; since the feminine of *kalos* is *kalē*, and there is hardly ever room for doubt whether a proper name in Greek is male or female, acclamations of male beauty can be clearly separated from those of female beauty. The great preponderance of male names accords with the preponderance of male figures, and with the fact that a male of citizen family could go freely about the city and compete in athletic or choral contests, whereas a female of citizen family was not on public view to a comparable extent. Among the individuals named as 'beautiful' in these inscriptions are some know to us from other sources, e.g. R997 'Euaion (*sc.* son) of Aiskhylos'; 'Euaion', according to a variant reading in the Suda (*αι* 357), was the name of the second son of Aiskhylos to the tragic poet. To deny that many, perhaps the great majority, of these inscriptions express admiration for the beauty of actual persons would be perverse; to assert that each of them declares the desire of the artist or his customer for homosexual relations with the person named would be extremely difficult to reconcile with the data as a whole, and we may find ourselves compelled to admit that the motivation of identical utterances was extremely variable.

It must first be observed that acclamations of beauty were not the earliest type of vase-inscription, nor were they, at any period, the only type. Before the end of the seventh century B.C. Corinthian and Attic vase-painters elucidated the mythological scenes which they portrayed by adding names, e.g. 'Herakles', 'Nessos', and sometimes in the sixth century this practice was extended by the naming of objects, e.g. 'lyre', 'lizard'. The filling of the blank spaces between figures by means of rosettes, lozenges, patterned diamonds, and the like had been a general characteristic of Greek vase-painting at an earlier date, and the writing of names took over this decorative function; it continued long after the Greek vase-painters had shaken off their *horror vacui* (small, neat, well-spaced letters characterise vase-inscriptions of the late sixth and early fifth centuries), but the fact that some inscriptions (e.g. B51*) are senseless sequences of letters reminds us that some vase-painters, at any rate, regarded lettering as an ingredient of composition and not as a means of communication. Potters' and painters' 'signatures' begin about 575 B.C.; a certain Sophilos provides us with the earliest surviving example, 'Sophilos painted me' (B6), and he labels his picture 'The (*sc.* funeral-) games of

---

is beautiful. Timoxenos is beautiful. Kharmides is beautiful.' The heading 'gods' occurs sometimes on state decrees; it is a verbal obeisance, the equivalent of prayer and sacrifice before the beginning of an undertaking, and does not mean that what follows is a list of gods or godlike persons.

Patroklos'. The vessel itself is, as it were, the speaker (as a tombstone may be inscribed 'I am the tomb of ... ' or a statue ' ... dedicated me'). Other utterances by vessels are: B109 'I belong to Taleides'; B454 'Greetings! Buy me!'; R90 'Drink me! I am capacious' (*lit.*, 'I have my mouth open'); R1039 'Invite me, so that you'll drink'.[14] The famous boast of Euthymides (R52), 'As never Euphronios', i.e. 'Euphronios never made one so good!' could be regarded as a proclamation by the vessel itself. A further category of vase-inscriptions consists of words which we have to imagine as spoken by the characters portrayed, e.g.: R463 'Stop it!' (cf. p. 6); R577* (heterosexual copulation) 'Keep still!'; R825 (a singer) 'For you and me ...'[15]

Since 'Achilles' written against a figure communicates 'This figure is a representation of Achilles', we have to consider the possibility of portraiture in vase-painting; not portraiture in the proper sense, for each painter adopted a standard face and figure (cf. p. 71), but in the sense that the attachment of a name to the painting of a youth could communicate 'This is the most beautiful youth I can portray, and ... is as beautiful as that!' The labelling of youths at a symposium in R904 as 'Euaion', 'Euainetos' and 'Kallias', all of whom occur in other vase-inscriptions as subjects of the predicate 'is beautiful', suggests (despite the late date of the vessel, *c.* 440 B.C.) that the hypothesis of idealised portraiture as an explanation of many *kalos*-inscriptions is at least worth exploring. It is not difficult to collect many plausible examples, e.g.: B218 (bride and groom in chariot) 'Lysippides is beautiful, Rhodon is beautiful'; B222 (women at a fountain) 'Sime is beautiful'; B434 (women at a fountain) 'Niko, Kallo, Rhodopis, yes, Myrte (?) is beautiful'; R78 (youthful wrestlers) 'The boy is beautiful, Leagros';[16] R90 (a boy athlete being crowned as victorious) 'Epainetos is beautiful'; R164 (youths) 'The boy is extremely extremely, Le[agros (?)' (*karta karta* is presumably a slip for *karta kalos*); R458* (a pin-up youth dressing) 'Aristarkhos is beautiful'; R514 (symposia) 'Diphilos is beautiful, Nikophile is beautiful' and 'Philon is beautiful';

---

14. B646 'Buy me and *euepolesei*' (Beazley [*AJA* 1950] 315) may be ' ... *eu e<m>-polesei<s>*', i.e. ' ... you'll be getting a good bargain' or '... you'll be doing well' (cf. LSJ); on any interpretation, there is a switch from the second person plural (in 'buy') to a singular.

15. *Soi kai emoi* happens to be the beginning of Mimnermos fr. 8.2 and of Theognis 1058; cf. R1053 (p. 10). In R125 *hipparkhokal* may be the opening words of a verse about someone called Hipparkhos, a well-attested *kalos*-name (*ARV* 1584). Even utterances intended as parts of the picture could be incised later; Beazley (*AJA* 1927) 348 cites a graffito *kuuu* beside the painted figure of an owl.

16. In Greek the two elements of the subject are commonly separated by the verb, giving the order S_1 V S_2. So constantly name$_1$ – verb – (*sc.* son) of name$_2$.

R569 (a woman embraces a youth enticingly) 'Hiketes is beautiful' (it is characteristic of the genre that in a scene of heterosexual love it should be a male whose beauty is acclaimed); R628 (men and youths courting women) 'Antiphanes is most beautiful' and 'Nauklea is beautiful'; R637* (men and youths courting boys) 'Hippodamas is beautiful'; R918 (a naked woman) 'Hediste is beautiful'; R1019 (a youth, a woman and a slave-girl) 'Timodemos is beautiful' and 'The bride is beautiful'; R1031 (a youth kneeling on one knee) 'Leagros is beautiful'.

It is also easy to make a long list of examples to which the hypothesis of idealised portraiture cannot apply because there is no one in the picture to whom the acclamation can refer: B94 (no picture) 'Theognis is beautiful, by Zeus!'; B202 (Herakles and a chariot) 'Mnesila is beautiful'; B214 (Herakles and Triton, horsemen and youths, a chariot fight) 'Mnesila is beautiful, Khoiros is beautiful' (there is no female figure to which the name Mnesila can refer, and although Khoiros could conceivably be one of the youths we should remember that *khoiros* is also a slang word for 'vulva');[17] B318 (a vine) 'Xenodoke [...] is beautiful'; B410 (a siren) 'Andrias is most beautiful'; B422 (Dionysos and satyrs) 'Sostratos is extremely beautiful'; R35 (a man titillating a woman) 'Antias is beautiful' and 'Eualkides is beautiful' (even if the man were one of these two, he could not be both); R70 (two naked women washing) 'Epilyke is beautiful. Helikopa' – so far so good, but then – 'Smikros is beautiful'; R132 (a naked woman with two olisboi) 'Hipparkhos is beautiful'; R438 (a man[18] vomiting) 'Leagros is beautiful'; R476 (a woman singeing her pubic hair) 'Panaitios is beautiful'; R742 (the birth of Erikhthonios) 'Oinanthe is beautiful'; R690 (Herakles and Apollo) 'Alkimakhos is beautiful, (*sc.* son) of Epikhares'; R691 (the North Wind and Oreithyia) 'Kleinias is beautiful'; R779 (the goddess Victory) 'Beautiful is Kharmides'; R887, R890 (a woman and her slave-girl) 'Diphilos is beautiful, (*sc.* son) of Melanopos'; R1023 (a satyr and a wineskin) 'Hiketes is beautiful'.

In cases of this kind the vessel is a medium carrying a message which does not appear to refer to anything on the vessel itself. Who composes the message, and to whom does he wish to communicate it? One could imagine that the erastes commissioned a vessel which would include an acclamation of his own eromenos, thus declaring his passion to his guests at a symposion; or that he commissioned it in order to give it to his eromenos. Some inscriptions would suit this

17. Cf. *AC* 63-65, Henderson 131f.
18. Klein 77 says 'Jüngling', but his illustration belies this.

hypothesis well, e.g.: B430 (a goddess mounting her chariot) 'Korone is beautiful, I love (*sc.* her)'; B442 (a chariot race) 'Nikon. Mynon. Hiketes seems to me beautiful'; R12 (a young athlete) 'Greetings, boy, you!' and 'Beautiful, yes!'; R369 (youthful dancers) 'Aristeides, you are beautiful' (or *ka*, anyway; the syllable *los* was omitted); R478 (a man and a youth) 'Aisimides seems beautiful to one who understands' (this is the probable interpretation of an oddly spelled word); RL16 (youths with javelins) 'Beautiful, dear' (*philos*; *sc.* 'to me'?) 'is Mikion'; cf. BB60 'Kleuikha is beautiful and dear (*philā*) to him who wrote (*sc.* this)'. The same hypothesis might be invoked to explain the occasional inscription *prosagoreuō*, 'I greet', 'I address', 'I accost', e.g. B358 (boxers), though in one case (R173), where a youth is masturbating in front of a herm, the word could as well be his jocular greeting to the ithyphallic statue.[19]

In a very large number of cases the person whose beauty is acclaimed is not named at all, but referred to simply as 'the boy' (or 'the girl'). Some of these inscriptions could be interpreted as referring to an idealised portrait within the picture itself, e.g.: R82* (a youth titillating a woman) and R247 (a youth in bed with a woman) 'the boy is beautiful'; so too R484 and R494* (pin-up youths) and R498* (a loping youth). However, as in the case of the inscriptions which contain names, portraiture of any kind is often ruled out, e.g.: R507 (a balding man copulating with a woman) 'the boy is beautiful'; R619 (a satyr and a maenad) 'the girl is beautiful'; R766 (Dionysos and a maenad) 'the boy is beautiful, the girl is beautiful'.

It may be an error to think of inscriptions of this kind as commissioned by erastai with particular eromenoi in mind. As we have seen, unsigned graffiti on walls, doors and rocks testified to the admiration felt by an unspecified number of unknown admirers for the beauty of preeminent young males, and we should perhaps think of the vase-painters as themselves choosing whether or not to include in a picture an acclamation suggested to them by the sentiment or gossip of the day. B322, of which the subject is an abstract pattern, constructs a conversation: 'Beautiful is Nikolas. Dorotheos is beautiful. I too think he is, yes. And another boy, Memnon, is beautiful. To me too he is beautiful (*sc.* and) dear' – or perhaps '... I too am on good terms with a beautiful (*sc.* boy)'. 'Pantoxena is beautiful at Corinth' on R912 and R913 (the former depicts Dawn and Tithonos, the latter the death of Orpheus) reminds us of the opening words of Aratos 1, 'Philokles the Argive is beautiful at Argos', and may be a statement about a well-known hetaira at Corinth, of a kind

19. For examples of 'I greet' cf. Beazley (1925) 35-7; Klein 63-5.

ἐκ Διὸς ἀρχώμεσθα . Zeus carries off Ganymede. This terracotta statuette, about a metre high, was made about 470 B.C.; the fragments of it have been found at various times during the last hundred years at Olympia.

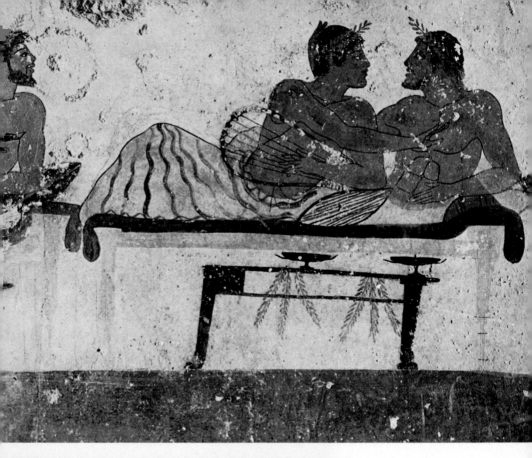

above A man tries to kiss a youth with whom he is sharing a couch at a party. This is part of a painting on the wall of a tomb at Paestum in southern Italy, datable to the early fifth century B.C.

B16 *left* A man courts a youth. The bird held by the youth is a courting gift.

B51 *facing page, above* Men copulate with women. Penetration is clearly anal, not vaginal.

B53 *facing page, below* The odd man out entreats a youth, who rejects him.

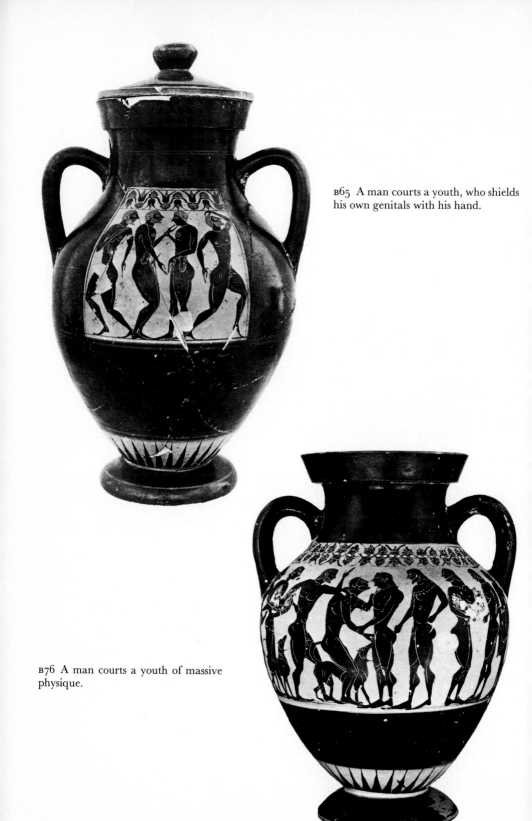

B65 A man courts a youth, who shields his own genitals with his hand.

B76 A man courts a youth of massive physique.

B80 Satyrs with characteristically over-developed genitals, glans exposed.

B114 A man and a youth copulate intercrurally.

B242 A sexually ambiguous abstract motif.

B250 Men court youths, and one pair copulates. The stag and the cockerel are courting-gifts.

B271 A man courts a youth, who holds a garland.

B342 A muscular youth resists a man's attempt to touch his genitals.

B370 Two satyrs, one with an equine penis, and a monumental phallos. Note the eye on the glans.

B462 Wrestlers. Note the funnel-shaped foreskin.

B470 Grape-pickers. Note the prominent genitals of the upper figures.

B486 A man and a youth copulate intercrurally.

B494 A bird suggestive of the phallos-bird (cf. R414).

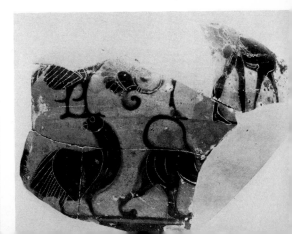

B502 A man courts a youth. For the garlands cf. B271. The dog may be a courting-gift.

B538 A man and a youth are wrapped in one cloak. We are probably meant to think of them as copulating.

B598 A man courts a boy, and a boy responds affectionately to a man's courtship.

B634 The pair on the left is a man and a youth (painted black), copulating intercrurally. Every other pair is a man and a woman.

BB16 A caricature of Zeus with his thunderbolt. The exposure of the glans is humorous.

BB24 *left* A hairy satyr masturbates while pushing a penis-substitute into his own anus.

C19 *above* An abstract motif suggestive of anus or (cf. R55) nipple.

C28 *below left* An abstract motif suggestive simultaneously of buttocks, thighs and female genitals.

C32 *below* An abstract motif suggestive of the female genitals.

CE33 A youth courts a woman, who restrains his hands.

CE34 One woman courts another. For the garlands cf. B271, B502.

R27 A youth embraces a responsive boy.

R55 *facing page* Theseus carries off Korone. Note their facial similarity, Korone's massive thighs, and the sparseness of pubic hair on Theseus.

R59 A youth embraces a responsive boy.

R82 A youth titillates a woman.

R177 Orestes kills Aigisthos. Note the position and shape of the sword.

R189 A youth puts a finger to the anus of another youth, probably as a jocular insult.

R196(a) Youths court boys, whose degree of resistance varies. Note that some are dark-haired and others blond.

R196(b) Youths court women.

R200 Youths at a symposium.

R207 One woman titillates another.

R219 A youth washes.

R223 The youth on the left, perhaps impatient at having to queue, importunes another youth.

R243 A group of youths engages in a complex homosexual activity.

R259 A phallos-horse.

R283 A man embraces a youth at a symposium.

R295 A man at a symposium seizes a fleeting opportunity to touch a boy's genitals.

R303 A youth embraces a girl.

R305 A boy athletic victor.

R313 Young athletes.

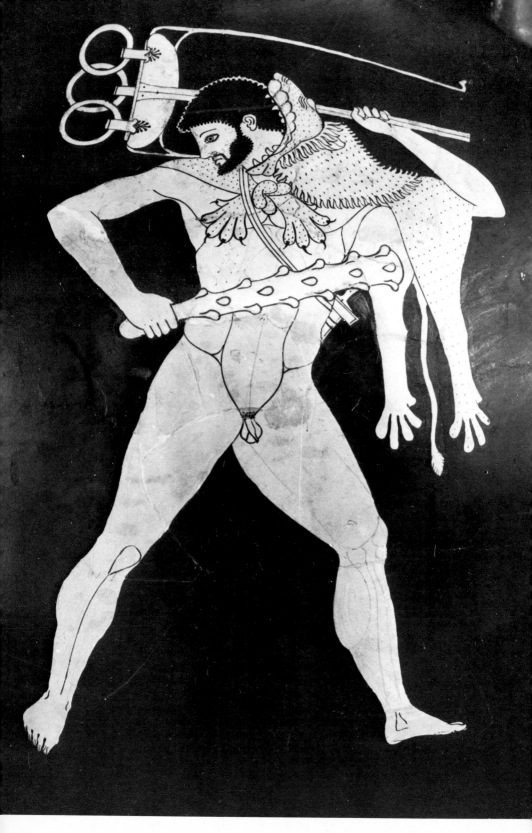

R328 Herakles. Note his musculature and (cf. R699) the smallness of his genitals.

R329 A satyr.

R336 A youth carries a heavy storage-jar.

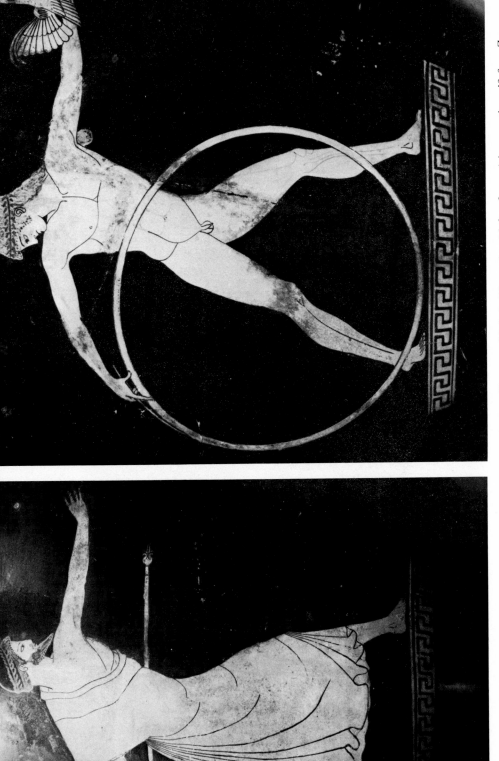

R348 Zeus pursues Ganymede (see Frontispiece). Ganymede is red-haired, and has no pubic hair. The cockerel (cf. B16, B250) is a courting-gift from Zeus.

R373 *above* A youth with a very small penis.

R406 *facing page and right* Poseidon pursues a youth.

R414 A woman carrying a phallos-bird uncovers a container full of phalloi; cf. R1071.

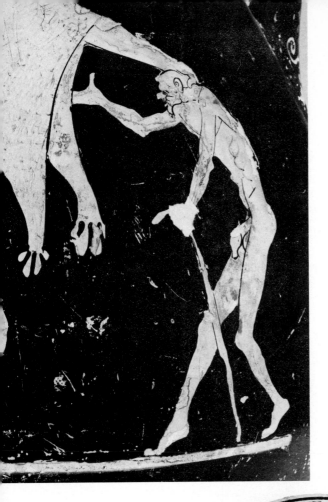

R422 Old Age (subdued by Herakles). His genitals are, by Greek criteria, as ugly as his face.

R454 A youth washes.

R455 A naked man with an unusual amount of body-hair.

R456 A man whose penis is much larger than that of the youth in R458.

R458 A youth dresses.

R462 A standing youth with small genitals and a seated man (vomiting) with larger genitals.

R471 A woman prepares to wash.

R472 A youth carries baskets on a pole.

R494 A youth in a relaxed pose.

R498 A hurrying youth. Note the prominence of his genitals.

R502 A man copulating intercrurally with
a youth. The hare is a courting-gift.

R520 A man and a boy get into position for intercrural copulation.

R543 A man copulates anally with a woman.

R545 The position of the woman suggests (despite the alignment of the man's penis) that portrayal of vaginal copulation is intended.

R547 A boy rejects a youth.

R573 *above* A man and a youth or boy get into position for intercrural copulation.

R603 *above* Zephyros carries off Hyakinthos. The painter has represented the deity's penis as somehow penetrating the clothing of the youth.

R577 *below* A man copulates anally with a woman.

R651 The penis of a boy is handled by an older male.

R659 Orpheus is killed by maenads. Note the facial similarity of male and female.

R682 A man titillates a woman. Note the masculine shape of her hips.

R684 A man courts a youth, who rejects him, brandishing a lyre. Cf. R682.

R699 Herakles overthrows Busiris, king of Egypt. The Egyptians are meticulously portrayed as circumcised. For the smallness of Herakles' penis cf. R328.

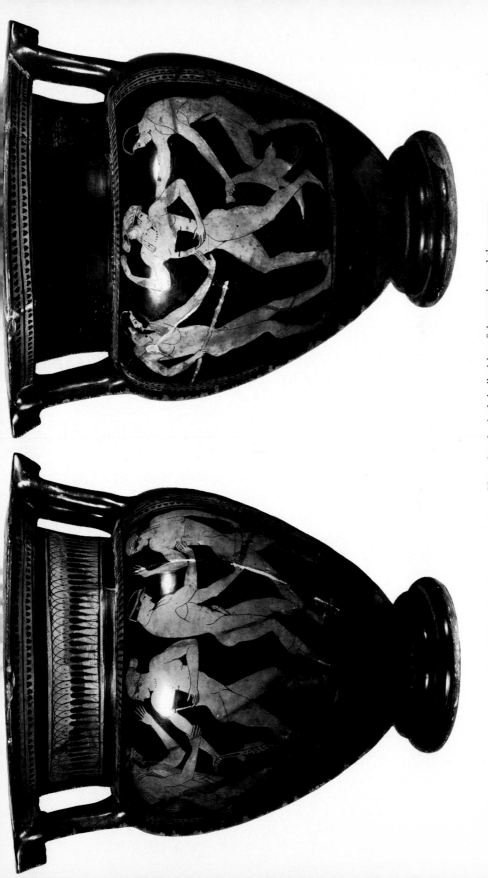

R712 Men and youths accost women. Note the physical similarities of the youths and the women.

R750 A youth and women. Note their facial similarity.

R758 Zeus and Ganymede; cf. R348.

R783 Apollo displays himself to a Muse.

R791 A man offers a cockerel to an unresponsive boy.

R829 Zeus lays hands on a struggling Ganymede.

R833 The same.

R851 A youth entreats an unresponsive boy.

R867 Men entreat a woman.

R934 A man tries to make the acquaintance of a youth during a sacrifice.

R954 A boy prepares to squat on the lap of another for anal copulation.

R958 A youth (on the right) stands in a relaxed pose. Note the female shape of his hips.

R970 A woman prepares to squat on the lap of a youth for copulation.

R1027 A youth dresses.

R1047 A boy washes. Note the prominence of his genitals.

R1071 A woman with a basket full of olisboi or phalloi; cf. R414.

RII27 Satyrs enjoy fellation and anal (or intercrural upside-down?) copulation.

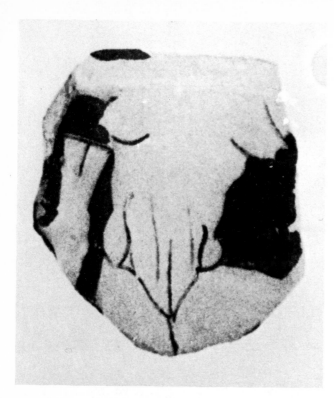

R1135 Female breasts and male hips on the same torso.

RS12 A winged youth of somewhat hermaphrodite appearance.

RS20 The figure on the neck of the vessel is unquestionably hermaphrodite.

which would be perfectly acceptable to the participants in an Athenian symposium even if they had little idea who exactly Pantoxena was. We may compare B326 'Mys is thought beautiful, yes!' and R160 'Philokomos is loved' (*philein*, perhaps referring to his popularity and not to an erotic relationship);[20] cf. also *IG* xii 3.549 (Thera) '...]s, I say, is beautiful [in the eyes of (?)] all (?)'. We may reasonably suspect that 'the boy is beautiful' was freely added to pictures by vase-painters (when it was regarded as something more than a sequence of letters constituting a decorative motif) because an Athenian host would not want his guests to think that he was unsympathetic to the pursuit of boys.

However, no comprehensive explanation will account for all *kalos*-inscriptions, for they do not always refer to sexually attractive humans, or even to humans at all. In a mythological scene, B697, the goddess Aphrodite and the hero Aineias are acclaimed in the '... is beautiful' formula;[21] so too the elderly Kadmos and Harmonia in R922; in R310 'you are beautiful' is painted beside the figures of Ajax and Hektor, and beside Apollo in R311. In B283 two different purposes are served by the inscriptions; the Trojan Paris (recognisable from his Asiatic dress) is labelled 'Paris is beautiful', but on the shoulders of the vessel we come back to earth with 'Teles is beautiful' and 'Nikias is beautiful', perhaps making the point 'the living youths Teles and Nikias are as beautiful as the legendary Paris'.[22] When the beauty of divine and heroic figures can be commemorated in this way, it is understandable that the Athenian Leagros should continue to be acclaimed as 'beautiful' for the best part of half a century;[23] he must have been of stunning beauty in his adolescence, and the vase-painters' continued use of the formula 'Leagros is beautiful' gave him something like proverbial status.

The case of Kadmos and Harmonia reminds us that *kalos* is a very general word indeed, applicable to any living being or manufactured

20. In Pl. *Smp.* 201c Socrates addresses Agathon as *ō philoumene Agathōn*, i.e. '... loved (*sc.* by everyone)'?

21. Cf. Ferri 98-100, Beazley (*AJA* 1941) 595, Schauenburg (1969) 49f.

22. R902 might seem at first sight to come close to evil omen; the legendary Aktaion, being transformed into a deer and torn to pieces by his own dogs, is labelled 'Euaion'. But *IGD* 62, 65, 69 makes a good case for supposing that Aiskhylos's son Euaion acted in tragedies, so that we might expect to find his name in pictures of mythological subjects.

23. Cf. Ferri 105, *ABV* 669, *ARV* 1591-4, Webster 65. Acclamation of Memnon (*ARV* 1599-1601) creates a problem. A handsome boy of that name is acclaimed in B322 (late sixth century), but the Memnon of legend was the handsomest man Odysseus had ever seen (Hom. *Od.* xi 522), and some red-figure acclamations refer to him.

object which is aesthetically attractive, and we have to consider the possibility that in some instances the painter uses it in praise of his own work ('This is a beautiful picture of ...') or to mean 'If you saw in real life the scene which I have portrayed, you would exclaim at the beauty of the persons concerned'. This seems likely in cases such as the following: B358 (boxers on one side, boys on the other) 'two beautiful men boxers' and 'two boy boxers'; R196* (youths, boys and women) 'beautiful', in the appropriate gender, beside nearly every figure. So too R251 (athletes); R778 (Paris's judgment between the goddesses who claimed each to be the most beautiful); R861 (a woman and youths); R926 (a naked woman); R946 (an old man, a youth and two women); R999 (a warrior and an Amazon). R1005, R1006 and R1007 show a male infant, and beside him 'Mikion is beautiful'; since *mīk-* means 'small', it is a very suitable nickname for him, but since 'Mikion' is also the name of a young athlete on RL16 (and cf. *IG* i² 924) we cannot be sure whether the inscription refers to the infant at all. *Kalos* could certainly be used of vessels themselves; explicitly in B650 'beautiful is the (*i.e.* this) jar'; B98 'I am a beautiful cup. Eukhros (*sic*) made me'; BB48 'I am the beautiful cup of the beautiful Gorgis'. Occasionally the word seems to be applied to some object which is part of the scene portrayed: R86 (woman and wineskin) *kalos* on the wineskin and '*kalos*, yes!' round the figure of the woman; R243* (youths in homosexual group-activity) *kala* (neuter plural) on a wineskin on the other side of the vessel – an approving comment on the good things of life, perhaps;[24] R465 *kalos* on an amphora on which a satyr is sitting, but also 'beautiful is the boy'; R474 *Khironeia* (the title of a poem) on a papyrus roll which a youth is reading, and *kalē* on the box from which he has taken it.[25] R1023 *kalos* on a wineskin carried by a satyr, but also 'Hiketes is beautiful'.[26] Since the Attic alphabet did not distinguish between omikron (short *o*) and omega (long *ō*) until the end of the fifth century,[27] the possibility that

24. In R1091 (youths) *kala* (neuter plural) is painted on a wineskin, *kalē* (feminine singular) on a laver. In R208 (youths playing 'kottabos' at a symposium) there is *kalos* on one cup, *kalon* on another; *kalon* is neuter singular, but the fact that vase-painters sometimes write *s* like *n* (e.g. R44, R110, R476, R1000) may perhaps absolve us from attempting a subtle interpretation of the message (let alone]*kalon*[in R551).

25. Cf. Ferri 128f.

26. Vase-inscriptions sometimes 'stray'; for example, 'Beautiful, yes!' beside Herakles and the lion in R239 probably reinforces 'Beautiful is Kharops' on another part of the surface. There is also an observable tendency to put words on vessels, wineskins, shields, etc., portrayed in vase-paintings (for example, Douris in R559 put the words 'O Douris!' on a cup in a youth's hand), and for this reason *kalos* on a wineskin may belong in sense with a *kalos*-inscription elsewhere in the picture.

27. There are sporadic exceptions, e.g. R997. Occasionally omega is written

the letters *KALOS* sometimes mean the adverb *kalōs*, 'well', has to be considered (a self-satisfied comment by the artist on his own work),[28] but it is not demonstrable except when accompanied by a verb, as in R377, 'I pour well', beside the figure of a woman pouring from a jug into a cup.

It has become obvious that there is no single and simple explanation of the *kalos*-inscriptions which will account for all the data; the use of lettering as a decorative motif, the adoption of clichés from male conversation, the acclamation of persons widely-known at any given time for their beauty, and comment on the content or artistic quality of a picture or any part thereof, are all moments in the history of the phenomenon, and every instance has to be considered on its merits. Caprice and arbitrariness on the part of the painter must be allowed to have played some part;[29] so must humour, as when an ugly satyr ('Stusippos' ~ *stūein*, 'erect the penis') is called 'beautiful' (R110) or the lame god Hephaistos (who bitterly contrasts himself with the handsome Ares in Hom. *Od.* viii 308-311; cf. *Il.* i 599f.) is acclaimed as beautiful on a Dionysiac scene (R950).[30] The compliment becomes empty when Socrates in Pl. *Phdr.* 235c refers to 'the beautiful Sappho' – he could not have known whether Sappho had been beautiful or not[31] – and the man who set 'Aphrodite is beautiful' and 'Good Fortune is beautiful' into a mosaic at Olynthos in the fourth century (there is no picture) was using 'beautiful' simply as an ingratiating word. Meleagros 66.5 does much the same in apostrophising 'You beautiful ships'. We would not, in my view, be justified in supposing that a vessel bearing a *kalos*-inscription, whether it names a youth or woman or leaves them nameless, was normally or even commonly a gift from erastes to eromenos or a conventionally recognised form of declaration by the erastes that at the time of purchase he was in love with a specific person. We are, however, justified in treating the quantity of the materials as evidence of Greek

---

consistently instead of omikron, e.g. R690, R691 (reversal of the normal functions of omega and omikron occurs also in some inscriptions of Thasos).

28. Ferri 100f. raises this point; Beazley (*AJA* 1950) 315 considers it in connection with B646, but (in that connection) rejects it for good reason.

29. Cf. Robertson (1972) 182.

30. R1017 acclaims as beautiful someone called 'Psolon'; the name is indecent (cf. p. 129). A fourth-century lamp from Gela (Milne 221) impudently declares itself the property of Pausanias *katapūgotatos*, 'the biggest *katapūgōn* of all'. R1147 substitutes *kakos*, 'cowardly', 'worthless' for *kalos*; cf. Klein 4, 169.

31. The statement of an anonymous biographer (*Oxyrhynchus Papyri* 1800 fr. I col. i 19-25, of Roman date) that she was far from attractive is probably derived from a poem in which she contrasted herself despairingly with someone else or repeated the words of an enemy or rival.

male society's preoccupation with the beauty of boys and youths, and the ubiquity of 'boy' and 'girl' – not 'youth', 'man'[32] or 'woman' – in the formulae reminds us (cf. p. 84) of the characteristic Greek conception of sexuality as a relationship between a senior and a junior partner. The repeated acclamations of named persons and the echo of ancient gossip which comes to our ears when we bring the iconographic and the literary evidence together (p. 8) should, if we reflect a little and use our imagination, tell us what it felt like to be a handsome boy in ancient Athens – or a boy not quite as handsome as the son of his father's enemy, or a boy with a snub nose, knobbly knees and a half-retracted foreskin.

Discretion is a more conspicuous feature of the vase-inscriptions than it may have seemed to be at first sight. The addition of 'Agasikrates is beautiful' to a scene of intercrural copulation in R31 is abnormally tactless in depicting explicitly what someone somewhere would like to do to Agasikrates, and it could even be taken to suggest that Agasikrates is easily caught (a similar scene in R1123 has the inscription 'loving-cup')[33]. B108 'Andokides seems beautiful to Timagoras' and (heterosexual) R426 'Aphrodisia is beautiful, in the opinion of Eukhiros' are acceptable enough compliments, particularly since Timagoras was the potter himself and thus professionally concerned with male beauty. 'Give me that promised between-the-thighs', painted on the bottom of B406,[34] is depersonalised (perhaps a coarse joke) by the fact that three different youths are acclaimed in the inscriptions on the main body of the vessel. RL40 'Gorgias loves Tamynis and Tamynis loves Gorgias' uses *philein*, and without knowing Gorgias and Tamynis no one could know whether their relationship was erotic or not.[35]

The early graffiti on Thera are less reticent; in *IG* xii.3.541 ' ...] is in love with [Ph]anokles' the subject of the verb must have been named. *Ibid.* 537 and 538b (1411) go a stage further; the former says

32. The anonymous boxers of R358 are an apparent exception, but (*lit.*) 'boxers men beautiful' (dual number) is formally distinct from (*lit.*) 'the boy beautiful' (with the definite article).

33. In B220 *philonse*, following 'Beautiful is Antimenes', is interpreted by Beazley (1927) 63f. as 'Philon you –', i.e. subject, object, then a meaningful, insulting silence, as if the verb were too improper to utter. Precisely such an insulting breaking-off occurs in Theokritos 1.105, where Daphnis is taunting Aphrodite with the fact that 'the cowherd' (i.e. Ankhises) copulated with her. However, 'if he loves you' is a possible interpretation of the letters; cf. n. 38 below.

34. Cf. p. 98. *Apodos*, 'give me what you promised' or 'give me back (*sc.* my gifts)' is part of a conversation between a man and a boy in R595.

35. Beazley's scenario (*AJA* 1927 352f.) is unforgettable.

'By (*sc.* Apollo) Delphinios, Krimon here copulated with a boy, brother of Bathykles', and the latter 'Krimon copulated with Amotion here'. The word used is *oiphein*, which is neither as slangy as 'screw' nor as coarse as 'fuck', for it occurs in the laws of the Cretan city of Gortyn ('*oiphein* by force' = 'rape'), but it is a very blunt word for sexual intercourse. The sex of the object, if it was stated at all, is not apparent from the surviving words of *ibid.* 536 'Pheidippidas copulated, Timagoras and Empheres and I copulated [...'. These utterances should not be regarded as solemn declarations of sanctified erotic relationships,[36] but as boasts, effusions and slanders of a kind familiar to us, seven centuries later, from the walls of Pompeii; recalling Athenian graffiti (p. 113), we should not imagine that Krimon, or whoever wrote no. 537, was on very friendly terms with the Bathykles over whose brother he triumphed.[37] A comparable spirit of malice underlies an Athenian graffito (*IG* i² 922) 'I do not *knēn* Lysanias (*sc.* son) of Khairephon'. The inscription is complete, and to whom 'I' refers is unknown; *knēn* is 'scratch', 'grate', 'tickle', and since Socrates in Xen. *Mem.* i 2.30 compares Kritias's homosexual desire for Euthydemos to a pig's desire to scratch itself against a stone[38] the graffito probably means 'I don't let Lysanias use me as he wishes to' – a hard-hearted joke against a lovesick Lysanias?

Exceptionally, we hear there the voice of the eromenos, even if the whole utterance is fictitious; it may be that we hear it also in *IG* i 924:

> Lysitheos says that he loves Mikion more than anyone in the city, for he is brave.

'Love' here is *philein*, certainly a possible word on the lips of an erastes, but also the appropriate word for the affection felt by an admiring eromenos (cf. p. 53); and *andreios*, 'brave', cognate with *anēr*, '(adult) man', suits the senior partner in the relationship rather than the

---

36. They are treated so by Bethe 449f., 452f., followed by Vanggaard 23f., 63f. 'The sacred place and the name of Apollo make it plain that ... we are being told about a sacred act' (Vanggaard) underrates the Greek use of oaths and overrates most people's reverence for sacred places. Cf. Semenov 147f., Marrou 367.

37. Cf. the herdsmen of Theokritos 5, discussed on p.104.

38. In R567, after 'Hermogenes is beautiful', the sequence of letters *eenemeknerine* may be *ēn eme knēi rīnēi*, 'if he'll scratch *me* with (*sc.* his) hard skin'; *rīnē* means 'rasp' or a fish with a very rough skin. Beazley (*AJA* 1960) 219 suggests *ēn eme enkrīnēi*, 'if he'll include *me* (*sc.* among his friends)'; so too Webster 45, but taking 'me' as the vessel and translating 'if he'll choose me'. Another verb, *knizein*, is cognate with *knēn* and overlaps it in denotation; in the sense 'provoke', 'stir up', 'trouble', 'tease' it could describe the action of a boy's beauty upon an erastes, but *knēn* is more appropriate for the action of the boy's body upon the penis of the erastes.

junior. The inscription would be a very striking declaration on the part of an eromenos if we could be sure that it was composed by Lysitheos himself and incised with his knowledge and consent; but of course we cannot be sure of that, nor indeed can be sure that the relationship between Lysitheos and Mikion was erotic rather than (for example) a deep sense of obligation and gratitude in consequence of a battle in which Mikion courageously saved the life of Lysitheos. If that is the explanation of the inscription, it loses its unusual character as an inscribed memorial, readable by passers-by for all time, of a homosexual relationship between two individuals who name themselves. There is no such indiscretion, in respect of the name of the eromenos, in a famous inscription (partly in verse) from late sixth-century Attica (*IG* i² 920):

> Here a man in love with a boy swore an oath to join in strife and woeful war.
>
> I (*sc.* the tombstone) am sacred to Gnathios of Eroiadai, who perished in battle (?).

On the other side someone has inscribed: ...]*thie* (?) *aiei speude*[*is* (?), i.e. 'Gnathios, you are always too hasty' (or '... you always try too hard'). The picture given by the relative or friend of the dead Gnathios who put these high-sounding words on the stone, a picture of a man going off to war to throw away his life or to win a glory which might evoke a response from the unnamed boy, reminds us of the flamboyant Episthenes in Xen. *Anab.* vii 4.7 (p. 51). There could be more to a homosexual relationship than 'scratching'.

B.   Predilections and Fantasies.

We have seen that the vase-painters often represented the erastes as fingering the genitals of the eromenos, and that a passage of Aristophanes makes a clear reference to this act (p. 96). Some other passages of Aristophanes reveal the importance attached by older males to the genitals of their juniors. In the contest between Right and Wrong in *Clouds*, Right laments the passing of the good old days when boys were hardy, disciplined and modest, and (973-8):

> When they were sitting in the trainer's, they had to put one thigh forward in order not to show anything cruel (*apēnes*) to those outside. Then, when a boy got up again, he had to brush the sand together and take care not to leave an imprint of his youth for his erastai. And no boy

in those days would anoint himself with oil below the navel, and so moisture (*drosos*) and down flowered upon his genitals as upon apples.

Apēnēs, an adjective predicated of Eros himself in Theognis 1353, means 'cruel' or 'harsh', and no attempt to translate it as 'indecorous' can be justified by evidence; Right's point is that the sight of the boys' genitals torments the spectators, just as beautiful women are 'pain to the eyes' (Hdt. v 18.4). His next sentence suggests that an erastes might brood longingly over the mark in the sand where the genitals of his eromenos had rested. The implication of the last sentence is disputed,[1] but Right's interest in the appearance of boys' genitals is not disputable. Old Philokleon in *Wasps* 578, listing the enjoyable perquisites of jury service, includes 'looking at the genitals of the boys' whose attainment of the age necessary for registration as full citizens had been questioned and referred to a lawcourt.

It would be surprising if the Greeks had no criteria for the aesthetic‧ judgment of male genitals, and the visual arts show us what these criteria were. In vase-painting, the characteristic penis of a young male (human, heroic or divine) is thin (sometimes notably thinner than a finger) and short (as measured from the base to the end of the glans), terminating in a long pointed foreskin, the axis of the penis and foreskin being almost always straight. The small penis is promised by Right in *Clouds* 1009-14 as one of the desirable results of a good old-fashioned education, together with a good colour, broad shoulders and big buttocks.[2] Examples of a short thin penis may be seen in R467 (youth), R716 (youth and boy), R942 (Eros and youth), R978 (youth), R1091 (youths), R1111 (youth), R1115 (young athlete), R1119 (youth arming); it is longer, but very thin, in (e.g.) B28 (Achilles), R164 (youths), R966 (youth). This small penis is combined as a rule with a scrotum of normal size, and the contrast is sometimes striking; the youth in R373* has a normal scrotum but a minute penis, and the youth's scrotum in R638 is massive. Ganymede in R348* has an unusually small scrotum, but the fact that he is there playing with a hoop suggests that the painter envisages him more as a child than as a youth. The painters do not normally contrast men with immature

1. My interpretation *ad loc.*, that *drosos* is Cowper's secretion, appearing when the boy's penis has been erected by titillation, is far-fetched (I am bound to agree with some reviewers on this), but no other interpretation so far seems to me to pay enough attention to the semantics of *drosos* or to explain why Right regards the beauty of '*drosos* and down' as incompatible with anointing below the navel. On the gulf between reality and the convention (p. 52) that the eromenos is not aroused cf. pp. 103, 204.

2. On big buttocks, which go with big thighs, cf. p. 70.

males by giving larger genitals to men, but persist with the ideal (e.g. R563); even a hero such as Herakles is no exception to this rule; in R328* he has very small genitals, and his large scrotum in RL28 is unlikely, in view of examples given above, to be a deliberate reference to his virility. Even giants (e.g. Antaios [R16] and Tityos [R675]), monsters (e.g. Argos [R367]) and legendary villains (e.g. Prokroustes [R315]) are spared the indignity of caricature in respect of their genitals.

Physical types of *homo sapiens* differ in penile size, as also in the angle of the penis at rest, and at any given period there are likely to be some correlations between geographical area and predominant physical type. Statistics based on sampling in modern Western Europe indicate an average penile length of 9.51 cm (measured to the end of the glans) and an average diameter of 2.53 cm.[3] These dimensions can be expressed as fractions of average stature, thickness of thigh, etc. Several considerations combine to suggest that in reality the Attic penis was not a particularly small fraction of other bodily dimensions. One consideration (by no means cogent physiologically, but artistically interesting) is that the erect penis, as depicted in vase-painting, is of normal size, and if it was exceptionally small when flaccid the extent of enlargement on erection is surprising. When a man or youth is depicted in a squatting position or in movement of such a kind that his genitals are visible below or behind the thigh, the penis is much larger than when a standing or seated figure is depicted; and if the painter adjusted the size of the penis to the position and movement of the person, there is no reason *a priori* to treat one of the two sizes as realistic rather than the other. In caricature and in the representation of satyrs a penis of great size, even of preposterous size, is very common, and it is a reasonable conclusion (though not, I admit, an inescapable conclusion) that if a big penis goes with a hideous face and a small penis with a handsome face, it is the small penis which was admired. The principal consideration, however, is that comparison of vase-painting with sculpture strongly suggests that in portrayal of many bodily parts the painter conventionalised far more than the sculptor; this is apparent in the length of the toes, the often unnatural flexibility of the finger-joints and (on occasion) the massive development of the thighs. Sculpture does not support the hypothesis that the Attic penis was particularly small. It leaves intact the presumption that exaggeration of any bodily feature of young males in vase-painting was exaggeration of what was admired, just as the impossibly long legs of young women in the drawings of modern dress-designers or their immense breasts in some

3. Cf. Dickinson 75, Masters and Johnson 191.

genres of popular art take to a 'logical' conclusion the tendency of men in the twentieth century to admire length of leg and size of breast in women.

A special feature of Greek art is the artists' interest in the foreskin, which the vase-painters, at least, often seem to treat as an entity separate from the penis; in R430, R521 and R585 it has clearly been painted with separate strokes.[4] Care in its portrayal is sometimes at odds with schematic treatment of the rest of the body, as in R4. Commonly it is so long that the end of the glans is hardly more than halfway from the base of the penis to the tip of the foreskin, e.g. R12 (young athlete), R231, R267, R966 (youths), R1067 (running youth). Sometimes it is a tube of constant diameter, sometimes tapered to a fine point (e.g. R1047*), but very often the slight constriction at the tip of the glans is meticulously portrayed; exaggerated, this gives a teat-shaped (e.g. R1027*) or funnel-shaped (e.g. B462*) foreskin.[5] This interest in the foreskin is not peculiarly Attic; in CP4 a centaur has a stocky penis crowned by a straight tubular foreskin almost as long, and other shapes of foreskin appear on CE28 (a splayed spout) and CP12, CP20 (a long tapering penis, the top lip of the foreskin projecting a little further than the bottom). Even when the penis is shown erect there is not, as a rule, any retraction of the foreskin, e.g. R192, R680 (youths); the foreskin on the erect penis of the youth in R970*, a moment before penetration, is very long and sharply pointed. Exceptions occur in scenes of heterosexual fellation (R156 and R223*) and the group-scene R243*; a foreskin is gaping in R518; in R898 the woman's fingers on the penis of the youth may be about to push his foreskin back.

Just as it is possible to infer from the faces of satyrs, ugly old men, barbarian slaves and comic burlesque what was thought beautiful, and what ugly, in respect of hair, eyes, nose and mouth, we can use the same material to distinguish disapproved from approved genitals. The disapproved penis is thick and long, sometimes far exceeding anything to be seen in real life, and tending to a 'club' shape, with a comparatively narrow base and a bulging glans. The contrast between the ugly man of R456* and the youth of R458* is instructive.[6] The

---

4. The pygmy in R752 has a foreskin so long that he could tie a knot in it without discomfort.

5. A satyr in R6 has a foreskin like an elongated lozenge, constricted at each end and bulging in the middle.

6. On a satyr in R329* the line of the corona is apparent on the outside of the penis, whereas it is invisible in the same artist's portrayal of a young athlete R326, despite the great similarity of the figures in all other anatomical features below the neck; it seems, however, to appear in the athlete of R332.

running satyr in B295 has a penis almost as long as his thigh (though by contrast with the club type it tapers gradually from a thick base and ends in a shapeless teat-like foreskin); cf. R446, a satyr whose large club-like penis, with short foreskin, swings as he moves, and R1075, bestial hairy satyrs with very thick penises. In R46 the bulging glans and foreskin of a satyr's erect penis form an 'onion dome'. Italiote fourth-century mythological burlesques represent comic actors wearing artificial genitals. In these cases the penis extends almost to the knee, and tends to be clubbed, e.g. RS141 (Hephaistos), RS147 (an old man) RS151 (Herakles and Iolaos), RS175 (a comic actor). A curl or twist on the foreskin seems sometimes to be treated as an ugly or ridiculous feature, e.g.: R422* (Old Age, hideous and bony, with an immense penis which curves downwards, the spout-like foreskin pointing at the ground); R962 (a satyr with a penis of normal size, but a foreskin curling down like a sharp hook); RS30 (a satyr with an upturned foreskin). Among the naked male figures of C10, who are probably minor supernatural beings, not ordinary men, one has a very large, thick penis with a short open foreskin; behind him is another with a long, pendulous penis of which the glans is completely exposed.

Exposure of the glans is common enough in sixth-century vase-painting when a satyr's penis is erect (a normal condition for satyrs), and almost invariable when he is masturbating; the glans may be painted reddish-purple (e.g. B394), and in frontal view the erect penis may reach as far as the middle of the satyr's chest. It is not always easy to decide at what stage between flaccidity and complete erection a satyr's penis is supposed to be. In B80* two of the satyrs engaged in pressing grapes have erections, and in the other three the penis is pendulous, but in all five the glans is exposed; in CP16, a scene which includes copulation and defecation, a fat hairy satyr has a penis hanging to his knees, again with glans exposed; and in B370* the penis of a dancing satyr, swinging forward, ends in a bifurcated exposed glans adorned with an eye. Red-figure vase-painting is more restrained in the depiction of satyrs' erections, assimilating them to human shapes and sizes,[7] but it was not unwilling to use the exposed glans as an element of coarse humour, as in R1141 (an ugly man defecating and holding his nose). The same feature appears sporadically as an element of caricature in Corinthian vase-painting, e.g.: C44, a comast squatting; C52, a slave working in a mine; C66, a branded and fettered slave sitting on the ground. So too in Boiotian black-figure of the classical period: BB16*, a frantic little pot-bellied

---

7. In R235 the erect penis of the satyr is of unusual type, gradually tapering to a point and undulating.

Zeus, and BB28, grotesque men in frightened poses. In the Corinthian examples the penis is very large, in the Boiotian not so large⸱ but distinctly clubbed.

There seems little doubt that in C52 and C66 the painters' intention was to portray circumcised slaves. Circumcision, practised throughout Egypt and Phoenicia, was familiar to the Greeks as a feature of visitors or slaves from the south-eastern corner of the Mediterranean, and in R699* it is exploited in a scene depicting Herakles' killing of the Egyptian king Busiris; the Egyptians have shaven heads and snub-noses, and the painter has taken care to expose their circumcised penises, the glans spotted, while Herakles' uncircumcised penis is half the width of the Egyptians' (barely, indeed, the size of his little finger). Herodotos expresses aesthetic disapproval[8] of the Egyptian practice (ii 36.3-37.2):

> Other nations leave their genitals as they were at birth, except for those who have learned from Egypt, but the Egyptians circumcise themselves ... And they circumcise their genitals for the sake of cleanliness, choosing to be clean rather than of seemly appearance.[9]

In comedy circumcision is denoted not, as in Herodotos, by the term *peritemnein* ('cut from off', used also of cutting off the ears and other forms of punitive mutilation) but by the adjective *psōlos* or the participle *apepsōlēmenos* ('with glans exposed'). Ar. *Birds* 504-7 puns on the two senses of *psōlos* in a joke about the Phoenicians, and in another passage (*Ach.* 155-61), in defiance of ethnological evidence,[10] he treats outlandish barbarians from Thrace as if they were circumcised:

> HERALD: Forward the Thracians whom Theoros has brought! DIKAIOPOLIS: Good God, what's this? THEOROS: An Odomantian host. DIKAIOPOLIS: What do you mean, 'Odomantians'? What's all this about? Who's peeled the Odomantians' cock? THEOROS: These men, if they're given two drakhmai (*sc.* a day) pay, will carry their arms in triumph over the whole of Boiotia. DIKAIOPOLIS: Two drakhmai – for these *apepsōlēmenoi*?

The context also points to 'circumcised' as the translation of *psōlos* in *Wealth* 265-7:

8. Cf. Hopfner 218-21.

9. *Euprepēs* is sometimes moral (and can mean 'specious', 'plausible') sometimes aesthetic; so of the youthful looking (and effeminate-looking) Agathon in Ar. *Thesm.* 192.

10. Greeks were well acquainted with Thracians, and the vase-painters never show them as circumcised.

He's come back here with an old man who's filthy, hunchbacked, wretched, wrinkled, bald, toothless, and, by God, I think he's *psōlos* too!

When males are represented in positions in which their genitals would in reality be concealed or partially concealed from an observer placed where the painter is, the genitals are forced on our attention by one device or another. The clothing, for example, may be diaphanous, especially if it is the skirt of a tunic, as in R39 (Achilles) – in R555 the cloak of Neoptolemos is diaphanous – or it may be unrealistically disarrayed, as in R23 (Herakles in combat with Geryon) and R699* (Busiris's Egyptians); or elements of profile and frontal view may be uncomfortably combined, as in R521 (a man with a girl-musician). In profile the penis is very often shown as projecting horizontally, even when it is small and certainly not erect, e.g. R667 (Eros), R894, R1027* (youths). If the figure is seated or lying back, the penis is shown pointing upwards, even when the legs are not so portrayed as to suggest that they are pressed together, e.g.: B176, reclining youth; B295, kneeling satyr; R48, seated youths; R136, crouching youths; R169, half-kneeling youth; R879, seated satyr; R1031, half-kneeling youth; RL44, RL56, RS8, RS24, RS44, RS48, RS121, seated – sometimes lolling – youthful deities and heroes. In RL56 and RS121 the penis is given a sharp upwards curl. Patroklos in R39, while his wound is being bound up by Achilles, sits on his right heel in such a way that his genitals rest on the upper surface of his foot; it is as if the painter were under a powerful constraint not to conceal the genitals. R216 is in some ways similar, on a humbler plane: a man shown in the act of climbing a wall, at the moment when his genitals are resting prominently on the top of the wall. Alternatively, when a male is seen in profile squatting, crouching, half-kneeling, jumping or in violent movement, the genitals may be partially visible below the thigh. In portraying such positions and movements the painter commonly makes the genitals wholly visible, and he makes them far larger, in proportion to the other dimensions of the body, than when a similar person is standing, sitting, lying down, walking or fighting. This is understandable in caricature or in the portrayal of satyrs – e.g. B226 (crouching), B310 (bending over), R754 (crouching), R1099 (position of scrotum and penis reversed!),[11] R1103 (headfirst into a jar). But the convention applies also to men and youths, e.g.: (men) B498 (dancing), R140 (bending over); (youths) B470* (sitting), B474 (bending over), R168 (dancing), R169 (half-kneeling), R498* (loping),

11. Cf. Lang no. 14.

R1055 (moving fast). R1047* is a remarkable instance: a youth or boy bends over, and his genitals stream behind him as if they were being torn from their moorings. R462* seems to offer a good contrast between the small penis of a standing figure and the large penis seen below the thigh of a sitting figure, but the issue is complicated by the fact that the former is a sober youth and the latter a vomiting man. In R420 the big blunt penis of Old Age is most unrealistically sticking back between his thighs. There are, of course, some breaches of the convention described: R263, where the genitals of a youth bending over are not visible; R450, youths jumping, with no exaggeration of the size of their genitals; R737, a youth half-kneeling; R770, a boy fleeing from Eros, the swirl of his cloak concealing his genitals; R845, Paris seated, his genitals concealed by clothing.[12]

Satyrs were a godsend to artists who felt impelled to give expression to exuberant penile fantasies (B35, in which a satyr's erect penis is as massive as his arm, is the ultimate exaggeration), and the uninhibited behaviour characteristic of comast-scenes provided other opportunities for celebrating the power of the penis. B678 is a fantasy rooted, I think, in that genre: a musician whose hands are fully occupied with the double pipe has a spontaneous ejaculation, and a bewildered bee dodges the bombardment. Progressive assimilation of satyric to human anatomy in the fifth century reduced the possibilities of fantasy, but left open the depiction of animals copulating (e.g. R871 [donkeys]; cf. B582 [pigs in charge of a woman]), balancing and weight-lifting tricks (e.g. R581, a satyr balancing a cup on his erect penis in a scene of riotous conviviality; cf. R275, a youth in a similar position but with a bowl on his stomach) and scenes of multiple sexual activity such as those to which reference has already been made in other connections. The domain of the penis, however, extended far beyond vase-painting, and provided the painters with themes which contained an element of fantasy even when treated representationally and served as a starting-point for a further stage of fantasy.

The very large, pendulous artificial penis worn by comic actors went out of use at Athens in the course of the fourth century, but it was normal wear on the comic stage in Aristophanes' time and, if the vase-paintings are a reliable guide, in fourth-century Italiote comedy as well. In satyr-plays the penis worn by the members of the chorus was erect, but (to judge from RL13) decorously small by the end of the

12. R62 is interestingly reticent; a youth on a bed, titillating a naked woman, has his cloak wrapped round his legs, and though it is obviously pushed up by an erection his genitals are hidden from us.

fifth century. The 'herm' which stood at almost every Athenian front door consisted of a square-section stone pillar surmounted by a head of Hermes and adorned, halfway down, with genitals, the penis erect (the figure of Priapos [cf. p. 105] was a Hellenistic innovation). Some Greek festivals, including the City Dionysia and the Rural Dionysia in Attica, included a procession carrying a phallos (i.e. a model of the erect penis) in honour of Dionysos and related deities,[13] one of whom, Phales, was the personification of tireless male sexuality (cf. p. 136). The treatment of fixed stones as phalloi is also attested in various localities.[14]

Some vase-paintings can be accepted as illustrations of these phenomena, but with intrusions of the supernatural, e.g.: C4, a phallos-stick wielded by a dancer; CE10, a satyr on the prow of a ship holds a big phallos, while a smaller male figure brandishes two, one projecting forward from his genitals and the other back from his buttocks; C58, a man wears an artificial penis, of great size, erect, strongly curved upwards and ending in a broad rim like a vase; C56, two men either side of a rock which resembles an erect penis, a ridge corresponding to the corona glandis; B370* and R94, phalloi fixed on the ground, the former with two cavorting satyrs and the latter heavily veined in a manner unusual in Greek art (though normal in Japanese erotic prints); B695, giant phalloi supported by a team of men and accompanied by gigantic beings, one certainly a satyr; R607, a fixed phallos, taller than a man, with two women; R695, a naked woman carrying a phallos as long as she is tall. Some of these phalloi (B370*, B695, R695) have a staring eye painted on the glans, and this is sometimes to be seen on an olisbos (R212, R414*); the strong marking of the rolled-back foreskin, in combination with the eye, gives the penis a 'head' and a 'neck', while in other cases (CE10, B695) exaggeration of the upper part of the corona turns the penis into a goad. The strong curve on the artificial organ is C58 is sometimes a feature of the herm as portrayed in vase-painting (e.g. R729, RL72, RS36); occurring also on satyrs (e.g. R317) and humans (R680),[15] it conveys the impression of great tension and has the effect of investing the penis with an impudent, aggressive personality of its own.[16] Hairy

---

13. Cf. Herter (1929) on these beings.

14. Cf. Herter (1938) 1688-1692.

15. On angles of erection and degrees of curvature cf. Dickinson 77f. and figures 105-8, 112-16.

16. To treat the penis as if it were capable of emotion and volition independently of the person of whom it is a part is a common device of pornographic literature; but of course pornography only 'works' – that is to say, succeeds in arousing the reader

centaurs in BB40 create a heraldic pattern with the curving, interlocked erect penises. Whether the vessel with a penis-like spout depicted in R593 (a woman – almost certainly a woman, not a youth – is drinking from it) was an article in common use is not known; in B219 the foot of the cup is in the form of penis and scrotum; C56 is slightly moulded into the form of a squatting man with penis erect (the dancers portrayed either side of the penis remind us of B370* and R607). In general the potters did not often yield to the temptation to make vessels in the form of genitals.[17]

'Surrealist' elements are very rare in Greek art, but an exception is the 'phallos-bird', which has the legs, body and wings of a bird but a neck and head in the form of a curved penis with the foreskin rolled back and an eye on the glans. In R414* a naked woman, uncovering a store of artificial penises, carries a small phallos-bird like a pet in her crooked arm, and in R416 and R1159 a plump little phallos-bird looks up from the ground, the stem of its neck rising from a breast like a scrotum. Much larger members of the species are ridden through the air by women (B386) or satyrs (R442). R259* shows us a horse whose neck turns into a sinuous human penis. A hint of these phallic creatures, discernible in the manner of portraying the neck and head, may be seen in B398 (siren), B570 (siren), B494* (a bird with a very short beak and a staring eye), B658 (a procession of animals), R171 (a hunting-dog with a collar-line), R352 (an eagle on the sceptre of Zeus).[18]

It may be legitimate (or it may not) to detect the artist's preoccupation with the penis at work in the configuration of scenes which have no overt sexual content. If the determinant was sometimes subconscious, it is hard to believe it was always so – as, for example, in R1087, where a tree behind a herm has a great curving branch which replaces the expected penis on the herm, and another branch which stands in the same relation to the tree as a herm's penis to a herm. The following examples have no obvious humorous intention, and *may* reveal unintentionally the 'penile fantasies' of their creators: R177*, Orestes, advancing to kill Aigisthos, holds a broad-bladed, curved,

---

sexually – in so far as it gives substance to ways of thinking and feeling which come easily to us.

17. For exceptions, see Boardman (1976) 288f. and *EG* 70f.; Herter (1938) 1968 describes some examples from the Neolithic period in the Aegean.

18. Here, and in the following paragraph, the reader is warned that by the time I had worked halfway through *CVA* in search of items in any way relevant to Greek homosexuality I was beginning to see penile imagery everywhere. On the possible relation of the phallos-bird to the cockerel and (more persuasively) on the cockerel as a symbol of male sexual aggression, cf. Hoffmann (1974) 204-213.

sharp-pointed sword in a position where it covers his genitals and appears to be projecting from him; R837, a spear, carried pointing half downwards, prolongs the line of a youth's penis, and its blade and blade-socket symbolise the glans and retracted foreskin; R821, a youth holds a long javelin so that it appears to pass through the genitals of another youth; B542, a Scythian with a bow, facing a hoplite, appears at first glance to be holding the hoplite's penis; B588, Iolaos holds his club so that it looks like his own erect penis, and Herakles, fighting the lion, appears to have his scabbard going up his anus (contrast B589); CW8, the shaft of a spear carried by a man arming, seems to penetrate the anus of a man bending over behind him, and in a scene of Theseus killing the Minotaur Theseus's sword prolongs the line of his penis; B39, the spear carried by a man on a boar-hunt goes as far as the buttocks of his companion, then reappears so that its blade is like a formidable penis on the companion, threatening the boar; B562, a man fleeing from a snake holds his stick so that he seems to be both erect and penetrated; R525, a dancing youth so placed over a triangular motif that he seems to be lowering his anus on to a sharp point. The precariousness of inferring subconscious preoccupations from configurations of this kind is obvious enough, and not least because most of the configurations are created by perfectly normal ways of carrying spears and swords and wearing scabbards, but further exploration of the topic might be rewarding.[19]

To say that Greek vase-painting was 'obsessed' with the penis would be to misuse a technical term which has already been devalued sufficiently, but the evidence considered in this section justifies the conclusion that Greek art and cult were extremely interested in the penis. It justifies also consideration of the hypothesis that the Greeks felt, however inarticulately, that the penis was a weapon, but a concealed weapon held in reserve.[20] That a youth or boy should have a straight, pointed penis symbolised his masculine fitness to become a warrior; that it should be small sharpened the contrast between the immature male and the adult male and assimilated this to the contrast between female and male; a small penis (especially if the existence of the corona glandis is not betrayed by any undulation in the surface of the penis) is an index of modesty and subordination, an abjuration of sexual initiative or sexual rivalry,[21] and the painters' adoption of the

19. Cf. Schneider on aspects (not sexual aspects) of the part played by spears on vase-paintings by Exekias.

20. In C62 (cf. p. 106) the foreskin of the black, dominant Tydeus is long and tight, whereas that of the white, defeated Periklymenos is loose and short.

21. The smaller the penis, the greater the drama when it becomes erect and the glans is exposed by spontaneous or manual retraction.

ideal youthful penis as the standard for men, heroes and gods is one item in their general tendency to 'youthen' everyone.[22]

Their interest in the female genitals, on the other hand, is minimal, R565 is unusual in deliberately bringing the vulva into view by putting it abnormally high. It is prominent in B51*, R462* and R1151, but played down in (e.g.) R528 and even in R531, a frontal view of a woman urinating, where a contrast with the treatment of the male genitals in R265 is striking. Better justice is done to the female genitals in the abstract motifs favoured by Corinthian vase-painters for small perfume-vessels, e.g. C22, C24, C32*, C40,[23] whereas a typical Attic decorative motif such as B242* is sexually ambiguous. It may be a mere coincidence that in the classical period Corinthian prostitutes and hetairai enjoyed an international reputation (Pindar fr. 122, cf. Pl. *Rep.* 404d) and 'Corinth' had something of the same connotations for an Athenian as 'Paris' for a nineteenth-century Englishman (cf. Ar. *Wealth* 149-52, fr. 354).

C. Comic Exploitation

Euboulos, a comic poet of the fourth century, said of the Greeks who spent ten long years in capturing Troy (fr. 120):

> No one ever set eyes on a single hetaira; they wanked themselves for ten years. It was a poor sort of campaign: for the capture of one city, they went home with arses much wider than (*sc.* the gates of) the city that they took.

The implication that the male anus serves, *faute de mieux*, like masturbation, when men are kept together without women for a long time is a humorous motif common to most cultures. A sixth-century vase (B53*) makes good use of it in showing three men busy with three women while a fourth man, having no woman, fruitlessly importunes an unfriendly youth. Much more positive attitudes, tolerant of the active homosexual partner and intolerant of the passive, are to be found in Aristophanes and other comic dramatists. A good starting-point is provided by the song with which Dikaiopolis in *Ach.* 263-279

22. The expression is Beazley's (*AJA* 1950 321).
23. C28* suggests the buttocks and thighs of a reclining woman seen (like the right-hand woman of R62) from behind; C19* is more like an anus than anything, but could possibly be considered a formalised nipple. Cf. the so-called 'pomegranate' vases (e.g. C15), which use the motif of the female breast.

addresses the deity in whose honour a phallos is being carried in procession:

> Phales, companion of Dionysos, fellow-reveller, roaming abroad by night, adulterer, *paiderastēs*, after five years I salute you, happy to return to my village, for I've made a truce for myself and I'm rid of troubles and battles and Lamakhos and all that!
> It's far nicer – O Phales, Phales! – to catch the pretty Thracian slave of (*sc.* my neighbour) Strymodoros collecting wood and stealing it from the slopes, and seize her round the waist and throw her down and stone her fruit – O Phales, Phales!

Paiderastiā is treated here as one appetite of the roguish, insatiable god who personifies the penis, together with adultery (illegal, but nice if one can get away with it) and a pounce on a pretty slave-girl caught in a lonely place; and all these ways of behaving belong with drunkenness, revelry and the delights of peace which the war years have restricted. A similar absence of distinction between homosexual and other pleasures is apparent in the words of Wrong, *Clouds* 1071-4:

> Just consider, my young friend, everything that's involved in being 'good' (*sōphronein*), and all the pleasures you're going to miss: boys, women, kottabos-games, good food, drinks, laughs. But what's the point of living, if you're done out of all that?

Wrong is an immoralist, and he goes on (1075-82) to describe in more detail how a man with the gift of the gab can outface even a husband who has caught him in adultery; the difference between him and Dikaiopolis lies not in any significant disagreement on the constituents of the agreeable side of life, but in the fact that he is in opposition to the austere Right over the upbringing of the young, whereas Dikaiopolis is a mature citizen who robustly voices the wish of the audience to forget for a while the valour and toil which confer fame and to have some fun instead. Euelpides and Peisetairos, the two elderly Athenians who in *Birds* have left Athens to seek a more agreeable life elsewhere, think the same. Euelpides, asked by the Hoopoe in what kind of city he would like to live, replies (128-34):

> Where I'd have no bigger troubles than this: a friend coming to my door first thing in the morning and saying, 'I beg you, you and your children have a bath early and come to my house, because I'm holding a wedding-feast. And you *must* accept; otherwise, don't you come round when things are going hard for me!'[1]

---

1. A humorous reversal of: 'I need your help; and if you won't give it now, it will be

Peisetairos caps this (137-42):

> Where the father of a good-looking boy will meet me and go on at me as
> if I'd done him a wrong: 'That was a nice way to treat my son,
> Stilbonides![2] You met him when he'd had a bath, leaving the
> gymnasium, and you didn't kiss him, you didn't say a word to him, you
> didn't pull him close to you, you didn't tickle his balls – and you an old
> friend of the family!'

Philokleon's pleasure in looking at boys' genitals (*Wasps* 578) is one
aspect of his uninhibited pursuit of his own comfort and advantage,
not (by Greek standards) incompatible with his designs on a slave-girl
(1342-81) or his enjoyment when his daughter fishes his jury-pay out
of his mouth with her tongue (608f.). At the end of *Knights*, where
Demos (the personification of the Athenian people) appears in all his
majesty, thanks to the defeat of his 'Paphlagonian slave' (Kleon) by
the Sausage-seller, we find (1384-91):

> SAUSAGE-SELLER: Now that that's settled, here's a folding-stool for
> you, and a boy (he's no eunuch) who'll carry it for you. And if you feel
> like it sometimes, make a folding-stool of him! DEMOS: Oh, joy! Back
> to the good old days! SAUSAGE-SELLER: You'll certainly say so when I
> hand over the Articles of a Thirty-year Peace[3] to you. Come on, now,
> Articles! (*Enter a group of pretty girls*). DEMOS; My God, they're lovely! I
> say – can I slip them a good long armistice?

These passages are not reconcilable with the supposition that
Aristophanes rejected the general Greek response to youthful male
beauty as a morbid or eccentric response deserving censure and
ridicule. They are entirely reconcilable, in the light of the fundamental
contradiction within the Greek homosexual ethos (pp. 82f.), with the
comic poets' invariably unfriendly treatment of males who submit to
the homosexual desires of others. There is no passage of comedy
which demonstrably ridicules or criticises any man or any category of
men for aiming at homosexual copulation with beautiful young males
or for preferring them to women.[4] Passages which have been regarded
as critical are:

---

no use your coming to me for help when you are in need and I am prosperous.'

2. The name of Peisetairos has not been revealed at this stage in the play; the name
'Stilbonides' is meant to suggest brightness (*stilb-*).

3. Literally 'Libations'; a diplomatic treaty was accompanied by the taking of
oaths and the pouring of libations to gods.

4. Henderson 218 lists ten men as 'active pederasts ridiculed by name in comedy'
(actually nine, because his no. 5 and no. 10 are the same person). On his no. 1,

(a) *Clouds* 348-350, on the shapes assumed by clouds:

> If they see a long-haired, wild man, one of the shaggy ones, like the son of Xenophantos, they make fun of his craziness and turn themselves into the shape of centaurs.

This has been discussed (p. 37) in connection with the 'wild men' of Asikhines i 52, and it was argued that the point of 'wild', 'long-haired', 'shaggy' and 'centaur' was not preference for males but headstrong pursuit of any attractive sex-object, male or female.

(b) *Wasps* 1023-8, where the poet boasts of his success and fame:

> And he claims that when he'd got a great name and was honoured among you more than any (*sc.* poet) had ever been, he didn't end up over-confident or get too big for his boots, or go round the wrestling-schools in a party, trying to seduce (*sc.* boys); and if an erastes, on bad terms with his own paidika, came to him (*sc.* the poet) and urged that the boy should be pilloried in a comedy, he's never yet done what he was asked by anyone (*sc.* like that); he kept his integrity, so as not to turn into procuresses the Muses with whom he deals.

Peace 762f. repeats the boast 'or go round ... seduce' in very similar words. The point here is not that trying to seduce boys is to be condemned as morally wrong, or that there should be no such people as erastai and their paidika, but that the poet was not so conceited as to think that his enhanced standing in the community would bring him sexual success nor so corrupted as to compromise artistic integrity by helping a friend, as a favour, to blackmail a boy. Substitute 'dancing-schools' for 'wrestling-schools' and 'girl' for 'paidika', and the point would remain entirely unaffected.

(c) Comic references to Misgolas's enthusiasm for musicians have

---

Agathon, see n. 5 below; no. 2, Alkibiades, is treated in comedy, and in the biographical tradition, as sexually unrestrained in all respects; in the case of no. 4, Kleon, the language is figurative, as Henderson says, and refers to Kleon's aggression towards everybody. There is no reason to believe that Autokleides (no. 3), one of the 'wild men' of Aiskhines i 52, was ridiculed for active homosexuality in the *Orestautokleides* of Timokles rather than for hybristic behaviour in general, that the joke in Ar. fr. 114 was against Meletos (no. 6) rather than against Kallias, or that the sexual word-play in *Knights* 1378f. is a hit at Phaiax (no. 7) himself; and to find sexual reference to Phainippos (no. 8) and Teisamenos (no. 9) in *Ach.* 603 is to miss the point of the passage, which is that conceited young men of the leisured class, with high-sounding names and extravagant habits, make a good thing out of military office.

been considered on p. 73. They no more entail general criticism of men for responding to male beauty than ridicule of an individual for a passion for claret would entail general criticism of human liking for drink.

Furthermore, there is no passage in comedy which demonstrably attributes an active homosexual role to anyone who is ridiculed for taking a passive role.[5] The only passage which can be seriously considered as an exception to this generalisation is *Clouds* 675f., where it is said of Kleonymos, ridiculed for womanishness (because he was a coward; cf. p. 144 below), that 'he had no kneading-trough, but kneaded up (*sc.* his bread) in a round mortar'. Bearing in mind Hdt. v 92.*η*.2, where Melissa's ghost tells Periandros that he 'put his loaves into the oven when it was cold' (i.e. had intercourse with her corpse), we might interpret *Clouds* 675f. as meaning that Kleonymos penetrated someone else's anus because a 'kneading-trough' (i.e. a vagina?) was not available to him. Since, however, *dephesthai*, the ordinary word for 'masturbate', is cognate with *depsein*, 'mould or soften by kneading', it makes better sense to suppose that the joke is that Kleonymos is rejected by women and reduced to masturbation (gesture with the comic phallos by the actor speaking the lines would remove any possibility of misunderstanding).[6]

Sexual opportunism and uninhibited arousal are characteristic of the comic stage. Dikaiopolis, who relishes the thought of his neighbour's slave-girl, ends the play gloriously drunk and propped up by two girls whose mouths and breasts excite him to erection (*Ach.* 1198-1221); he has a wife (132, 245, 262), but no one remembers her. Demos in *Knights* 1390f. immediately reacts to the attractive Articles of Peace by asking if he can have intercourse with them; Trygaios in *Peace* 710f., presented with the supernatural Opora in marriage, asks straight away 'Do you think it'll do me any harm, after so long, to stick it into her?' When the Nightingale appears to Peisetairos and

---

5. Henderson 218 takes *Thesm.* 254 as meaning that Agathon's feminine clothes 'smell of little boys' penises'. But the point is that the Old Man, in affected tones, exclaims 'Oh, my dear, what a *delicious* perfume ...' and adds, in a different tone, '... of prick!', because Agathon, who has worn the dress, is male. The diminutive *posthion* is patronising and contemptuous.

6. We never have independent evidence for stage action, but it is legitimate to point out ways in which figurative language can be completely clarified by action. Henderson 200, 214, takes the image in *Clouds* 676 to mean 'buggered' (active, presumably). His generalisation about satyrs grasping their penises in vase-paintings is on the whole true (cf. p. 97 above), but has no relevance to the unusual picture (B118) which I cited in my comment *ad loc.*

Euelpides in *Birds* 667-9 Peisetairos says 'You know what? I'd like to do her between the legs!' He threatens the goddess Iris in similar terms (1253-6):

> And if you give me any trouble, I'll start off by sticking the legs of Zeus's messenger (*i.e.* you) in the air and doing Iris herself between the legs, so that you'll be surprised how an old man like me can raise a cockstand like a battering-ram.

Enthusiastic acceptance of the provision of brothels for travellers (*Frogs* 113) and of prostitutes and persuadable female musicians and dancers at dinner-parties (*Ach.* 1091, *Frogs* 513-20) did nothing to make brothel-keepers respectable or to turn words such as *pornē* and *laikastria* into terms of respect and endearment; equally, a liking for dalliance with a handsome adolescent boy did nothing to diminish the seducer's contempt for the seduced. *Euruprōktos*, literally, 'having a wide arse', is a common abusive term in comedy, and, as we have seen from Euboulos fr. 120, its literal meaning was kept in view. Ar. *Clouds* 1085-1104, where Wrong compels Right to admit that *euruprōktoi* are in a majority at Athens among speakers in the courts, poets, politicians and the audience at large, grows out of 1083f., in which Right points out that if a young man is caught in adultery he will become *euruprōktos* because (cf. p. 106) a radish will be forced up his anus by the offended husband. The passage ends with Right's despairing cry to the audience, *ō kīnoumenoi*, 'you who are stirred'; *kīnein*, 'stir', 'move', is a slang equivalent of *bīnein*, 'fuck', used in the active voice or in the passive according to whether the subject is the sexually active or the (male or female) sexually passive partner.

In the opening scene of *Thesmophoriazusae*, when the old man has declared that he does not know who Agathon is, Euripides says (35) 'Well, you've fucked him, but perhaps you don't know him', implying that the effeminate Agathon has functioned as a male prostitute in the dark. When Agathon has declined to help Euripides, intoning a rhyming distich (198f.),

> It is right not by inventiveness to withstand misfortune, but by submissiveness,[7]

the angry old man cries (200f.):

---

7. Literally 'inventings ... undergoings'; a person's *pathēmata* are what happens to him, what is done to him, and the contrast between 'doing' (*poiein, drān*) and 'undergoing' (*paskhein*) has obvious sexual applications, whence the Latin term *pathicus* for a passive homosexual.

And you, you *katapūgōn*, are wide-arsed – not just in words, but in submissiveness!

A moment later, when Agathon explains that he cannot go in disguise (as Euripides wants him to) to the meeting of the women, for it will be suspected that he is seeking to make love with them by stealth, the old man pours scorn on him (206):

What, 'make love by stealth'? Trying to get fucked, more likely!

Similarly (*ibid.* 50), when Agathon's servant has said 'For the poetic genius of our overlord Agathon is going to ...', the old man puts in 'Going to what? Why, is he going to get fucked?' The sausage-seller in *Knights*, portrayed as brought up in the gutter, illiterate and shameless, sums up his way of life (1242): 'I sold sausages and I was fucked[8] a bit'. The standpoint of Aristophanic comedy, adopted by its principal characters and choruses, is normally that of middle-aged, even elderly, citizens, resentful of the bright, energetic, disrespectful young men who seem to them (increasingly, of course, as one gets older) to dominate the assembly and to be elected to military and administrative offices. They express this resentment by speaking of the young as 'fucked' (Eupolis fr. 100.2, indignant at such creatures in office) or 'wide-arsed', as in Ar. *Wasps* 1068-70:

I reckon my old age is superior to the ringlets of a lot of young men, and the way they hold themselves,[9] and their *euruprōktiā*.

The man in the street consoles himself with the thought that those who run his life politically and order him about are in fact his inferiors, no better than prostitutes, homosexually subordinate. When Kleon in *Knights* 877 claims, apparently with reference to a successful prosecution of the same nature as Aiskhines' prosecution of Timarkhos,

I put a stop to those who were being fucked, by crossing Gryttos off (*sc.* the citizen-list)

the Sausage-seller retorts (878-80):

8. LSJ treats the imperfect tense *bīneskomēn* not as passive but as 'middle', with active sense; but for the Sausage-seller to say 'I fucked a bit' would be pointless in the context, since most people do, and he is answering a question on what skill or craft be practised when he grew up. Cf. also n. 12.

9. On effeminate or affected stance and movement cf. p.72.

Well, that was a bit much, arse-watching and putting a stop to them that were being fucked. It must have been jealousy that made you do it; you didn't want them to turn into politicians.

Plato Comicus fr. 186.5 expresses the same attitude to politicians, and 'Aristophanes' is made to enunciate with deadpan delivery in Pl. *Smp.* 191e-192a:

> While they are boys ... they (*sc.* the products of an original 'double male'; cf. p. 62) love men and like lying beside men and being embraced by them; and these are the best of the boys and youths. ... The evidence for that is that it's only such boys who, when they grow up, turn into real *men*[10] in politics.

An anonymous verse (*Com. Adesp.* fr. 12), 'everyone long-haired is pollinated' is an expression of class antagonism, since long hair (cf. p. 78) was regarded as characteristic of wealthy and leisured young men.

The word *katapūgōn*, used in the old man's vilification of Agathon in *Thesm.* 200, is cognate with *pūgē*, 'buttocks', and in at least one other passage of comedy unmistakably connotes a passive homosexual role: *Knights* 639, where the Sausage-seller takes the fart of a *katapūgōn* as an omen. The anatomy of the anus is altered by habitual buggery,[11] and there are modern jokes which imply (rightly or wrongly) that the sound of farts is affected by these changes. Whether *katapūgōn* ever connoted an active role in homosexual copulation is doubtful. In *Ach.* 77-9, when the envoy back from Persia has explained that 'the Persians only respect those who can eat and drink the most', Dikaiopolis comments 'And we (*sc.* only respect) *laikastai* and *katapūgones*'. *Laikazein* is 'fuck',[12] *laikastria* 'whore', and *-tēs* is a common agent-noun suffix; *laikastēs* should therefore denote a man

---

10. On expressions such as 'Be a *man!*' and 'We need a *man!*' cf. *GPM* 102. Symonds 44 and Karlen 30 seem not to observe the sarcasm of the passage of *Smp.*

11. Cf. D.J. West 27f.

12. Many verbs which have an active form in the present tense have a middle form in the future; but in other verbs the middle form of the future can have a passive sense. *Laikasomai*, the future corresponding to the present *laikazō*, is designated middle by LSJ, but (*a*) in the only passage in which an active sense in the future is absolutely required (*Knights* 167, 'You'll imprison [*sc.* anyone you like], you'll fuck in the Town Hall') the manuscript tradition very strongly favours the second person active form (*-seis*, not *-sei*), and (*b*) wherever the form is middle, the passive sense is required, e.g. Straton *CGF* 219.36 *ou laikasei?* = 'Get fucked!' or 'Fuck you!'. Kephisodoros fr. 3.5 *laikasomai ara* = 'Well I'll be fucked!', 'I'm fucked if I'll put up with that!' (the noun which follows it is not its object, but a self-contained incredulous repetition of a word from the previous line).

who penetrates others, and there would be a certain symmetry in *Ach.* 79 if the two words meant respectively 'fornicators' and 'buggers'. However, the graffiti exhibit a feminine *katapūgaina* (cf. ˙p.113), and comedy affords several instances of *katapūgōn* and its cognates used as very general words of abuse and contempt. In *Clouds* 529 Aristophanes refers to the moral and the immoral youth who contended in his early play *Banqueters* as 'the *sōphrōn* and the *katapūgōn*', almost 'the well behaved and the badly behaved'. Right calls Wrong 'shameless and *katapūgōn*' in *Clouds* 909, and when the woman to whom Lysistrata puts forward her plan for a sex-strike turn pale at the thought of such deprivation, she exclaims (*Lys.* 137) 'What a miserable bloody lot (*pankatapūgon*) we women are!' Ar. fr. 130 calls vegetable dishes and light food *katapūgosunē* ('a load of rubbish') compared with a good joint of meat. Similarly in *Clouds* 1327-1330, when Strepsiades has been beaten up by his son in a quarrel over the merits of Euripides as a dramatist, he calls his son 'burglar' and *lakkoprōktos*, 'tank-arse', as well as 'parricide'. Compare Kephisodoros fr. 3.4, a character abused by another as *lakkoprōktos* because he wants a special scent for his feet, and Eupolis fr. 351.4, where drinking too early in the day is characterised as *lakkoprōktiā*.

It must be emphasised that when a comic poet uses words such as *euruprōktos*, *lakkoprōktos* and *katapūgōn* of a named person (e.g. *Clouds* 1023, *Wasps* 687), we do not as a rule know whether it is important to him that the audience should interpret the word as a charge of passive homosexuality rather than as a charge of worthlessness, inferiority or shamelessness in general.[13] *Wasps* 84 (Philoxenos *katapūgōn*) is unusual in that the same man is stigmatised as 'not male' in *Clouds* 686f. and as 'female' in Eupolis fr. 235. Even when we can be sure what the specific charge is, we cannot know whether it is true,[14] any more than we know in the case of the people named in graffiti. Linguistic usage in this area is a reflex of the contempt felt by the dominant for the subordinate. There is a suggestion of homosexual penetration as an act of aggression in the first scene of *Thesmophoriazusae*, where the old man, after hearing the pompous proclamation of Agathon's slave, describes himself (59-62) as one who is 'ready to channel his cock into your foundations and your precious poet's', or where he says in

13. *Contra* Henderson 210, whose use of words such as 'evil' and 'wicked' (rather than 'worthless' or 'useless') seems to me inappropriate.

14. The argument 'There must have been something in it, or Aristophanes would never have got away with it' can only be propounded by those whose acquaintance with the political practice of our own time is very limited indeed; in any case, it begs the question, since we do not know *in the case of any individual passage* what a comic poet or orator 'got away with'.

Agathon (157f.) 'When you're writing a satyr-play send for me, so that I can collaborate standing (*estūkōs*, 'with an erection') right behind you'.

Agathon was an exceptionally good-looking man (Pl. *Smp.* 213c) who in his earlier years had been the paidika of Pausanias (Pl. *Prt.* 315de) and continued in this relationship well into adult life; he must have been in his thirties at the time of *Thesmophoriazusae*. Euripides calls him (191f.) 'good-looking, fair-skinned, shaved, with a woman's voice', and the scene is full of jokes against his effeminacy in bodily form (31-3), clothing (136-40) or both (in 98 he reminds the old man, on his first appearance, of the hetaira Kyrene). It is likely enough, given his unusual relation to Pausanias, that Agathon cut his beard close in order to retain the appearance of a young man whose beard is beginning to grow, and extremely unlikely that he went so far as to shave it off ('shaved' in 191 can refer to the body rather than the face, and the humour extracted from his possession of a razor [218-20] is founded on the fact that the razor was an article of female toiletry). His unwillingness to grow out of the eromenos stage into sexual dominance will have been sufficient reason for Aristophanes to treat him as 'fucked'; whether he declined an active heterosexual role, and whether he wore feminine clothing, we do not know.

In the Athens of Aristophanes the supreme effeminacy was cowardice on the battlefield; Eupolis's comedy *Astrateutoi* ('men who have not been on military service') had the alternative title *Androgunoi* ('women-men'). A certain Kleonymos, ridiculed in *Ach.* 88, 844, *Knights* 958, 1293 as bulky and greedy, was believed to have discarded his shield in order to run away faster, and for this he was pilloried in comedy over a period of at least ten years, from *Knights* 1372, via *Clouds* 353-5, *Wasps* 15-23 and *Peace* 446, 670-8, 1295-1301, to *Birds* 289f., 1470-81. Consequently his name is turned into a feminine 'Kleonyme' in the discussion of substantival declension in *Clouds* 670-80. Kleisthenes has an even longer run (twenty years) as a comic butt. His offence – at least, the only offence with which we have any grounds for charging him – was possession of a face on which a good beard would not grow. The old man in *Thesm.* 235, looking at himself in a mirror after his beard has been shaved off, exclaims 'It's Kleisthenes I'm seeing!' Kleisthenes is coupled with a certain Straton in early plays; Dikaiopolis in *Ach.* 119-24 pretends to recognise them in the eunuchs accompanying a Persian noble,[15] and they are 'beardless boys' in fr. 430 (cf. *Knights* 1373f.). The womanish appearance of Kleisthenes is the basis of a joke in *Clouds* 355; in *Birds* 829-31 it is assumed that he

15. Cf. Dover (1963a) 8-12.

weaves, like a woman, instead of bearing arms; and in *Thesm.* 574-81 he officiously comes to the women at their festival, as their friend and champion ('as is clear from my cheeks') to tell them of Euripides' scheme. With *Lys.* 1092 a new note comes in: the Athenian representative, desperate for a peace-treaty and an end to the wives' strike, declares that otherwise 'we'll have to fuck Kleisthenes'. The final stage is reached in *Frogs* 48 and 57, where the notion of Kleisthenes as 'mounted' by Dionysos (who supposedly longs thereafter to have him again) is spun out of a *double entendre*.

The exploitation of any kind of effeminacy for the purpose of jokes about passive homosexuality accords well with the uniform tendency of Aristophanic comedy to leave no sexual potential unrealised, to express heterosexual relationships in the most direct physiological terms, and to speak of other emotions in concrete imagery; fear, for example, is often described in terms of its effect on the bowels.[16] Homosexual eros, in this ambience, is treated simply as a desire for anal penetration, as when in *Thesm.* 1115-24 Euripides (to the bewilderment of the Scythian policeman) pretends that he is Perseus and that the old man arrested and fastened to a board is Andromeda:

EURIPIDES: Come, maiden, give me your hand, that I may touch it. O Scythian! There are weaknesses in all men, and I myself am seized with eros for this maiden. POLICEMAN: I don't envy you. Still, if his arse were twisted round this way, I wouldn't object to your taking him and buggering him. EURIPIDES: Why do you not allow me to release her, Scythian, and fall with her into the bed of marriage? POLICEMAN: If you're really keen on buggering the old man, bore a hole in the board and go up his arse from behind.

Fine distinctions between male prostitution and homosexual eros are submerged in Aristophanes' reduction of both alike to the same bodily act. In *Peace* 11, where the great dung-beetle brought home by Trygaios is being fattened so that he may bear his owner up to Olympos, one of the slaves in charge of the feeding asks the other for a dung-cake 'from a *hētairēkōs* boy; the beetle says he wants one well rubbed'. Later, when Trygaios needs to return to earth from Olympos, his beetle has decided to stay there, and Hermes explains (724) that it will 'feed on the ambrosia of Ganymede'; ambrosia being the food of the gods, the faeces of the immortal boy will naturally be composed of it, and we are brutally reminded of what Zeus does to Ganymede. A differentiation between prostitution and eros,

16. Cf. Taillardat 151-220.

important to the social and political standing of those involved in homosexual relationships, is in effect denied by a moralising passage, *Wealth* 153-9:

> KARION: Yes, and they say that boys do just the same (*sc.* present their buttocks), not for the sake of their erastai, but for money. KHREMYLOS: Not the good boys, only the *pornoi*; it isn't money that the good ones ask for. KARION: What is it, then? KHREMYLOS: One asks for a good horse, and another for hunting dogs. KARION: Maybe they're ashamed to ask for money, so they dress up their bad behaviour in a (*sc.* different) word.

Generalised hostility to boys who play the role of eromenoi appears also in *Knights* 736-40, where the sausage-seller compares old Demos to 'those boys who are eromenoi' (he does not say '*some* boys ...'); rival politicians are, as it were, rival erastai of Demos, who, however, rejects good men and gives himself to 'lamp-sellers and cobblers and shoemakers and tanners'. A scornful attitude to eromenoi may always have existed in some sections of Athenian society, and one black-figure vase (B614) gives us a glimpse of it. A homosexual courting scene (the eromenos has accepted a cockerel) is accompanied by the letters *arenmi* and *idoren* (or *iaoren*?). If the correct interpretation is *arrēn eimi*, 'I am male', and *idou arrēn*, 'Behold, male!', we recall the frequent comic idiom in which a second speaker repeats a word used by the previous speaker and prefaces it with an indignant or contemptuous *idou*, e.g. *Knights* 343f., 'I can speak, too ...' – '*Idou*, speak!' The comment 'What do you mean, *male?*' will then express the painter's view of the eromenoi in the courting scenes which his public liked.[17] It is conceivable that the occasional attachment of the feminine adjective *kalē* to a male name in vase-paintings is sarcastic, but some of these cases can be explained as thoughtless repetition from a proper use of the feminine in another inscription on the same vase (R356, R655, R990) or as a reference to a female in the picture (R385); there are also cases of the masculine *kalos* with feminine names and pictures of women (R152, R917) and (R1139) an inscription 'the girl is kalos' – the painter absentmindedly completed the inscription with the formula most familiar to him – without any picture.

An interesting example of contrasting romantic and cynical treatment of one and the same eromenos is furnished by the case of Autolykos. This is the young athlete who figures in Xenophon's

17. However, 'Look! Male!' is a possible interpretation; cf. 'Look! A swallow!' on R78 (Kretschmer 231).

Symposium, the eromenos of Kallias, invited to dinner together with his father, modest, shy (1.8, 3.13), possessed of a beauty which overawed all the guests (1.9-11). Eupolis in 421/0 produced a comedy entitled *Autolykos* in which the youth and his parents, Lykon and Rhodia, were targets of ridicule and abuse, Rhodia as a promiscuous adulteress. In this play Autolykos was designated 'Eutresios' (fr. 56), which literally denotes an inhabitant of Eutresis in Arkadia but is also clearly meant to suggest 'easily penetrated' (*trēma* is a slang term for the vagina). Whether the alleged homosexual prostitution of Autolykos to Kallias was a central motif of the play, we do not know; the political relationships involving Kallias and Lykon, affected by the public adulation accorded to athletic success,[18] may well have been more important, but so far as the evidence goes it shows that the same homosexual love-affair could be looked at in different ways.

The assumption that all homosexual submission is mercenary, and with this a total silence on the possible emergence of extreme devotion, courage and self-sacrifice from a homosexual relationship, is analogous to another characteristic feature of comedy, the assumption that all holders of administrative offices feather their own nests, and with that silence on the possibility of public spirit, integrity and devotion to duty on the part of existing officials. *Lys.* 490, arguing that 'we are at war because of money' and charging 'Peisandros and those who aim at office' with pursuing bellicose policies in order to give themselves the chance to steal public funds, leaves it open to the audience to believe that there exists a better kind of politician, and so *ibid.* 578, where Lysistrata advocates getting rid of organised political corruption, but the tone is different in *Birds* 1111, 'If you've been appointed to some minor office and want to make a bit on the side ...', *Thesm.* 936f., 'Prytanis, I beseech you by your right hand, which you are wont to hold out, palm upwards, if anyone offers you money ...', and *Wasps* 556f., where Philokleon describes a defendant as saying, 'Sir, pity me, I beg of you, if[19] you yourself ever got away with a bit when you held office or when you were buying food for your messmates on campaign!' Dikaiopolis in *Ach.* 594-619 wins over the chorus in his contest with Lamakhos by furious denunciation of military commanders and diplomatic envoys as running away from the hard life at home (601, 71f.) in their anxiety to hold office (595)

18. The Autolykos of myth was a great thief and cheat (Hom. *Od.* xix 394-8) and the subject of a satyr-play of Euripides which contained (fr. 282) a diatribe against athletes.

19. The formula 'If you yourself were ever in my situation, treat me as you would have wished to be treated' is common; cf. *GPM* 271f.

with a prospect of high pay (597, 602, 608); the same resentment underlies the portrayal of the Athenian envoys who have been away in Persia for twelve years, drawing good pay and living in luxury (65-90), or at the court of a Thracian king (134-41). In *Wasps* 691-6 Bdelykleon tries similarly to arouse resentment against young public prosecutors who, he alleges, in addition to getting good pay take bribes from defendants, share the money out between themselves, and 'fix' the cases, while the old juror is anxious for his miserable jury-pay. In *Clouds* 1196-1200 Pheidippides explains a point of legal procedure to his father as designed to allow magistrates to steal the litigants' deposits. Other passages extend this general accusation of dishonesty to the citizen-body as a whole; cf. *Birds* 115f., where Peisetairos is talking to the Hoopoe, who was once human: 'You owed money once, just like us; and enjoyed not paying it back, just like us!' As for military commanders in the field, *Clouds* 579f. assumes that an expedition which they announce is 'senseless'; *Peace* 1172-90 complains that commanders are the first to run away in battle but never tire of messing about with the call-up lists, so that the individual soldier (the countryman, that is; things go better for the townsman [1185f.]) never knows from one day to the next where he stands.

The reader who turns from Plato to comedy is struck not only by the consistent comic reduction of homosexual eros to the coarsest physical terms but also by its displacement from the centre to the periphery of Athenian sexual life; for comedy is fundamentally heterosexual. In *Lysistrata* there is, of course, a special motive; the success of the sexual strike of citizens' wives organised by the heroine turns upon the absence of significant alternatives to marital intercourse, so that homosexuality must be relegated if the plot of the play is to cohere. The same applies to prostitution; and having chosen to portray marital relations essentially in terms of erection of the penis, Aristophanes must also ignore the fact that male tension can be reduced by masturbation (whereas clear references to female masturbation are permitted [105-110, 158f.]). Similarly, the wives' opportunities for intercourse with lusty slaves, a motif which occurs in *Thesm.* 491f., must be suppressed in *Lys.* in order that the comic potentiality of sex-starved women may be fully exploited (125-39, 215f., 706-80), and female masturbation is suppressed in *Thesm.* 473-501 (cf. *Lys.* 403-23) where the adulterous inclinations of women are the focus of humour; it is never Aristophanes' purpose to compose a social survey for the instruction of posterity.[20] In *Ecclesiazusae* the take-over of the state by the women, their consequent assumption of sexual

20. Cf. *AC* 160f.

initiative, and their rule that the old and ugly must be gratified before the young and pretty, are not allowed for a moment (cf. 611-50, 707-9, 877-1111) to raise in the men the notion that homosexual relations might prove a less exacting alternative. Here too it is easy to find decisive dramatic reasons.

In plays which are not about women the sexual element in the triumph of the hero is heterosexual: Dikaiopolis gets girls at the end of *Acharnians*, the presentation of the Articles of Peace to Demos in *Knights* supervenes as climactic upon the presentation of the boy who can be a 'folding-stool', Philokleon's enthusiasm for the good things of life in *Wasps* leads him to steal a girl, Trygaios in *Peace* marries Opora and presents Theoria to the Council, and Peisetairos in *Birds* marries Basileia. For the chorus of *Acharnians* the return of peace signifies the enjoyment of women (989-99; cf. Trygaios in *Peace* 894-905), not of boys. It would not be true to say that homosexual relations were never the central subject of a comedy, for in the fourth century we hear of a *Paiderastēs* produced by Antiphanes and a *Paiderastai* by Diphilos, not to mention comic treatment of the Ganymede legend by Alkaios Comicus, Antiphanes and Euboulos and of the Khrysippos legend (cf. p. 200) by Strattis, but it happens to be true of the extant plays, Menander's as well as Aristophanes'. This fact puts us on the track of what may be an important distinction at Athens between rich and poor.

It is obvious enough that strict segregation of the wives, daughters, wards and widowed mothers of Athenian citizens was practicable only to the extent to which the head of a household could afford to keep enough slaves for the running of all errands, the performance of all work outside the house, and the execution of his orders for its internal regulation. Among the rich, a young man's opportunities for love-affairs with girls of his own class were minimal, and if he was to enjoy the triumph of leisurely seduction (rather than the flawed satisfaction of purchase) he must seduce a boy. Among the poor, where women often had to go to market and sell their produce or handiwork (the bread-woman of *Wasps* 1389-1414 is clearly [1396f.] of citizen status; cf. *Thesm.* 443-58), or where they had to work in the fields, segregation could not be strict.[21] The poor but upright farmer of Eur. *Electra*, nominally married to Elektra, has no slaves, and though he is naturally disapproving when he finds Elektra talking to two strange men, it is part of the life of such a family that the wife should go out alone to get water (70-6). The girl in Ar. *Eccl.*, waiting for her boy-friend, sings (912-14) 'I'm left all alone here, because my mother's

21. Cf. *GPM* 209-13.

gone off somewhere else'. No doubt the poor tended to assume that what the rich did must be worth doing, and the herdsmen in Theokritos 5 boast equally of homosexual and heterosexual success (86-9), but – to put the matter cautiously and beg no questions – it is likely that when sex-objects of types A and B are both available some people will choose A, and certain that when there is only B no one can choose A. The central characters of comedy are not poor men, but they are not notably rich either, and most of the audience whose sentiments and attitudes Aristophanes intended his characters and choruses to voice will have known more than the rich about the possibilities of heterosexual seduction offered by rural or urban life at a comparatively modest social level. Apart from the cost of strict segregation and the cost of winning over a desired person by impressive gifts, leisure too was a prerequisite for courtship, especially if many days of patient watching in the gymnasium and many conversations about art and war and life were needed in order to make oneself admirable and interesting in the eyes of a boy whose sexual arousal could not be counted on as a contributory factor. The personages we meet in Plato virtually all belong to a leisured class, some of them to the richest and noblest families in Athens, whereas in Aristophanic comedy it is a compliment to call a man *ergatēs*, 'hard worker', 'good worker' (*Ach.* 611); the same word is used of the poor farmer in Eur. *El.* 75. In *Peace* 632 the countrymen, men of good sense (603) and good morals (556), the salt of the earth, sufferers from war (588-97) and the saviours of peace (508-11), are 'the *ergatēs* folk', and Trygaios himself boasts (190f.) of being 'a skilled cultivator of vines'. A hard-working man, even a poor man, can marry, because the condition of his marrying is not that a girl should fall in love with him but that he should be chosen by her father (and should not be so repulsive to her that she enlists her mother's sympathy and frustrates her father's intentions). But falling in love and pursuing the object of one's love are a luxury, a diversion of time and effort from profitable work to an activity which, even if successful, will do nothing to feed and clothe the lover. Hence the sentiment of Akhaios fr. 6:

> There is no eros of the beautiful in an empty stomach; Aphrodite is a
> curse to the hungry.

This was later cast into more succinct form (Eur. fr. 895), and it is the basis of the joke in Men. *Heros* 15-17. Gorgias in Men. *Dysk.* 341-4 says that he has never fallen in love, and cannot, since the troubles which already beset him leave him no respite, and one of the countrymen in Theokritos 10, who is lagging in his work as a reaper and has left his own vegetable-patch unweeded, is asked by his unfeeling companion (9) 'What is an *ergatēs* man doing longing for what is out of reach?' His desire is for a girl, not a boy, but since the vocabulary and symptoms of eros are the same in both cases it is not difficult to see how the ordinary Athenian citizen, however ready to identify himself as a man of property with his social superiors,[22] could also pride himself that he wasted no time on homosexual love-affairs such as occupied idle young men who had more money than was good for them.

The 'comic hero' of Aristophanes does not fall in love; Opora and Basileia are not the goal of the ambitious schemes of Trygaios and Peisetairos respectively, but the unexpected bonus of political triumph, and however passionate and enduring the eros which we may expect the hero to feel towards his prize henceforward, it will be the product of sexual relations, not their cause.[23] Young men in New Comedy, on the other hand, do fall in love – indeed, the happy outcome of love-affairs which are assisted by good fortune to win through against serious odds is a mainstay of the genre – but only with young women, and we have to consider the possibility that the sentiment of audiences in the late fourth century, receptive towards heterosexual eros and tolerant even of its excesses, was beginning to sweep homosexuality under the carpet. Many considerations tend against this supposition; certainly explicit allegations of homosexual prostitution were by no means unknown in the comedy of Menander's time (cf. p. 99). Menander's preoccupation is with families and the relations between generations, not with the activities of young men which, having no relevance to marriage and inheritance, belong outside a familial context. It is however observable that a general inhibiting respectability becomes the norm in different art-forms at different times, and we do not always know why it operates when and where it does.[24] In vase-painting, for example, the physique of satyrs, except for their faces, becomes humanised at the beginning of the fifth century; in the fourth, even their faces are affected, so that only horse's ears and a modest tail distinguish a satyr from a human youth (RL20, RL56, RS97). Fearsome legendary beings become disappointingly tame quite early in the classical period (cf. p. 7), indistinguishable from

22. Cf. *GPM* 34-45.

23. The assumption that shared sexual experience is the foundation upon which the mutual sexual passion of the partners is built rather than the goal towards which their pre-existing passion moves is widely adopted in societies which segregate boys and girls and put the responsibility of arranging marriages on parents.

24. Even non-phallic herms begin to appear in the late fifth century; cf. Lullies (1931) 46.

comely humans in face and identifiable only by schematised attributes: Harpies (R774), Raving Madness (R902), the Furies (R932, RS179). Yet in caricature and burlesque the hideousness becomes exaggerated, not diminished, in later vase-painting; it is as if the demarcation of genres were being sharpened. This is just as well; the participants in the threesome of R898, who should be afire with lust and jollity, all wear the doleful and soppy expressions with which the later vase-painters attempted to convey spiritual depth, and this mixture of genres is not impressive.[25]

Down to the early fifth century the painters sometimes chose to portray disgusting subjects: a man wiping his anus (R291), an explosion of diarrhoea at a party (B120), copious drunken vomiting (R519); in R265 a squatting youth simultaneously urinates and defecates on the ground, and the painter has made his penis loll to one side lest our view of the faeces be obscured. Vomiting and urination have obvious enough associations with drunken festivity, and urination also has anatomical associations with sex. Defecation, on the other hand, is rather forced upon us in connection with drink, dancing and sex in black-figure vase-painting, e.g.: B90, a man on each side of the vessel reclines, happily masturbating, while under each handle a dog defecates (a satirical comment on masturbation?); B330, a participant in a komos defecates; B394 (cf. B346), a satyr in a squatting position, defecating and masturbating; BB8, one comast masturbating while another defecates; C70, a satyr on the ground at a drunken party drinks from a wineskin and defecates; CP16, a row of figures which includes two dancers and a hairy satyr with an immense pendulous penis contains also a man defecating and a man penetrating a woman from behind. This is the coarse language of the archaic iambic poets and of Attic Old Comedy translated into visual terms, but it ceased to be fashionable in vase-painting well before Aristophanes was born, and by the time he brought the constipated Blepyros on stage in *Eccl.* 311-72 the area of the arts which was licensed to portray any or all of the bodily activities which people enjoy performing had already become severely restricted. Irredeemably disagreeable subjects, such as mutilated and decomposing flesh, were always eschewed, though what was not only disagreeable but powerful and frightening enough to be part of the fabric of great events – the horrible Furies of Aiskhylos's *Eumenides*, the wound of Philoktetes, the death-agony of Herakles – was used by the tragic poets to good theatrical effect. The irregular pattern in which inhibition crept over the arts between the latter part of the sixth

25. Cf. *EG* 124.

century and the end of the fourth suggests a multiplicity of causes, among which we should reckon the dissemination of attitudes which were popularly regarded as philosophical and the tendency of stable cultures to develop canons of refinement which can be defined and applied without too much intellectual effort; the consequence of both was a disinclination to acknowledge openly the true status of the uncompromisingly physical element in our lives. The treatment of homosexuality by Hellenistic poets, grafting a new sensual gusto on to the 'romantic' tradition inherited from earlier poetry, suggests that the suppression of homosexual affairs in Menander should not be considered in itself sufficient evidence for a significant general change of direction in public tolerance of them.

D.   Philosophical Exploitation

To ask whether Plato responded homosexually to the stimulus of male beauty more intensely than most Athenians of his social class in the late fifth and early fourth centuries is to ask a question of very limited relevance to the history of philosophy or the history of homosexuality; the cogency of a philosophical argument, its power over the imagination, its moral and social value and its influence over subsequent thought do not depend on the sexual orientation of its proponent, and when (as in classical Athens) anyone is free to declare the intensity of his own homosexual response the homosexuality of a philosopher is not even a biographical datum of importance. To ask the same question about Socrates is much more useful, so far as concerns the history of philosophy, for if we could answer the question we would know more than we do at present about the relation between the teaching and influence of Socrates and the portrait of Socrates presented by the only philosophical writers of the period whose work survives intact, Plato and Xenophon. Apart from a curious remark by Aristoxenos (fr. 55) that Socrates had a strong heterosexual appetite and indulged it (but 'without injustice', i.e. without adultery or violence), we are virtually deprived of independent evidence bearing upon the sexuality of Socrates (it is an aspect of his life on which Aristophanes' *Clouds* is silent), and in what is said below about the relationship between homosexuality and Socratic philosophy 'Socrates' means the Socrates portrayed in Plato and Xenophon. In Plato's *Laws*, the last work he wrote, Socrates is replaced by an anonymous Athenian, and the doctrines and arguments propounded by that character will be designated Plato's without more ado. In the context of the present enquiry the most important aspect of Socrates is his exploitation of the Athenian homosexual ethos as a basis of metaphysical doctrine and philosophical method. Condemnation (explicit in *Laws*, foreshadowed in *Phaedrus*) of the consummation of homosexual desire as 'unnatural' is not quite as important historically as might appear at first sight,[1] since the contrast between 'nature' and the laws and conventions of society had been discussed – in general terms, without specific reference to homosexuality – before Plato was born,[2] and in praising the ability to resist temptation to bodily pleasure Plato was fully in accord with Greek moral tradition.[3]

We encounter Socrates in a strongly homosexual ambience; some of Plato's earlier dialogues are set in the gymnasium, Socrates' youthful friends are commonly – one might say, normally – in love with boys, and he fully accepts these relationships: Ktesippos and Kleinias in *Euthydemos*, Hippothales and Lysis in *Lysis*, the allusion in *Meno* 70b to Menon's erastes Aristippos, the teasing of Glaukon as *erōtikos* in *Rep.* 474d-475a, and compare the report in *Parmenides* 127b that Zenon has been the paidika of Parmenides. In his sympathetic conversation with the lovesick Hippothales Socrates uses the language to which we became accustomed (pp. 44f.) in reading between the lines of the Lysianic 'speech of the non-lover' and Pausanias's speech in Plato's *Symposium*. On hearing that Hippothales writes poems in praise of the family of Lysis, Socrates asks him (*Lys.* 205d-206a):

> Are you composing and singing an encomium on yourself before you've won?
>
> It's not in *my* honour, Socrates, he said, that I'm composing and singing.
>
> You don't *think* so, I said ... If you catch a paidika of such quality, what you have said and sung will do you great honour and will in reality by encomia on a victor, because you will have got (*tunkhanein*) such a paidika. But if he gets away from you, the greater the encomia you have pronounced on your paidika, the greater the blessings which you will be seen to have lost, and you will be despised.[4] So, my friend,

1. A surprising amount of thought and feeling has been devoted in our own time to the question whether homosexual relations are 'unnatural', and, if so, in what sense. Since I observe that any community encourages behaviour which it regards as probably conducive to an eventual situation of a kind desired by that community and discourages behaviour which seems likely to hinder the development of such a situation, and since the absence of any clear correlation between 'nature' and desirability seems to me self-evident, I cannot engage with any enthusiasm in debates about the naturalness or unnaturalness of homosexuality. Cf. also p. 67.

2. Cf. *GPM* 74f., 255-7.

3. Cf. *GPM* 175-80, 208f.

4. We might have expected 'the more downcast you will be' or 'the more you will be

anyone who knows what he is doing in *ta erōtika* refrains from praising his eromenos until he has caught him, because he is apprehensive about how things may turn out. What is more, beautiful boys are filled with pride and conceit when they are praised and glorified. Don't you think so?

Yes I do, he said.

And the more conceited they are, the harder they are to catch?

That is likely.

Well, what sort of hunter would you think a man who in hunting roused his prey and made it harder to catch?

Obviously, a poor sort.

The unnamed friend who meets Socrates at the opening of Plato's *Protagoras* asks him (309a):

> Where have you come from, Socrates? Well, I suppose it's obvious: from chasing (*lit.*, 'hunting with hounds') around after Alkibiades' beauty?

— to which, indeed, Socrates takes no exception; but (cf. p. 159) the conversation is due to take an unexpected turn. When it is proposed at Agathon's party that all the guests should make speeches in praise of Eros, Socrates welcomes it in so far as (*Smp.* 177d) '*ta erōtika* are the only subject I claim to understand'. Compare Xen. *Smp.* 8.2, 'I can't think of a time when I wasn't in love'; he is described in Pl. *Smp.* 216d as 'always excited by the beautiful', and his reaction in *Phdr.* 227c, on hearing that Lysias has composed a speech urging a boy to favour a non-erastes, is 'I wish he'd said "favour ordinary older people" like me and most of us!' In *Chrm.* 153b he qualifies his description of the beauty of Kharmides by saying, 'I'm nothing to go by ... because pretty well *all* youths of that age seem beautiful to me, but ...', and we see the force of the 'but' when Kharmides has sat down between Socrates and Kritias (155c-e):

> Then I just didn't know what to do, and all the confidence that I'd previously felt, in the belief that I'd find it easy to talk to him, was knocked out of me. When Kritias told him that I was the man who knew the cure (*sc.* for headache), and he looked me in the eye – oh, what a look! – and made as if to ask me, and everyone in the wrestling-school crowded close all round us, that was the moment when I saw inside his cloak, and I was on fire, absolutely beside myself ... All the same, when he asked me if I knew the cure for his head, I did somehow manage to answer that I knew it.

---

pitied', but a Greek was greatly concerned with the effect of success or failure on his standing in society; cf. *GPM* 226-9, 235-42.

If we translate this scene into heterosexual terms, so that Socrates' glimpse inside the cloak of Kharmides becomes a glimpse of the breasts of a young woman of extraordinary beauty, as she leans forward to ask an unaffected question,[5] we come as close to seeing through ancient Greek eyes as we are likely to come.[6]

There is nothing in these utterances of Socrates, as quoted – and all the quotations have been terminated short of the developments which require the reader to think again about any premature conclusions he may have drawn – at variance with the language and sentiments of males who desired and sought orgasm in bodily contact with younger males. But Socrates does not go on to disguise copulation under layers of metaphysical flannel; from the experience which he shares with his contemporaries he draws different conclusions, and he is so far from calling eros by other names that he calls many other things[7] by the name of eros. It was never difficult in Greek to use 'eros' and cognate words figuratively when their object was not an individual human; one may, for instance, *erān* victory, power, money, one's homeland, or a homecoming.[8] Socrates uses 'erastes' figuratively (e.g. *Rep.* 501d), but sometimes couples this with literal usage, as in *Gorgias* 481d, where he calls himself 'erastes of Alkibiades and of philosophy' and his interlocutor Kallikles erastes of 'two (*sc. dēmoi*), the Athenian *dēmos* ('people', 'assembly') and (*sc.* Demos, son) of Pyrilampes' (cf. p. 111); he compares Kallikles' inability to contradict or thwart the Athenian people with his inability to oppose Demos, and he finds philosophy, 'my paidika', much less capricious and unstable than his human

---

5. Cf. Wender 78f.

6. Among those of us whose orientation is mainly or entirely homosexual, some may see clearly enough through Greek eyes already, and in any case it would not help them to imagine Kharmides a girl; I have made the assumption that the difference of heterosexual stimulus between sight of the female face and sight of the breasts is greater than the difference of homosexual stimulus between sight of the male face and sight of the torso. We may be intended to understand, however, that Socrates glimpsed Kharmides' genitals, not his torso.

7. I say this not because I have failed to understand the Socratic doctrine of eros, but because I do not share Socrates' assumptions and therefore reject his doctrine in its entirety. This rejection in no way inclines me to a cynical view of Socrates' own behaviour. Those who are so much more afraid of being deceived in one particular way than in others as to maintain with a knowing smirk that Socrates buggered Alkibiades can be as amusing unintentionally as Lucian (*Philosophies for Sale* 15) is intentionally, but their sense of proportion is open to criticism; even if they are right, they have not discovered anything about Socrates which deserves a fraction of the attention deserved by (e.g.) *Chrm.* 161c, 163e, 166cd, *Smp.* 201c, *Grg.* 472ab.

8. Eur. fr. 358, in which children are commanded to *erān* their mother, is deliberately daring in language, but is so obviously not a command to feel incestuous desire for one's mother that there is no risk of misunderstanding.

paidika, Alkibiades (481d-482a). Again, when he says (Xen. *Smp.* 8.41) that he is consistently 'fellow-erastes with the city' of those who are 'of good quality by nature and zealous in the pursuit of virtue' he so blends personal eros with the public's affection and admiration for the brave and wise and upright as to call in question the extent to which sensual response to bodily beauty plays any part in his own eros. He does not hesitate, in fact, to use 'erastes' of a devoted admirer of an older person's wisdom or skill; hence an aristocratic family of Thessaly are 'erastai' of the sophist Gorgias (*Meno* 70b), the 'fans' of the sophists Euthydemos and Dionysodoros are their 'erastai' (*Euthd.* 276d), and when he introduces Hippokrates to the eminent Protagoras (*Prt.* 317cd):

> Suspecting that Protagoras wanted to show off to Prodikos and Hippias that erastai of his had come to the house, I said, 'Well, why don't we invite Prodikos and Hippias and those with them to come and listen to our discussion?'

These passages may be jocular, in a way familiar to us throughout the literary presentation of Socrates (cf. Pl. *Smp.* 216e and the joke about 'procuring' pupils for philosophers in Xen. *Smp.* 4.62), but when a certain Aristodemos is described in the opening scene of Plato's *Symposium* (173b) as 'erastes of Socrates more than anyone at that time' we may well feel that 'erastes' is so freely used in the Socratic circle that the boundary between the serious and the playful or between the literal and the figurative is overrun. This is possible if, and only if, it is very well understood within that circle that eros is not a desire for bodily contact but a love of moral and intellectual excellence.

The famous tale told by Alkibiades in Pl. *Smp.* 216c-219e is intended to illustrate Socrates' own relationship with the young Alkibiades. Convinced that his beauty, of which he is very proud, has excited Socrates' desire, and no less convinced that Socrates is a man of remarkable quality, from whose wisdom and guidance he can profit, Alkibiades decides that he will *kharizesthai* Socrates (217a). He therefore creates, with increasing indiscretion, opportunities for Socrates (whose behaviour he expects to follow the normal pattern of erastai) to ask him for bodily favours: he dismisses his attendant slave when he meets Socrates (217ab), he invites Socrates to wrestle (217bc) and to dinner (217cd), 'for all the world as if *I* were an erastes with designs on a paidika'. Finally, despairing of less direct methods, he detains Socrates after dinner until late at night, goes to bed in the same room, and sends away his slaves (217d-218b). Then (218cd):

I thought it was time for me to cease my roundabout approach and say freely what was in my mind. So I nudged him and said 'Are you asleep, Socrates?'

'No, no' he said.

'Do you know what I think?'

'No, what?' he said.

'In my opinion' I said 'you have been the only erastes worthy of me, and you seem to me to be hesitant to say anything about it to me. Now this is my feeling about it: I 'think it silly of me not to grant you that favour and anything else you might want from my property or my friends. Nothing is more important to me than to become the best man I can, and I don't consider anyone can do more than you to help me in that. I would be much more ashamed of the judgment of intelligent people if I didn't grant you a favour than of the judgment of the stupid majority if I did.'

Socrates replies that if Alkibiades really sees in him a 'beauty' of the kind he describes, he (Alkibiades) is getting the best of the bargain in offering bodily beauty in exchange (218e-219a). Encouraged to believe that the 'shafts' which he has loosed have 'wounded' Socrates, Alkibiades without more ado gets on to Socrates' bed, puts his cloak over them both, and lies down with his arms round Socrates (219bc). Socrates makes no sign of being aroused, and in the morning they part, Alkibiades mortified at the insult to his beauty (219d) but overcome with admiration for the control exercised in Socrates by rational principle over the demands of the body; this *karteriā*, 'endurance', is the quality which he displayed also on campaign at Poteidaia, showing no sign of intoxication however much he drank, and going about in icy weather without sandals, wearing only the cloak he wore at Athens (219e-220b).

The notion that there are unseen beauties far excelling the visible beauty of bodies is used to good dramatic effect at the opening of *Protagoras* (309b-d):

Have you come from him (*sc.* Alkibiades)? And how's the young man getting on with you?

Very well, I thought, especially today. He said a lot in my defence, coming to my support. In fact, I've just left him. But I must tell you an extraordinary thing: even though he was there with me, I didn't pay any attention to him, and I kept on forgetting him.

What can have happened of such importance affecting you and him? You're not going to tell me you've met someone else more beautiful – not here in Athens, anyway!

Oh, yes, much more.

Really? Citizen or foreigner?

A foreigner.

Where from?

Abdera.

And did you think this foreigner was so beautiful that he actually seemed to you more beautiful than the son of Kleinias (*sc.* Alkibiades)?

How can the height of wisdom fail to appear more beautiful?

Why, you've come from meeting somebody *wise*, Socrates?

The wisest man of our time, surely – I assume you count Protagoras the wisest.

Eros for wisdom is more powerful, and more important to Socrates, than eros for a beautiful youth; in Xen. *Smp.* 8.12 he treats it as better to be in love with the qualities of a person's soul than with the attributes of the body. It does not follow logically from this that homosexual copulation should be avoided, unless one also believes that any investment of energy and emotion in the pursuit of an inferior end vitiates the soul's capacity to pursue a superior end. Socrates does believe this, and therefore forbids homosexual copulation, as is clear from his own conduct with Alkibiades and from *Rep.* 403b, where 'right eros' in the ideal city permits the erastes to touch his paidika 'as a son' but to go no further than that. Pausanias in *Smp.*184b-185b came to the conclusion that in the pursuit of virtue and wisdom it is permissible to render *any* service and offer *any* favour (cf. p. 91), a principle which the young Alkibiades followed in his vain attempt to seduce Socrates; but in *Euthd.* 282b Socrates himself makes a significant addition:

For the sake of this (*sc.* acquisition of wisdom) there is nothing disgraceful or objectionable in subordination or enslavement to an erastes or any person, in complete readiness to perform *any* service – *of those services which are honourable* – out of zeal for becoming wise.

According to Xen. *Mem.* i 2.29f. enmity between Kritias and Socrates arose from the following incident:

He saw that Kritias was in love with Euthydemos and wanting to deal with him in the manner of those who enjoy the body for sexual intercourse. Socrates tried to dissuade Kritias, saying that it was mean and unbefitting a good man to importune his eromenos, in whose eyes he wishes to appear a man of merit, by beseeching him as beggars do and asking for charity, and that too when what he asks is not a good thing. Kritias took no notice and was not dissuaded. Then, it is said, Socrates, in the presence of Euthydemos and many other people, said that he thought Kritias was no better off than a pig if he wanted to scratch himself against Euthydemos as piglets do against stones.

In another moralising story (Xen. *Smp.* 3.8-14) we are told that on hearing that Kritoboulos had kissed Alkibiades' son Socrates said that kissing a beautiful youth could turn a free man into a slave; he compares a kiss to the bite of a poisonous spider, which may drive a man out of his mind. Xenophon's Socrates lacks the sensibility and urbanity of the Platonic Socrates, but there is no doubt that both of them condemn homosexual copulation.

Why then does Socrates attach such importance to the combination of bodily beauty with good qualities of mind and character (Pl. *Chrm.* 153d, 154e, 158b, *Smp.* 209b), instead of saying outright that bodily beauty is irrelevant? Why, indeed, does he speak so often (cf. p. 155) as if his own heart were almost continuously thumping at the sight of beautiful youths and boys?

Plato's Socrates believes that particular persons, animals, things, artefacts, acts and events which constitute our sensory experience, all possessing definable duration and location in space and all subject to change and decay, give us faint and fitful glimpses of a different world, a world of everlasting, unchanging entities, 'forms' or 'ideas', accessible to systematic reasoning (progressing towards logically irrefutable 'knowledge') but not perceptible by the bodily senses (upon which only indefinitely corrigible 'opinion' can be founded). The relation between forms and particulars is never defined; it can be said that the former are 'present in' the latter or that the latter 'participate in' the former. The ultimate cause, towards which all rational explanation progresses, is Good itself; qua form, it is the goal of reason, and qua Good it is the goal of desire. Hence to perceive it is to love and desire it, and error blinds us to it; reason and desire converge upon Good, and in its vicinity fuse together. Eros is treated in the *Symposium* as a force which draws us towards the world of eternal being, of which Good is the cause, and in *Phaedrus* (245b, 265b) as a 'madness' inspired by deities, Aphrodite and Eros (rather as falling in love, an experience which happens to us without conscious design on our part, was popularly regarded [e.g. Xen. *Smp.* 8.10, 8.37] as god-sent). According to the doctrine expounded in *Phaedrus* (and elsewhere in Plato, but not in the *Symposium*)[9] the soul of any individual person existed always, before it was joined with the body of that person in the world of 'Becoming', and it once 'perceived' the forms in the world of 'Being'. The strength of my own impulse to pursue Good

9. It was not Plato's practice to reconcile what he said in a given work with what he had said in a previous work; it is therefore seldom possible to decide when he has changed his mind and when he is exploring different aspects of the same problem in different imagery.

through philosophy and to maintain the pursuit despite all·adversity and temptation depends less on the opportunities which present themselves to me in my life than on the length of time which has elapsed since my soul was acquainted with the world of Being and on its vicissitudes between that time and its conjunction with my body (*Phdr.* 250e-251a).

From these metaphysical beliefs a prescriptive schema of sexual values is derived. Response to the stimulus of bodily beauty is a step in the direction of absolute Beauty, an aspect of Good.[10] The 'right approach to *ta erōtika*', as described by Diotima (the Mantinean woman – real or imaginary – from whom Socrates in the *Symposium* professes to have learned about eros),[11] is (*Smp.* 211c-e):

> Beginning from these beauties (*i.e. the beautiful particulars which we perceive by the senses*), to ascend continually in pursuit of that other Beauty, going, as it were, by steps, from one to two and from two to all beautiful bodies, and from beautiful bodies to beautiful pursuits ('practices'), and from these to beautiful studies, and from studies to end in that study which is a study of nothing other than that Beauty itself ... If you ever see it, it will not seem to you beautiful in the sense that gold and clothes and beautiful boys and young men are – though now you are excited when you see *them*, and you are ready, as many others are too, so long as you see your paidika and are always with him, to go without food and drink, if that were possible, simply gazing on him and being with him. What are we to think a man would feel if it were open to him to see Beauty itself, genuine, pure, uncontaminated, not infected with human flesh and colour and all that mortal trash, but to see divine Beauty itself, unalloyed?

What happens when I meet another person who combines beauty of body and beauty of soul to an even greater degree than my existing eromenos? Diotima's doctrine implies that I have a duty to prefer Y to X, at whatever cost in agony to myself and to X, if it is clear that Y is a better instrument for the attainment of metaphysical enlightenment. Plato's argument is easy enough to follow so long as we keep 'eros' in Greek, but is he talking about love? There is no reason to suppose that

10. Cf. Robin 220-6.

11. 'Diotima' is a genuine Greek woman's name (and 'Diotimos' a very common man's name). We have no evidence outside the *Symposium* for a female Mantineian religious expert called Diotima, and in any case it is unlikely that any such person taught Socrates a doctrine containing elements which, according to Aristotle, were specifically Platonic and not Socratic. Plato's motive in putting an exposition of eros into the mouth of a woman is uncertain; perhaps he wished to put it beyond doubt that the praise of *paiderastiā* which that exposition contains is disinterested, unlike its praise in the speech of Pausanias.

Plato did not experience or did not understand love, for he may well have come to believe that love for another person as an end rather than as a means, however intensely he felt it, was a malfunction or deficiency in his own soul.[12] He certainly perceived the difference between the eros which he praises and what is commonly regarded as love, for having given Aristophanes the argument that eros is the individual's response to his 'other half', the recognition of 'affinity' being an essential part of its joy (*Smp.* 192b),[13] he makes Diotima explicitly reject this view (205de):[14]

> There is an argument that those who are in love are those who seek the other half of themselves; but my argument is that eros is not eros of half or of whole, except in so far as that may be *good* ... Surely people do not embrace what is their *own*, unless one calls good 'akin' and one's 'own' and bad 'alien', for there is nothing with which men are in love other than *good*.

When Socrates had finished speaking, Aristophanes 'tried to say something, because Socrates had referred to his argument' (212c), but his protest was never uttered, for just then the drunken Alkibiades arrived at Agathon's house. The description of erotic response in *Phaedrus* 251a-c is more dramatic than anything in Diotima's exposition – shuddering, sweating, fever, pain and joy together, religious awe – but the response is still the recognition of something in the eromenos other than the individual eromenos himself; the end lies in the world of Being, and however intense the love generated between erastes and eromenos, each is a means.

Throughout *Symposium* and *Phaedrus* it is taken for granted that eros which is significant as a step towards the world of Being is homosexual. In this respect Diotima's standpoint coincides with that of Pausanias's speech, and although Phaidros's speech includes Alkestis's devotion to Admetos and (with reservations) Orpheus's love for Eurydike as exemplifications of conduct inspired by Eros (179b-d), he makes much of a homosexual example (Achilles and Patroklos [179e-180b]), and his generalisations about eros are all cast in homosexual terms (178c-179a, 180b). Procreation, as explained by

---

12. Cf. Vlastos 27-33.

13. In Pl. *Lys.* 221e-222a it is argued that one's eros is a response to that which is 'akin' to oneself, and cf. *Phdr.* 252c-253c; but there is an important difference between seeking a unique individual who is complementary to oneself (and thus the right 'recipe') and seeking someone who resembles oneself to the extent that both resemble something outside and above them.

14. Cf. Dover (1966) 47-50; den Boer 48f.

Diotima, is an expression of the desire of mortal bodies to achieve a kind of immortality, and is shared by mankind with the animals (207ab); anyone, she remarks, would rather compose immortal poems or make enduring laws than procreate mere human children (209cd), and the generation of rational knowledge is the best of all manifestations of the human desire for immortality. Those men who are 'fertile in body' fall in love with women and beget children (208e), but those who are 'fertile in soul' transcend that limitation (209a), and the 'right approach' is open to them alone. Similarly in *Phaedrus* the man whose soul has long forgotten its vision of Beauty wishes only to 'go the way of a four-footed beast ... and sow children ... and is not ashamed to pursue pleasure contrary to nature' (250e).[15] Here heterosexual eros is treated on the same basis as homosexual copulation, a pursuit of bodily pleasure which leads no further (on 'contrary to nature', cf. p. 167), and in *Symposium* it is sub-rational, an expression of the eros which operates in animals. The eros commended in *Phaedrus* begins with a homosexual response, but the 'charioteer' of the soul, driving a noble horse and a wicked horse, has to prevent the wicked horse, on sighting a beautiful boy, from making indecent propositions on the spot (254a). The language in which the 'capture' (253c) of the eromenos is described is highly erotic: at first sight the charioteer experiences a 'tickling' and a 'pricking of desire' (253e; cf. Ar. *Thesm.* 133, where Agathon's seductive music gives the Old Man a 'tickling under the bottom'), the erastes follows his eromenos about 'in the gymnasium and elsewhere' (255b), the eromenos is so overcome with gratitude for the benevolence of the erastes that he embraces and kisses him, wants to lie down with him, and is disposed to refuse him nothing (255d-256a), and if their philosophical zeal is deficient they may in an unguarded moment yield to temptation (256cd). This lapse will not destroy their eros or render it valueless, for the good in it is not undone,[15] but the erastes and eromenos who have withstood temptation to the very end are superior; they have successfully

15. Vlastos 25 n. 76 argues that 'four-footed beast' does not refer to heterosexual intercourse at all, but I do not agree with him (despite *Laws* 841d – where, incidentally, concubines are mentioned in the first instance as recipients of seed, and males are tagged on) that *paidosporein* was intended by Plato, or understood by his readers, to mean no more than the ejaculation of semen. Given Greek modes of copulation (cf. p. 100), the heterosexual reference of 'four-footed beast' is clear enough, and Plato's point is that the man in whom the vision of Beauty is dim pursues only bodily pleasure.

16. When Plato refers to the lapsed pair as 'having exchanged the greatest pledges' (256d) he does not mean their copulation but the rest of their relationship, in which they resemble those who do not copulate.

'enslaved' the source of moral evil within them and 'liberated' the forces for good (256b).

It is easy enough to see why Socrates should handle a doctrine of eros predominantly in homosexual terms: in his ambience, intense eros was experienced more often in a homosexual than in a heterosexual relationship, and it was taken absolutely for granted that close contact with a beautiful, grateful, admiring young male was a virtually irresistible temptation. It is equally easy to see why an eros which perpetually restrained itself from bodily gratification should be homosexual: it was after all the prescribed role of women to be inseminated, whereas popular sentiment romanticised and applauded the chastity of an eromenos and the devotedly unselfish erastes. Why eros should play so conspicuous a part in a metaphysical system is not so obvious, but the most succinct explanation is to be found in *Phdr.* 250d, where it is observed that beauty is the only one, of those things which are *erastos*, 'attracting eros', which can be directly perceived by the senses, so that the sight of something beautiful affords by far the most powerful and immediate access we have to the world of Being. There is a further consideration: philosophy, as understood by Socrates, was not the product of solitary meditation, to be communicated by a spell-binding orator (or a guru) to a throng of silent disciples, but a co-operative process involving question and answer, mutual criticism and the eliciting of perceptions by one person from another. The climactic section of Diotima's speech in the *Symposium* envisages the 'procreation' of rational knowledge of the world of Being by an elder in a young male (209b), a process of 'procreation in a beautiful medium' (cf. 206b) of which the literal begetting of progeny by heterosexual intercourse is the gross and material counterpart (206c). The erastes tries to educate the eromenos (209c; cf. Xen. *Smp.* 8.23), and '*paiderastein* rightly' (211b) is philosophical education. At this point we might ask why, granted that from a methodological standpoint co-operation in discussion and criticism marks a considerable advance on lecturing *ex cathedra*, there should be such remarkable emphasis on the relationship between a senior and a junior partner rather than on partners of equal age and status. This in fact is the point at which we may decide that the sexual behaviour of leisured Athenians in the late fifth and early fourth centuries had a decisive influence on the form in which Socratic philosophy was realised; not an influence on its basic assumptions – the existence of a world of Being, the accessibility of that world to reason, its dependence upon Good[17] – but on its treatment of the

---

17. These are assumptions, not conclusions for which anything that we could

patient education of a younger male, to whose beauty one responds with a more intense and powerful emotion than to anything else in life, as the most direct road to philosophical achievement.[18] The sexual similes (*Smp.* 211d) or imagery (*Rep.* 490b) which Plato is apt to use when he speaks of the soul's vision of ultimate reality force upon us an analogy between the ecstasy with which 'true' eros rewards philosophical perseverance and the ecstasy of genital orgasm, the reward of persistence in sexual courtship. In modern literature we are more likely to find metaphysical language applied to sex than sexual language to metaphysics; in both cases, the analogy is facilitated by the sensation, not uncommon in orgasm, that one's individual identity has been obliterated by an irresistible force. To speak in this way of Plato is not to 'reduce' metaphysics to physiology; it is simply to recognise that whereas both the identification of assumptions and the scrutiny of the validity of deductive processes founded thereon are the business of a philosopher, it is for the biographer to explain the existence of the assumptions.

In *Laws*, composed at the end of Plato's life, he is no longer in the mood for compromise or tolerance such as he shows for the pair who 'lapse' in *Phaedrus*. The theme of homosexuality in *Laws* is first broached in 636a-c, where (in connection with temperance and restraint) the Athenian speaker declares that the pleasure of heterosexual intercourse is 'granted in accordance with nature', whereas homosexual pleasure is 'contrary to nature' and 'a crime caused by failure to control the desire for pleasure'. Later, the theme of sexual legislation as a whole is introduced (835c) with a reference to the magnitude of legislator's problem in controlling 'the strongest desires'. The absence of excessive wealth imposes certain limits on licence (836a), and the community is always under rigorous supervision by its magistrates, but (836ab):

> In what concerns erotes for male and female *paides* and of men for women and women for men, which have had innumerable effects on individuals and on whole cities, how can anyone take adequate precautions?

After a further reference (on the lines of 635e-636a) to the bad

---

seriously call evidence is offered; and that they are assumptions Plato makes clear enough, not pretending to demonstrate what he has not demonstrated. Cf. p. 11 n. 20.

18. In *Phdr.* 249a the only type of soul which is said to 'return whence it came' in less than ten thousand years is that of 'him who has philosophised or has been a *paiderastēs* with (= in conjunction with) philosophy'. Whether 'or' here means 'that is to say' is disputable (cf. T.F. Gould 117 and n. 74), but even if it does not the eschatological status of philosophical *paiderastiā* is still remarkable.

example set by Sparta and Crete (the Athenian's interlocutors in *Laws* are a Spartan and a Cretan; cf. p. 186), the speaker passes specifically to homosexual relations (836c-e):

> Anyone who, in conformity with nature, proposes to re-establish the law as it was before Laios,[19] declaring that it was right not to join with men and boys in sexual intercourse as with females, adducing as evidence the nature of animals 'and pointing out that (*sc.* among them) male does not touch male for sexual purposes, since that is not natural, he could, I think, make a very strong case.

No one, continues the Athenian, could argue that the law should take a benevolent view of homosexual relations, for they do not implant courage in the soul of the 'persuaded' or self-restraint in 'the persuader'; the latter is open to blame as failing to withstand the temptations of pleasure, and the former as 'mimicking the female' (836de). The Athenian's proposal is that the religious sanctions which already operate against incest, so that 'not so much as a desire for such intercourse enters most people's heads' (838b), should be extended to sexual legislation in general (838e-839b):

> That is precisely what I meant in saying that I had an idea for reinforcing the law about the natural use of the intercourse which procreates children, abstaining from the male, not deliberately killing human progeny or 'sowing in rocks and stones', where it (*sc.* the seed) will never take root and be endowed with growth, abstaining too from all female soil in which you would not want what you have sown to grow. This law ... confers innumerable benefits. In the first place, it has been made according to nature; also, it effects a debarment from erotic fury and insanity, all kinds of adultery and all excesses in drink and food, and it makes men truly affectionate to their own wives.

Athletes abstain from sex for the sake of the physical fitness which will bring them victory in games (839e-840b); should we not then expect of our young people (asks the Athenian) that they should control their passions for the sake of victory over pleasure?[20] The law must declare (840de):

> Our citizens should not be inferior to birds and many other species of animals, which are born in large communities and up to the age of procreation live unmated, pure and unpolluted[21] by marriage, but when

19. The mythical inventor of homosexuality; cf. p.199.
20. On identification of the self with reason cf. *GPM* 124-6.
21. Many of us may think (as I do, for one) that there is nothing to be said in favour

they have arrived at that age they pair, male with female and female with male, according to their inclination, and for the rest of their time they live in a pious and law-abiding way,[22] faithfully adhering to the agreements which were the beginning of their love.

Eventually the Athenian proposes two alternative laws on 'sexual intercourse and all that has to do with eros' (841e), the first alternative more rigorous than the second (841de):

> Either, among those of good citizen stock and free status, no one should touch anyone except his own wedded wife, and should not sow unacceptable and illegitimate seed in concubines, nor unfruitful seed in males, contrary to nature; or we could ban intercourse with males entirely, and if a man had intercourse with any woman except those who have entered his house with the religious rites of marriage ... and failed to conceal this from all men and women,[23] by prescribing that he should be debarred from the award of official honours we should, I think, be regarded as making a sound prescription.

The theme of nature, anticipated by *Phdr.* 250e, is conspicuous in all these passages, as well as in 636a-c, and Plato appeals to the animal world to establish what is natural and what is not. This argument is weak, if only because Plato knew virtually nothing about animals (the generalisation in *Smp.* 207b that animals sacrifice themselves for the protection and feeding of their young, true of some species, is untrue of many others), but Plato would not regard it as equally open to adversaries who might wish to argue (e.g.) for aggressive individualism; the ingredient of reason (in his view) differentiates human nature from animal nature, but in respect of an irrational activity such as sexual intercourse humans and animals can be treated together. Plato's main concern is to reduce to an unavoidable minimum all activity of which the end is physical enjoyment, in order that the irrational and appetitive element of the soul may not be encouraged and strengthened by indulgence, and to this end he is prepared to deploy arguments of different kinds, including a prudential argument (the strengthening of the marital bond, which necessarily contributes to the like-mindedness, and therefore to the

---

of the habitual use of words such as 'pure', 'clean' or 'innocent' to mean 'non-sexual' or 'sexually inactive', but this usage was not begun by Plato; it is firmly rooted in Greek religious belief and practice.

22. The formula '*hosios* and *dikaios*' in commonplace in oratory; cf. *GPM* 248.

23. In *Laws* 841b it is treated as desirable that we should be ashamed of our sexual activity, whether legitimate or not, and should conceal it, in order that its inevitable reduction will then diminish the power of sexual desire over us.

strength and stability, of the ideal community) and an appeal to nature which may perhaps exploit a feeling that the processes of the non-human world manifest obedience to commands issued by the gods. While prohibiting homosexual relations because they go beyond what nature shows to be adequate in sexual pleasure, he does not express an opinion on the naturalness or unnaturalness of the desire to perform the prohibited acts; it is to be presumed, in accordance with the sentiment of his time, that he would regard the desire as an indication that the appetitive element of the soul is insufficiently disciplined,[24] and would say that such a soul desires homosexual copulation only as one among many pleasurable sensations.

Condemnation of homosexual acts as contrary to nature was destined to have a profound effect on the history of morality, but it should be noted that Plato's most distinguished pupil treated the question cautiously. In *Nicomachean Ethics* 1148^b 15-9^a 20 Aristotle distinguishes what is naturally pleasurable (divisible into 'pleasurable without qualification' and 'pleasurable to some animal species or some human races, but not to others') from what is pleasurable without being naturally so. In this latter category he puts (a) things which are pleasurable because of 'deficiencies' or 'impairments' in those who find them so, (b) things which become pleasurable through habit, and (c) things which are found pleasurable by bad natures. Corresponding to each of these three sub-categories is a 'disposition': (a) 'bestial' (i.e. 'sub-human') dispositions, exemplified by a woman who cut open pregnant women and devoured the foetuses; (b) dispositions which result from disease, including insanity; (c) dispositions which are 'disease-like or as a result of habituation'. These include pulling out one's hair, eating earth, and (literally):

> moreover, the (*sc.* disposition?) of sexual intercourse for males; for they come about (*i.e.* the pleasure in such actions comes about) for some by nature and for others through habituation, as, for example, for those who were first outraged (*hubrizein*) when they were boys. No one could describe as 'lacking in self-control' those for whom nature is the cause,[25] any more than (*sc.* we so describe) women (*lit.*) because they do not mount sexually but are mounted.[26]

24. On the tripartite soul, here and elsewhere, I have over-simplified somewhat (cf. Guthrie iv 422-5); the essential point is that to Plato relaxation of the control of reason within the soul creates a 'power vacuum' into which lust and greed will make haste to move.

25. The principal question in this portion of the *Ethics* is the nature of the inability to refrain from doing what one believes to be wrong.

26. *Opuiein* means 'marry' in some dialects, but we need a more down-to-earth translation for it in Attic and Hellenistic Greek, yet not too coarse a word.

Perhaps distaste for the subject has prevented translators and commentators from discussing the curious words 'the of sexual intercourse for males' and has induced them to translate it as 'pederasty', 'faire l'amour avec les mâles', etc. If that translation were correct,[27] Aristotle would be saying that subjection to a passive role in homosexuality when young disposes one to take an active role when older. This would be a strange thing for a Greek to say; it would also be strange for a Greek to suggest that pleasure in an active homosexual role is 'disease-like' or unlikely to be experienced except in consequence of involuntary habituation; the example of the passive sexual role of women as naturally-determined behaviour which cannot be reproached as a lack of control over bodily pleasure indicates that Aristotle's mind is running on the moral evaluation of sexual passivity; and – a near-decisive consideration – if we assume that Aristotle is speaking of passive homosexuality only, the exclusive preoccupation of the pseudo-Aristotelian *Problemata* iv 26 with the passive role is more readily intelligible. The writer asks:

> why some men enjoy being subjected to sexual intercourse,[28] some of them while at the same time performing it, and others not.

The writer explains that seminal fluid does not always and necessarily form in the genital system, but may be secreted – though not in great quantity, and not under pressure – in the rectum; wherever it is secreted, that is the part whose friction creates sexual enjoyment.

> Those who are effeminate by nature ... are constituted contrary to nature; for, though male, they are so disposed that this part of them (*sc.* the rectum) is necessarily defective. Defect, if complete, causes

27. Grammatically, 'sexual intercourse with males' would be possible; cf. Kühner-Gerth i 427f.

28. The writer uses the passive *aphrodīsiazesthai*, which is distinct in meaning from the active *aphrodīsiazein*. To the best of my belief the only passage in which *aphrodīsiazesthai* appears to have an active sense is *Problemata* iv 27, where the writer asks why people who desire *aphrodīsiazesthai* are ashamed to admit it, whereas no one minds admitting to a liking for food and drink. The answer he gives, that a desire for food and drink is a necessity if we are to keep alive, whereas 'desire for sexual intercourse' is 'a product of surplus', i.e. a desire to get rid of something, is strange, for one might have expected him to use the argument of the preceding section and say that people are ashamed to admit to a defect; if, on the other hand, the text is wrong, and we should read the active instead of the passive, so that the question is simply why people are embarrassed at admitting to a liking for sexual activity, everything is plain sailing. If the text is wrong, the cause of the error will be the preoccupation with the passive role in the long preceding section.

destruction,[29] but if not, perversion (*sc.* of one's nature). The former does not occur (*sc.* in the matter which we are considering), for (*sc.* if it did) the man would have been a woman. It therefore follows that they must be distorted and have an urge in a place other than (*sc.* that of) procreative ejaculation. For that reason they are insatiable, like women; for the liquid is small in quantity, does not force its way out, and quickly cools down.

Having offered this bizarre physiological explanation, the writer continues in language which recalls the elliptical statement of Aristotle:

Some undergo this experience also as a result of habituation. For whatever they do, it comes about that they take pleasure in that and ejaculate their semen in that way. So they desire to do the things through which this happens, and the habit becomes increasingly like nature. For that reason those who have been accustomed to be subjected to sexual intercourse not before puberty, but at the time of puberty, in consequence of recollection arising in them when they are so dealt with, and pleasure with the recollection, and because (*sc.* they become) as if naturally (*sc.* so disposed) through the habit, desire to undergo (*sc.* intercourse); for the most part, however, the habit arises in those who are as if naturally (*sc.* so disposed). If (*sc.* a man) is lustful and soft, all these developments come about more quickly.

The writer's concept of nature is not difficult to understand: a male who is physically constituted in such a way that he lacks something of the positive characteristics which distinguish male from female, and possesses instead a positively female characteristic, suffers from a constitutional defect contrary to nature, and a male who through habituation behaves in a way which is a positive differentia of females behaves as if he had such a defect. There is no sign in the sexual discussions which make up Book IV of the *Problemata*, or in Aristotle, or indeed in Plato, that a genital response to the bodily beauty of a younger male was regarded as a defect or impairment of male nature, no matter what view was taken of the duty of the law to prevent gratification of the desire aroused by this response.

---

29. Not death, but an obliteration of the characteristic form of the species, in this case the male human. Robinson and Fluck 41 wrongly believe that the writer is referring to injury to the anus through penetration.

E.   Women and Homosexuality

That female homosexuality and the attitude of women to male homosexuality can both be discussed within one part of one chapter reflects the paucity of women writers and artists in the Greek world and the virtual silence of male writers and artists on these topics.

People in love are jealous of rivals, and people who are not in love but whose security depends on their retention of someone else's sexual interest have equally strong grounds for anxiety and jealousy when this security is threatened by a diversion of sexual interest. Whether Greek women had a special animosity against male eromenoi, we do not know. We should expect that hetairai and would-be hetairai did, and in individual cases resentment, contempt and mortification may have given an extra dimension to the jealousy felt by a woman (let us put ourselves in the place of Ionis in Kallimakhos 11 [p.65] or imagine the feelings of either of the girls in R62 if she saw the young man's eyes fixed on a passing boy), but in general the pursuit of eromenoi was characteristic of the years before marriage (cf. Anon. *HE* 33.5 [p. 66], Meleagros 84, 87:5), so that wives will comparatively seldom[1] have had grounds for fearing that their husbands were forming enduring homosexual attachments.[2] Yet Kritoboulos's hyperbolic praise of his eromenos Kleinias (Xen. *Smp.* 4. 12-16) is uttered by a young man who is newly married (*ibid.* 2.3). In Theokritos 7.120f., where Simikhidas prays that the young Philinos, by whose attractions his friend Aratos is tormented, may himself suffer the torment of unrequited love for another, we hear a rare and interesting note of malice:

> Can't you see? He's riper than a pear (*i.e. past the eromenos stage, and no use to you any more*), and the women say, 'O dear, Philinos, your pretty flowers are dropping!'

1. Cf. p. 62.
2. In Eur. *Medea* 249 Medeia, complaining of the miserable lot of women, says that whenever a husband feels that he has had enough of his home he can go out and recover his spirits 'turning either to someone *philos* or to someone of his own age'. Since Wilamowitz's condemnation of the line it has been customary for editors to delete it as an interpolation by a prudish Byzantine schoolmaster who wished to prevent his pupils from entertaining the idea that a husband might recover his spirits by sexual intercourse with someone other than his wife. This notion, however unrealistic, receives superficial support from the fact that *hēlika*, 'of his own age', does not scan; but the plural *hēlikas*, conjectured by a Byzantine scholar, does, and with that slight emendation we can keep the line; by 'someone *philos*' (and by implication younger) Medeia means to imply an eromenos.

Xen. *Hell.* vi 4.37 relates an incident of unusual type: Alexander, tyrant of Pherai, had quarreled with his paidika and had imprisoned him; his wife begged for the release of the youth, whereupon Alexander executed him, and was subsequently murdered by his aggrieved wife. It sounds as though Alexander suspected a love-affair between his paidika and his wife, and he may have been right. The attributes which made a young male attractive to erastai were assumed to make him no less attractive to women; Pentheus, sneering at Dionysos in Eur. *Bacchae* 453-9, treats his good looks, long hair ('full of desire') and fair skin as particularly captivating to women. When goddesses fall in love with mortal males, as Aphrodite did with Adonis, Dawn with Tithonos or the Moon with Endymion, they react like older males; vase-paintings which depict Dawn and Tithonos assimilate Tithonos to Ganymede or to anonymous eromenoi courted by men, and the portrayal of Adonis described in Theokritos 15.84-6 gives him 'the first down spreading from his temples', so that he resembles a youth at the age which some erastai found most seductive (cf. Pl. *Prt.* 309a, *Smp.* 181d). Hylas, the eromenos of Herakles, captivates the water-nymphs and is pulled down into the water by them (Theokritos 13. 43-54).

Classical Attic literature refers once, and once only, to female homosexuality: 'Aristophanes' in Pl. *Smp.* 191e derives *hetairistriai* from that category of original double beings who were all female. The word is not attested elsewhere, any more than its masculine analogue *hetairistēs*, though Pollux (vi 188) found the latter in an Attic source (unspecified); it clearly means a woman who stands in a relationship to another woman comparable to a male relationship of *hetairēsis* (cf. p. 20), and it may acquire a derogatory nuance from *laikastria*, 'whore', though that is by no means certain, since Pl. *Euthd.* 297c introduces us to *sophistria* as the feminine of *sophistēs* in the sense 'ingenious', 'resourceful'. We have a Hellenistic epigram (Asklepiades 7) on two Samian women who

> are not willing to enter upon the (*sc.* practice?) of Aphrodite according to her rules, but desert to other things which are not seemly ('not *kalos*'). Mistress Aphrodite, be an enemy to these fugitives from the couch in your domain!

This hostility, on the part of a poet who elsewhere (37) declares the strength of his own homosexual desire, is striking; that he treats a woman who rejects male lovers as a 'deserter' and 'fugitive' and as disobedient to the 'rules' (*nomoi*) of Aphrodite suggests the possibility that the complete silence of comedy on the subject of female

homosexuality is a reflex of male anxiety. There are such things as
'taboo' subjects which the comic poets did not try to exploit for
humorous purposes; the plague of 430 B.C. is one, and menstruation[3]
is another. At Sparta, on the other hand, according to Plu.
Lyc. 18.9, 'women of good repute' (*kalos kai agathos*)[4] 'were in love
with girls', i.e. had a female counterpart of the male erastes/eromenos
relationship. CE34*, an archaic plate from Thera, shows two women
apparently courting; one puts her hand to the face of the other, and
both hold garlands. Vase-paintings in which two women are wrapped
in one cloak should probably be associated not with two males
similarly wrapped (or partially veiled by a 'backcloth'; cf. p. 98) but
with scenes in which the number of women may exceed two and they
may not be facing each other but facing all in one direction.[5] An
exceptional Attic red-figure vase (R207*) shows a kneeling woman
fingering the genital region of another woman.

The strongest expression of female homosexual emotion in Greek
literature is to be found in the poetry of Sappho, earliest and most
famous of the few female Greek poets. She was a native of the city of
Mytilene on the island of Lesbos, and active in the first quarter of the
sixth century B.C.; like her equally famous contemporary and
compatriot, Alkaios, she composed lyric poetry predominantly for
solo performance. The evidence for her homosexuality is fragmentary
in the literal sense: only one of her poems survives complete (quoted
by a literary critic of the Roman period), the rest being represented by
scraps of ancient copies, in which a complete line is a rarity, and by
later writers' quotations of short passages, individual lines or phrases.
The evidence is also fragile and ambiguous: Sappho's Lesbian dialect
created problems in transmission which are reflected in corruption of
the text, understanding of crucial passages is often frustrated by the
absence, unintelligibility or doubtful interpretation of the words
needed for resolution of problems, and although biographical
statements made about her by commentators of Hellenistic or Roman
times were founded ultimately on what is denied to us, access to her
work in its entirety, we do not know the processes of inference which
underlie a given statement – and we do know the *horror vacui* which led
ancient biographers to treat mere possibilities as established facts.

---

3. Philetas *HE* 1.5 may refer ('things not to be spoken of by a man'); cf. Hopfner
332, and Hesiod's dictum (*Works and Days* 753f.) that is baneful for a man to wash in
water in which a woman has washed.

4. On the meaning of this term, often simply 'good' when applied to a male citizen,
cf. *GPM* 41-45.

5. Cf. Guarducci and also Schauenburg (1964).

Comment on Sappho's erotic relationships with women does not begin, so far as the extant evidence goes, until Hellenistic times. At least six comedies entitled *Sappho* were produced in classical Athens, and in one of these Diphilos (fr. 69f.) made the Ionian poets Arkhilokhos and Hipponax her *erastai*. In Antiphanes' play (fr. 196) she propounded riddles (like the legendary Kleobouline, or the Sphinx). We do not know anything about the Sappho-plays of Ameipsias (fr. 16), Ephippos (fr. 24), Amphis (fr. 32) and Timokles (fr. 30), but Epikrates fr. 4 names her, together with some minor poets, as an author of *erōtika* (*sc.* songs). Menander (fr. 258) spoke of her as falling in love with Phaon, the legendary ferryman of great beauty (cf. Plato Comicus fr. 174 and Servius on Vergil *Aeneid* iii 279), 'hunting' him, and committing suicide in despair.[6] Hermesianax at the end of the fourth century referred (fr. 7.47-50) to Alkaios and Anakreon as rival *erastai* of Sappho; Dioskorides 18, associating her with eros of the young in general, imagines her honoured by the Muses, Hymen (the god of marriage) and Aphrodite (as – in particular – the lover of Adonis). Although no one who speaks of Sappho's eros for her own sex can be dated with complete certainty before the Augustan period (Horace *Odes* ii 13.5 and Ovid *Tristia* ii 365), a fragment of a biography (*Oxyrhynchus Papyri* 1800 fr. 1 col.i 16f.) which remarks that 'she is criticised by some as being licentious (*ataktos*, 'disorderly', 'undisciplined') and *gunaikerastria*', i.e. '(female) erastes of women', may well be using early Hellenistic material. Certainly it refers a few lines later to Khamaileon, who wrote a monograph on Sappho, in which, incidentally, he mentioned (fr. 26) the idea that Anakreon fr. 358 (cf. p. 183) expresses desire for Sappho, and he apparently lent his authority[7] to an interpretation of a stanza in Sapphic style (*PMG* 953) as a reference to Anakreon. Klearkhos (frr. 33 and 41) said something about Sappho, and a certain Kallias of Mitylene, perhaps as early as the third century B.C., is also known to have written a commentary on her poems.

There is at any rate no doubt that some of Sappho's poems address women in the language used by male *erastai* to their *eromenoi*; in late antiquity Maximus of Tyre (xviii 9) compares her relationship with girls to Socrates' relationship with handsome youths, and Themistios xiii p. 170d couples Sappho and Anakreon as giving 'unbounded praise' to their *paidika*. A recently published fragment of a commentary (*SLG* S261A), speaking of Sappho as 'educating the best'

---

6. Cf. Nagy on Sappho's own treatment of the Phaon myth.

7. Unless Athenaios 599d 'and he says that Sappho said ...' is a careless expression for (cf. 599c) 'and he says that some say that Sappho said ...'.

(feminine plural) 'not only of her compatriots but also of those from Ionia', gives an interesting turn to Maximus's analogy. The fragment goes on to say that Sappho was 'in such high favour with the citizens that Kallias of Mytilene said in [...', and thereafter there is only part of the name of Aphrodite to afford us any clue to what Kallias said. In what, if anything, did Sappho 'educate' Lesbian and Ionian girls? Most obviously, in that in which she herself excelled, poetry and music, establishing a female counterpart to a predominantly male domain; there would be a certain improbability in supposing that Lesbian girls of good family were sent by their parents to a school of sexual technique, but none in supposing a school[8] which enhanced their skill and charm (charm is within the province of Aphrodite) as performers in girls' choruses at festivals. If in the generation after Sappho there were other women poets in the Eastern Aegean, Lesbian tradition will have regarded them as pupils of Sappho; for what it is worth — and that is very little, except as an indication of the form of the Sappho-legend in much later times – Philostratos *Life of Apollonios* i 30 names a Pamphylian woman Damophyla as a 'disciple' of Sappho and as having had girl disciples of her own, like Sappho. Kallias will probably have based his statement about 'high favour' on tradition as he knew it, not on evidence giving direct access to the sentiment of the Lesbians in Sappho's lifetime.

To return, however, to Sappho's own language. In fr. 16.15 her delight at the sight of Anaktoria exemplifies the generalisation '*I* say that the most beautiful sight on earth is that which one loves (*erātai*)'; she declares to Atthis (fr. 49) 'I was in love (*ēramān*) with you long ago', and blames her (fr. 131) for turning against Sappho and 'flying to Andromeda' instead. Compare also fr. 96, 'she remembers gentle Atthis with desire (*hīmeros*)'; 'Aphrodite' and 'Persuasion' occur later in the poem, in unintelligible contexts. In fr. 94 Sappho describes her great grief at parting from someone who is female, as feminine pronouns, adjectives and participles show (lines 2, 5, 6f.); she recalls occasions on which the two of them were together, scented and wearing garlands (the usual concomitants of drinking and festivity). Lines 21-3 say:

And on soft beds tender [...]
you expelled desire (*potho*[   ) [...

---

8. The notion of Sappho as a 'schoolmistress' now attracts a certain amount of ridicule, a reaction against earlier attempts to play down the sensuality of her poetry, but in the Greek world those who could not only did but also taught.

The Homeric expression 'when they had expelled eros of drink and food' in the sense 'when they had satisfied their desire for …' indicates that to 'expel' desire is to satisy it. But whose desire? In Homer the verb is in the middle voice, i.e. 'expelled from themselves', 'satisfied their …', and in Sappho fr. 94 it is active, suggesting that it was someone else's desire which the addressee of the poem satisfied. Yet in another Homeric passage, *Il.* xxiv 227, 'when I had expelled (*sc.* my) eros of lamentation', the active voice is used although the middle would have scanned as well. However, whether it was Sappho's desire or the addressee's which was satisfied (by bodily contact, common sense would suggest)[9] on soft beds, in the context of Sappho's grief-stricken farewell it is more appropriate that she should be speaking of relations between the two of them than of the addressee's relations with men.

Two well-preserved poems, frr. 1 and 31, are of the greatest importance. In fr. 1 Sappho appeals to Aphrodite for help, reminding her of a previous occasion on which help was forthcoming. On that occasion (lines 14-24):

> With a smile on your immortal face you asked me what had happened to me this time, why I was calling on you this time, and what I most wished, with heart distracted ('insane', *mainolās*) to be done for me (*or* 'to obtain'). 'Whom this time am I to persuade' (*then an unintelligible phrase*) 'to your love (*philotēs*)? Who wrongs you, Sappho? For even if she[10] flees, soon she will pursue; and if she does not accept gifts, yet she will give; and if she does not love (*philein*), soon she will love even unwilling.' Come to me now too …

9. Fr. 99.5 is tantalising, but perhaps not important; it presents us with *olisb*[*o*]*dokois*[, in a very badly damaged context. The word, 'receivers of the olisbos', recalls the satyr's name 'Phlebodokos' (p. 103), 'receiver of the vein', i.e. '… of the penis', and if on the strength of a double-ended olisbos, portrayed in R223* (cf. Pomeroy 88), we assumed that the olisbos was not merely used in female homosexual relations in the archaic and classical periods but used primarily for that purpose, we would naturally treat the passage as relevant to Sappho's homosexuality. Since, however, the olisbos is associated essentially with solitary female masturbation, Sappho may here be speaking derogatorily, or relating someone else's derogatory description, of a female enemy who, she alleges, can find no partner.

10. In the Greek text the phrase *kai ouk etheloisa*, 'even unwilling', using the feminine participle, is the only indication of the sex of the person whom Aphrodite is asked to influence. The metre requires — ∪ ∪— x (*–ai* and *ou–* coalesce); unfortunately, 'be willing' in Lesbian dialect is always *thelein*, never *ethelein*, and the disyllabic negatives *oukhi* and *ouki* are not as yet attested in that dialect, which has only *ou* and *ouk*. Among emendations designed to restore linguistic normality, some (e.g. Knox 194, Beattie 183) have the effect of removing the only indication that the desired person is female.

Pursuit, flight, gifts and love are familiar ingredients. The complaint of the erastes that his eromenos 'wrongs' him (*adikein*) – that is to say, does not requite the love of the erastes in the manner or to the extent desired by the erastes[11] – occurs in Theognis 1283 ('O boy, do not wrong me!'). A notable feature of Sappho's poem is the inclusion of her own name, which shows that she is not composing a poem both for an imaginary situation and for a fictitious *persona*.[12] A second and more important feature is that a marked degree of mutual eros is assumed: the other person, who now refuses gifts and flees, will not merely yield and 'grant favours' but will pursue Sappho and will herself offer gifts. This obliteration of the usual distinction between a dominant and a subordinate partner is contrary to what the evidence for Greek male homosexuality would have led us to expect. In a heterosexual context Theokritos 6.17 says of the sea-nymph Galateia's desperate attempts to arouse the sexual interest of the Cyclops 'she flees one who loves, and when one does not love she pursues', and Sappho might conceivably have meant by 'pursue' no more than 'try to attract', but Theokritos's line has the flavour of a proverb (cf. 11.75, 'Milk the [*sc.* ewe] that's here. Why pursue one who [*masculine*][13] flees?') and may not originally have had a sexual reference at all.

Fr. 31 runs as follows:

He seems to me to be equal to gods, that man who is sitting[14] facing you and hearing your sweet voice close by, and your lovely (*hīmeroeis*, 'desire-attracting') laugh. That, I swear, set my heart fluttering in my breast. For whenever[15] I look at you briefly, then it is no longer in my power to speak. My tongue is fixed(?)[16] in silence, and straightway a subtle fire has run under my skin, and with my eyes I see nothing, and my ears hum, and cold sweat possesses me, and trembling seizes all of me, and I am paler than grass, and I seem (*a word is missing here*) within a little of being dead. But all is to be endured (*or* 'has been endured?'),

11. Cf. Gentili (1972) 63-6; but however one applies the Greek concept of equilibrium and reciprocity to erotic relationships, it must also be remembered that evaluative words such as 'wrong' are instruments by which we try to make other people do what we wish, justly or unjustly (cf. *GPM* 50-6, 181f., 217).

12. Cf. Dover (1963b) 201-12 on the danger of treating Greek lyric poetry as autobiography, and Lefkowitz on fr. 31.

13. In generalisations masculine forms stand for masculine and feminine together; cf. p. 66.

14. Literally, 'whoever is sitting'; the indicative mood precludes 'whoever (*sc.* at any time) sits' and points to 'inasmuch as he is sitting ...', 'because he ...', a possible meaning for 'whoever' in Greek.

15. 'When', Page (1955) 19 (cf. ibid. 29 n.1 and Devereux (1970) 24), which to the English-speaking reader suggests 'now that ...'; but cf. n. 21 below.

16. Cf. Devereux (1970) 23f.

since even (?) (*the next word is not intelligible, and the quotation ceases*) ⌊ ...

Occasions on which a man sits facing a (presumably young) woman and talks to her may well have been more numerous and varied in archaic Lesbos than in classical Athens; if the object of Sappho's emotion is the bride at a wedding, the poem is exceedingly unlikely to be a wedding-song;[17] but that by no means precludes the possibility that Sappho is expressing the emotion aroused in someone by the wedding of a girl with whom that person is in love. Whether the man is 'equal to gods' because his beauty and strength are superhuman, or because he is unimaginably fortunate to have engaged the sexual interest of the girl, or because he does not (as a mortal might be expected to do) faint when confronted with the girl's beauty,[18] is disputed. Since it is precisely the intonations of speech and laughter which, by appearing to a jealous person to betray an unexpected intimacy between two other people, act as a detonator of intolerable emotional stress, I doubt whether 'equal to gods' here connotes imperturbability, and I prefer[19] to take it as an indication of fear of loss and despair at the impossibility of competing with the man. 'Set my heart ...' is in the aorist tense in accordance with a common Greek idiom: the speaker communicates the fact that he is in an emotional state by saying that it came upon him, *sc.* a moment before speaking.[20] The 'I' of the poem glances frequently and repeatedly at the girl (hence 'whenever I look ...') in the wild hope of disproving by sight the inference she drew from sound, but that inference is only confirmed.[21]

17. Cf. Page (1955) 30-3.

18. So Marcovich 20f., 29; cf. Anon. *HE* 13.3f. 'If upon looking at him you were not subdued by the flames of desire, you must be a god or a stone'; but the connotations of 'equal to a god' in archaic and classical literature are not indifference and immunity but size, beauty, majesty, strength and exultation.

19. Subjectivity is not easily excluded in the interpretation of Greek lyric poetry, and the reader is warned that in my eventual decision between alternative treatments of this poem there is a larger element of subjectivity than I usually (if I perceive it in time) allow myself. Cf. n. 21 below.

20. Cf. Kühner-Gerth i 164.

21. Marcovich's interpretation of the sequence is: (a) 'your voice and laugh originally excited my heart with love for you', (b) 'subsequently, whenever I look at you, I faint (etc.)'; '*for* whenever ...' justifies by expansion the fact communicated in 'excited my heart'. The strength of Marcovich's case (and the weakness of Devereux's and mine) is: (i) the verb which I have translated 'excited' is almost certainly used by Alkaios fr. 283.3f. of the effect of desire for Paris on Helen's heart, even though it is used elsewhere in early Greek poetry of the effects of fear, and (ii) 'whenever ...', or 'every time that ...' is certainly a correct translation, and I do not feel entirely confident that a Greek hearer would understand 'whenever (*sc.* during this temporary situation) I glance at you'. I do, however, feel (and here I avoid the word 'think') that

The ancient writers who quote the poem, Plutarch and Pseudo-Longinus, treat the physical symptoms which Sappho describes so fully as a manifestation of her eros for the girl;[22] so they are, in the sense that if she had not been in love with the girl she would not have experienced such symptoms, but collectively they amount to an anxiety-attack,[23] and the fact that she feels towards her male rival not a malice which would express itself in depreciation, but the hopeless envy which a mortal feels towards a god, accords with a homosexual orientation.[24]

Strong and apparently erotic response by a woman to the beauty of another woman is not confined to the poetry of Sappho;[25] it exists also in some *partheneia*, 'songs for choruses of virgins', composed (by male poets) and performed at a variety of festivals in many parts of the Greek world. Pindar in the first half of the fifth century composed some, of which we have two sizable fragments and some scraps, but the genre is especially associated in our own day with the early[26] Spartan poet Alkman, thanks to the survival of nearly seventy legible lines of one of his *partheneia*, fragments of others, and interesting fragments of ancient comments on them. His fr. 3 says (61-81):

] with desire that weakens the limbs, and her look melts (*sc.* me?) more than sleep and death. And not without reason is she (*i.e.* 'her effect'?) sweet (?). But Astymeloisa does not give me any answer.

'That, I swear ...' describes the shock-wave which hit the speaker when she heard the tone of voice in which the girl spoke to the man, and 'for whenever ...' explains why 'He seems to me ...'.

22. Plutarch *Dial.* 763a describes Sappho's emotion as recurring 'when her *erōmenē*' (feminine) 'has appeared to her'; Beattie (1956) 110f. adopts an alternative emendation of line 7 which gives 'when I look upon (*sc.* this situation)' and opens the possibility that Sappho is in love with the man and jealous of the girl.

23. Cf. Devereux (1970) 18f.

24. Devereux's reference (22f.) to 'phallic awe' is treated by Marcovich 20 as 'pushing' the hypothesis of Sappho's jealousy '*ad absurdum*'; but there is an important difference between statements which are absurd because they are irreconcilable with facts and facts which are absurd but are the subject of truthful statements. Experience has compelled me to believe that some elements in Freud's psychodynamics are true and the common-sense assumptions which conflict with them untrue. On the subject of 'phallic awe' and 'penis envy' (cf. Slater 45-9) I am not in a position to contribute an opinion of my own, but I beg the reader to distinguish between (a) the truth or falsity of a statement, (b) the goodness or badness of the fact, or the hypothetical goodness or badness of the factoid, communicated by that statement, and (c) the goodness or badness of the consequences of believing the statement. 'Earthquakes are common in Turkey' suffices to illustrate the difference between (a) and (b), and the difference between (a) and (c) is thrust upon us by developments in 'genetic engineering'.

25. Cf. Diels 352-6.

26. Late seventh and early sixth century; cf. M.L. West (1965) 188-94.

Holding a garland, like a star falling through the glittering sky, or a
golden shoot or soft down [   ] she passed with long steps
[   ] moist beauty of the lovely (?) locks of Kinyras, which
dwells upon the hair of girls. [   ] Astymeloisa in the host
[   ] darling to the people [   ] having won
honour(?) [

                                                                          ]
in the hope that [   ] might come (*third person*) close and take (*sc.*
her? me?) by the tender hand; quickly would I become her suppliant [

It is possible for a chorus of girls to sing verses composed from a
standpoint other than their own, or to sing a narrative in which they
report the direct speech of some other person, and caution is required
in interpreting a passage such as the above, where the context is
missing. Unfortunately we may find ourselves in deeper trouble when
we do have the context. The extant portion of the great *partheneion* of
Alkman (fr. 1) follows a portion in which a myth was related and a
summary moral drawn; the chorus then goes on to sing of itself and of
a number of individual girls by name. It is not easy to make any
statement about the interpretation of the poem which will be both
useful and non-controversial, and anyone who reads it will see why.[27]
It is composed for a chorus of ten girls (98f.); it refers to a certain
Hagesikhora as 'my cousin' (52f.); it praises her hair (51) face (55)
and ankles (78; a conventional epithet); it also praises Agido (39-49),
who is 'like the sun'; and it rounds off a list of names with (73-7):

> Nor will you go (*feminine participle*) to (*sc.* the house) of Ainesimbrota and
> say 'Would that I could have Astaphis', and 'would that Philylla would
> look at me!' and 'Damareta' and 'lovely Vianthemis'.[28] It is Hagesikhora
> who distresses (*teirein*) me.

The language is erotic; even *teirein*, though it often denotes the action
of pain and suffering, is used by Hesiod (fr. 298) of the effect upon
Theseus of his eros for Aigle, and in any case it is not easy to see in
what other sense a girl so praised for her beauty could 'distress' those
who praise her.

Whether the girls for whom Alkman composed this *partheneion* came
all from one family depends on how we interpret the fact that, singing
collectively, they call Hagesikhora 'my cousin'; one of the unknown
factors is the degree of kinship denoted by the word 'cousin' (*anepsios*)
in the Spartan dialect.[29] There were many cults in which functions

27. Translations are available in Page (1951) 21f. and Bowra (1961) 45f.
28. I have adopted the punctuation of M.L. West (1965) 199f.
29. Cf. Bowra (1961) 47.

were restricted to sections of the community regarded as having each a common ancestor more recent in date than the legendary ancestor of the community as a whole. But since it was also very common for the size of a chorus in any part of any festival to be specified, the formation of a chorus for a given occasion entailed selection, whether all the participants came from the same kinship-unit or not. The Greeks naturally wished any performance at a festival to sound good and look good, and in selecting a chorus the ostensible purpose (no matter how often frustrated by favour, enmity and intrigue) would be to pick those who combined to the highest practicable degree beauty, grace and skill. This fact forms an interesting link between Sappho and Alkman. We know that in Sappho's time there were beauty contests of women on Lesbos, for Alkaios fr. 130.32 says:

> ... where the Lesbians (*feminine*) go, with trailing dresses, having their bodily form (*phuā*, 'growth') judged (*or* 'trying to get a decision on ...' *or* 'trying to have ... chosen'), and all around resounds the wondrous noise of the sacred cry of women each year.

Beauty contests of women, and of men too, were held also in Elis (Theophrastos fr. 111).[30] Who judged? To praise someone's beauty is (whether we like it or not) a sexual act, and for that reason it is unlikely that in any Greek community women of citizen status were displayed for the appraisal of men and the award of prizes to named individuals on the citerion of sexual arousal; Plu. *Lyc.* 14.4 regards Sparta as unusual in even permitting young men to be present as spectators at the performance of *partheneia*. If, however, girls were praised by women and other girls in extravagant and uninhibited terms, they could enjoy the reassurance which their male counterparts received unstintingly. The relations between participants in a female chorus or between teacher and pupils[31] in music and poetry may thus have constituted an overt 'sub-culture', or rather 'counter-culture' in which women and girls received from their own sex what segregation and monogamy denied them from men.[32] The language in which these

30. I think Nilsson 1674 is right in connecting such contests with selection for ritual purposes. Athenian contests in 'manliness' (*euandriā*) involved adult soldiers, not good-looking youths.

31. Sappho fr. 213 seems (to judge from an ancient commentator's paraphrase) to have said that 'Pleistodika will share with Gongyla the title of "yoke-fellow of Gorgo" '; the word used is found in poetry both in the sense 'spouse' and in the sense 'comrade'. The names of Gongyla and Gorgo occur elsewhere in Sappho. What is implied by 'yoke-fellow' we do not know, but it suggests a nexus within Sappho's circle rather than a convergence upon her.

32. For this suggestion I am entirely indebted to an unpublished paper of Dr Judith Hallett. On parallelism of male and female social groups cf. Merkelbach.

relationships were expressed hardly suffices to tell us whether Sappho, the girls of Lesbos and the members of Alkman's choruses sought to induce orgasms in one another by bodily contact. Sappho fr. 94 (p. 175) and Plu. *Lyc.* 18.9 suggest that they did, and that the male population of Lesbos and Sparta in the archaic period knew very well that they did; outside the Socratic circle it cannot have been very common for a Greek to hear erotic language and not suppose that those who used it took pleasure in genital acts when the opportunity presented itself. If I am right in suggesting that in Attic art and literature female homosexuality was, for all practical purposes, a taboo subject (p. 173), an important variation between regions and periods becomes apparent; variation of this kind will be discussed in Chapter IV Part A. The late date at which adverse comment was passed on Sappho's homosexuality may be explicable by reference to the part played by Athenian social, moral and cultural attitudes (not forgetting the increasing importance of philosophical preoccupations in educated Athenian society of the fourth century) in determining Hellenistic moral criteria.[33]

One other consideration is relevant to this question. In discussing Greek female homosexuality I have avoided the words 'lesbian' and 'lesbianism', and for a good reason.[34] In antiquity 'Lesbian women' could connote sexual initiative and shamelessness (cf. Pherekrates fr. 149, where it is taken in the sense *laikastriai*);[35] Hesykhios λ 692 defines *lesbiazein* as 'fellate' (cf. Suda 306), and when Philokleon in Ar. *Wasps* 1345f. says to the girl whom he has brought home from a party 'I got you away pretty smartly when you were just going to *lesbiazein* the guests' he is obviously not referring to any conceivable homosexual propensities on the girl's part but simply translating 'flirt with the guests' into the coarse and extreme terms regularly adopted in comedy.[36] In Lucian's *Dialogues of*

33. On the growth of inhibition and sexual respectability in the fourth and third centuries B.C. cf. p.151.

34. Cf. Kroll (1924) 2100. Symonds 71 misstates the facts about the term 'Lesbian'.

35. *Laikastria* is a derogatory word, and in imagining that the speaker comments on a proffered gift of Lesbian women 'with satisfaction' Gentili (1973) 126 overlooks the sarcasm of 'That's a fine gift!' (cf. Eur. *Cyclops* 551 and Denniston 128).

36. To say, as Giangrande does (131f.), that 'Lesbian' necessarily implied fellation to the exclusion of other sexual modes goes a little beyond the evidence; some references to 'Lesbian' behaviour in comedy were so interpreted by later commentators on comedy, and I am sure they were right in some of these cases, but the comic passages themselves do not justify so narrow an interpretation (cf. in particular Ar. *Eccl.* 920, with Ussher's note *ad loc.*). It is also misleading to say (Giangrande 132) that the verb *khaskein*, 'applied to girls in amatory contexts, is the *terminus technicus* denoting eagerness to *fellare*'. It means 'open the mouth', and fellation is impossible without opening the mouth, but that is not the kind of thing

Prostitutes 5 (written in the third century A.D.) we hear of a very masculine homosexual woman from Lesbos (she has a shaven head under a wig), but her equally homosexual companion, with whom she sets on a girl, is from Corinth, and if there is significance in Lucian's choice of cities it is probably that both Lesbos and Corinth (cf. p. 135) had a reputation for sexual enterprise. The only ancient text in which there is a *prima facie* association between Lesbos and homosexuality is Anakreon fr. 358. The poet sings of his desire for a girl who

> since she is from the noble island of Lesbos, finds fault with my hair – it
> is white – and gapes after another (*feminine*).

Since 'hair' (*komē*) is a feminine noun, this may be understood with 'another', whether it means '(*sc.* someone's black hair) other (*sc.* than mine)' or, with a reference to the Lesbians' reputation for fellation, '(*sc.* someone else's black pubic hair) other (*sc.* than the white hair on my head)'.[37] It is however possible both that Anakreon means to represent the girl as homosexually interested in another girl[38] and also that 'Lesbian' did not, in his time or at any other time in antiquity, have a primary connotation of homosexuality. So long as we think of the world as divided into homosexuals and heterosexuals and regard the commission of a homosexual act, or even the entertaining of a homosexual desire, as an irrevocable step across a frontier which divides the normal, healthy, sane, natural and good from the abnormal, morbid, insane, unnatural and evil, we shall not get very far in understanding Greek attitudes to homosexuality. If Lesbian women had a reputation (perhaps the creation of Athenian humorists at the time of the wars between Athens and Mytilene in the sixth century) for shameless and uninhibited sexuality,[39] they are likely to have been credited with all such genital acts as the inventive pursuit of a piquant variety of pleasure can devise, including homosexual

---

that 'technical term' normally implies. Figuratively, '*khaskein* to ...' or '... at ...' denotes besotted admiration, desire or expectation of any kind.

37. Giangrande 132 wishes the antithesis to be between 'my *head*-hair' and 'my *other* hair', but the antithesis offered us by the Greek, using the emphatic possessive adjective *emos*, is between '*my* hair' and '*other*'.

38. I would be very surprised indeed if M.L. West (1970) 209 is right in thinking that the girl is 'deep in trivial conversation with her friend' rather than sexually interested in a direction which makes it impossible for Anakreon to arouse her sexual interest in him.

39. When Didymos discussed (Seneca *Epistles* 88.37) 'whether Sappho was a whore (*publica*)' he did not mean 'Could she have been a heterosexual whore as well as, or

practices together with fellation, cunnilinctus, threesomes, copulation in unusual positions and the use of olisboi.

---

rather than, a homosexual lover?' but 'Was she a shameless woman ready for *any* kind of sexual behaviour?'

IV

Changes

A. The Dorians

Some Greek communities which spoke closely related dialects
believed themselves to share a common ancestry, and the three most
important groupings of this kind were the 'Dorians' (e.g. Sparta,
Argos, Corinth and the cities of Crete), the 'Aeolians' (Boiotia,
Lesbos) and the 'Ionians' (Athens and most of the Aegean islands and
cities of the Aegean coast of Asia Minor). A colony planted near or far
naturally belonged to the same grouping as its mother-city; hence, for
example, Syracuse was Dorian because its mother-city was Corinth.
The three groups do not constitute an exhaustive division of the Greek
world, for substantial regions – such as Phokis, Elis and Arcadia – were
neither Dorian nor Aeolian nor Ionian.

The most widely accepted generalisation about Greek homosexuality at the present time is that it originated in the military
organisation of Dorian states (so that its diffusion throughout the
Greek world was a product of Dorian influence) and that in the
classical period overt homosexual behaviour was more acceptable in
certain Dorian regions (notably Sparta and Crete) than elsewhere.
The first part of this generalisation is not refutable and may be true,
but the evidence for it is not as cogent as is commonly believed and
asserted. The second part of the generalisation might possibly be true,
but it has to contend with a significant body of contrary evidence; the
difficulty of assessing the evidence lies in the fact that Greeks, like
other people, passed judgments in accordance with the emotion
engendered by examples present to their minds at the moment of
speaking, and in the notorious disparity between professed attitudes
and actual behaviour.

The generalisation is largely founded on two passages of Plato's
Laws, where the three speakers are an Athenian, a Cretan and
Spartan. In 636ab, responding to the Spartan's claim that the military
organisation of communal messes and physical training contribute to
sōphrosunē, the Athenian says:

These gymnasia and messes ... seem also to have undermined a law which is old and in accordance with nature: I mean the pleasure which man and beast alike have in sexual intercourse. For this your cities above all should be blamed, and all such cities as make use of gymnasia. ... We must reflect that when the natural forms of female and male come together for procreation, the pleasure in this act seems to have been granted them in accordance with nature, but that enjoyed by males in intercourse with males or by females in intercourse with females seems to be contrary to nature, a crime of the first order, committed through inability to control the desire for pleasure. We all blame the Cretans for having made up the myth of Ganymede ...

The Spartan is embarrassed, and turns the conversation on to the restraints imposed upon drunkenness at Sparta. When in due course the Athenian comes back to sexual legislation in detail (cf. p. 165) he says (836b):

In many other respects Crete as a whole and Sparta give us a good deal of solid support in our attempt to make laws differing from the way most things are, but in the matter of eros – we're by ourselves (*sc.* and can therefore speak in confidence) – they are completely opposed to us.

It must be said at once that Plato was not a historian either by trade or by temperament, and even if he intended to imply that homosexuality began in Crete and Sparta and spread thence over the Greek world, we are not obliged to respect his authority; neither he nor any other Greek of the classical period was in a strong position to discover how a social usage was diffused two or three centuries earlier.[1] The belief that the Cretans invented *paiderastiā* was certainly held and expressed by Timaios (F144) not long after Plato's time, and Ekhemenes, a Cretan historian of uncertain date, argued (F1) that it was not Zeus who carried off the beautiful Ganymede, but Minos, the legendary king of Crete. In implying that at the time of writing *Laws* Sparta and Crete were exceptional in the degree of approval which they extended to homosexuality, Plato deserves a hearing; so far as concerns Crete, he is supported by Aristotle, *Politics* 1272^a 23-26, where Cretan 'intercourse with males' is treated as a practice designed to prevent over-population. It will be advisable to consider first the evidence for regional variation in homosexuality during the classical period and

---

1. No relevant documentary evidence existed; a combination of statements by archaic poets about traditions in their time would constitute evidence worth considering, but we have no reason to suppose that there was a sufficiency of such statements.

only then (taking into account the uncertainties inherent in extrapolation from later to earlier periods) theorise about the origins of the homosexual ethos.

(i) Linguistic usage.

Among interesting entries in lexica of late antiquity and the early medieval period we find: Hesykhios κ 4080 'in the Cretan way: to use paidika'; λ 224 'lakonize:[2] use paidika' (cf. Suda λ 62); λ 226 'in the Lakonian way: penetrate; *paiderastein*; offer themselves (*feminine plural*) to visitors, since the Lakonians guard their women less than any other people'; μ 4735 '*kusolakōn*: Aristarkhos says that Kleinias was so called because he lakonized with the *kusos*, and they called using paidika "lakonizing" ' (cf. κ 4738 '*kusos*: buttocks or vulva', and cf. Photios s.v. *kusolakōn*); χ 85 Schmidt 'khalkidize: used of those who *paiderastein*'; cf. Suda χ 42 'khalkidize: *paiderastein*, since among them (*sc.* the inhabitants of Khalkis) the eros of males was practised'. A fairly high proportion of such words come from Attic comedy, but Hesykhios only rarely names the sources of what he (following Hellenistic commentators) lists and explains. Suda λ 62 adds 'Aristophanes in the second[3] *Thesmophoriazusae*' to the explanation of 'lakonize', and there could be no doubt in any case (even without the name of Aristarkhos, who commented on some plays of Aristophanes) that *kusolakōn* as an epithet of Alkibiades' father Kleinias[4] came from a comedy. As we can easily see by taking passages from extant Aristophanic plays and imagining them reduced to bare phrases without a context, there is room for disagreement on what a given humorous term means. Against the simple inference that the Athenians of the central classical period applied 'lakonize' not only (as they did) to imitation of Spartan dress and routine and adoption of pro-Spartan policies[5] but also to participation in homosexual copulation, and the further inference that they were right in believing such conduct to be specially characteristic

2. In this chapter, for all practical purposes, 'Lakonian' = 'Spartan'; and 'Theban' virtually = 'Boiotian', in so far as Thebes was the dominant partner in the Boiotian federation.

3. So far as our evidence goes, the lost play of Aristophanes entitled *Thesmophoriazusae* had nothing in common with the extant play of that name.

4. On the type of joke 'Alkibiades the son of Kusolakon' (a hit at Alkibiades, not at his actual father Kleinias) cf. Dover (1964) 36.

5. In Pl. *Grg.* 515e Kallikles refers to Athenian 'Lakonizers' as 'the men with cauliflower ears' (cf. *Prt.* 342b). The Socratic circle contained some, notably Kritias, who admired Sparta and were prepared to betray Athens, but we do not seem to encounter in Plato people who imitated Spartan austerity and dirt (Ar. *Birds* 1282f. refers to a 'craze for Sparta', but does not associate it with any particular class of the population).

of Sparta, one must set two quite important considerations. One is that, as we have seen, an allegation of ready submission to homosexual penetration was always derogatory, the kind of thing one says of an enemy, and Sparta and Athens were enemies, with only brief interludes of peace, in the lifetime of Aristophanes and his contemporaries. The second is that Photios adds to his explanation of *kusolakōn* 'for that is how Theseus used Helen,[6] according to Aristotle'.[7] Coupled with the statement of Hagnon of Tarsos *ap.* Athenaios 602d that 'before marriage it is customary for the Spartans to associate with virgin girls as with paidika', it seems that Aristotle mentioned the idea that Theseus and Helen (abducted by Theseus as a child) 'invented' anal intercourse, and since Helen was a Spartan heroine the original sexual meaning of 'lakonize' will have been 'have anal intercourse', irrespective of the sex of the person penetrated. 'Khalkidize', so far as the evidence goes, associates the Ionian city of Khalkis in Euboia with homosexuality less ambiguously than 'lakonize' associates Dorian Sparta. A source not named by Athenaios (601d; Athenaios thinks of the people of Khalkis as *daimoniōs* enthusiastic about *paiderastiā*, like Misgolas in Aiskhines i 41) claimed that Ganymede himself had been a Khalkidean and snatched up by Zeus in the neighbourhood of Khalkis; and Plu. *Dial.* 761ab cites from Aristotle (fr. 98)[8] a song popular at Khalkis:

> O boys, you who possess charm and noble lineage, do not begrudge good men converse with your beauty! For together with courage Eros who dissolves the limbs[9] flourishes in the cities[10] of the Khalkideans.

(ii) Extant comedy.

In the reconciliation scene of Aristophanes' *Lysistrata*, when Athenian and Spartan representatives, reduced to a miserable condition by the sex-strike of their wives, are impatient for a settlement, the Athenian says (1103) 'Why don't we summon Lysistrata, who alone can reconcile us?' and the Spartan replies 'By the twin gods, summon Lysistratos too, if you like!' When negotiations are completed, the Athenian says (1173) 'Now I want to strip off and work the land!' – a clear enough sexual allusion, given the context – and the Spartan chimes in 'And I want to do the

---

6. An emendation, virtually certain, of a name which does not make sense.

7. Whether the philosopher Aristotle or his contemporary (?), the historian Aristoteles of Khalkis, we cannot be sure.

8. Cf. n. 7.

9. *Lūsimelēs*, making a man feel weak at the knees.

10. The plural embraces Khalkidean colonies as well as the mother-city.

manuring first!' Before drawing the conclusion that Athenians and Spartans are here contrasted as heterosexual *vs.* homosexual, we should reflect that Aristophanes could perfectly well have put both these jokes into the mouth of a speaker of Athenian or any other nationality, given that the Athenian in 1091f. has said 'If someone doesn't reconcile us pretty quick we shall have to fuck Kleisthenes!', and that heterosexual anal intercourse was common (to judge from the vase-paintings; cf. p. 100) at Athens. The second joke, however, has an additional point if the Spartans were regarded as the 'inventors' of anal penetration (cf. above).

(iii) Ritualisation in Crete.

Ephoros, writing in the mid-fourth century, gives a remarkable account (F149) of ritualised homosexual rape in Crete. The erastes gave notice of his intention, and the family and friends of the eromenos did not attempt to hide the boy away, for they would have been an admission that he was not worthy of the honour offered him by the erastes. If they believed that the erastes was unworthy, they prevented the rape by force; otherwise they put up a good-humoured and half-hearted resistance, which ended with the erastes carrying off the eromenos to a hide-out for two months. At the end of that period the two of them returned to the city (the eromenos was known, during this relationship, as *parastatheís*, 'posted beside ...' or 'brought over to the side of ...') and the erastes gave the eromenos expensive presents, including clothing which would thereafter testify to the achievement of the eromenos in being chosen; he was *kleinos*, 'celebrated', thanks to his *philētōr*, 'lover'. We do not know how general this usage was in the cities of Crete; we look in vain for the relevant terms, or for any other indication of the ritual, in the Law-code of Gortyn, where the prohibition of ordinary rape (II 1-17) is similar to that of Athenian law in not differentiating between male and female victims, though the penalty is financial only.[11] Nor, of course, do we know how old the Cretan ritual was in Ephoros's time. Cretan convention agreed with Spartan (cf. p. 202) in regarding courage and moral character, not good looks, as the attributes which attracted the erastes, but there is no evidence from any other Dorian area for the procedure described by Ephoros,[12] and it would be prudent to treat it as a special local

11. Cf. Willetts 10.

12. Bethe 456f. discerns analogies to the Cretan ritual in two of Plutarch's *Love Stories*: one (no. 2), that Arkhias of Corinth, the reputed founder of Syracuse in the eighth century B.C., tried to kidnap his eromenos Aktaion, who was unfortunately torn to pieces in the resultant fight between his friends and Arkhias's; the other (no.

development irrelevant to the problem of the origins of the homosexual ethos.

(iv) Elis and Boiotia.

The most striking feature of the Athenian's criticism of Crete and Sparta in Plato's *Laws* is negative: it is contradicted not merely by what some people thought about Khalkis but by what Plato puts into the mouth of Pausanias in *Symposium*, and Plato's contemporary Xenophon, very well acquainted with Sparta and having experience of commanding troops drawn from many different parts of the Greek world, agrees with Pausanias, not with the anonymous Athenian of *Laws*. Pausanias says (*Smp.* 182ab) that homosexual eros meets with unqualified approval in Elis and Boiotia – neither of which, incidentally, was Dorian – and with unqualified disapproval in 'many parts of Ionia and elsewhere', but at Athens and Sparta public attitudes are 'complicated'. Xenophon in *Smp.* 8.32f. makes Socrates, with explicit reference to Pausanias, accept the prevalence of overt homosexuality in Elis and Boiotia as a fact ('it is their custom, but at Athens disgraceful'), and in *Lac.* 2.12f. he himself differentiates Sparta both from Elis and Boiotia and, at the other extreme, from places where 'they absolutely prevent erastai from talking to boys'. The Spartan practice is indeed 'complicated' as Xenophon describes it (2.13):

> If a man who was himself what a man should be admired the soul of a boy and tried to make a perfect friend of him and associate with him, he (*sc.* the original legislator, Lykourgos[13]) commended that man and regarded this (*sc.* association) as the best kind of education; but if anyone clearly had an appetite for the boy's body, he laid it down that this was utterly shameful, and he brought it about that at Sparta erastai abstained from sexual relations with their paidika no less than parents from their children and siblings from one another. That some

---

3), that the Spartan governor of Oreos in Euboia seized a youth and killed him when he resisted rape. The Aktaion story, however, arises out of the normal habit of brawling over eromenoi (cf. pp. 54-7), and the other story, incorporated in a more detailed story of two young Spartans who raped and murdered the daughters of their host, is intended to illustrate the atrocious oppressiveness of Spartans towards foreigners over whom they had power. Marriage was ritualised at Sparta as a ravishment (*harpagē*), according to Plu. *Lyc.* 15.4, but it would be perverse to suppose that this emerged from a homosexual practice of Cretan type, rather than the reverse.

13. Lykourgos was regarded by the Spartans as their legislator; when he lived, and how much of Spartan classical usage went back to his time, are matters of dispute. It is also of some significance that Xen. *Lac.* 14 regards the Spartans of his own time as falling far short of what Lykourgos intended.

people do not believe this does not surprise me, for in many cities the
law does not oppose desire for boys.

A system which encourages something called 'eros' but treats its
bodily consummation as incest is all very well as a philosophical
construction, such as we encounter in the picture of ideal eros in
Plato's *Phaedrus*, but its operation is likely to open a gulf between what
is said and what is done. Whether this gulf was in fact opened at
Sparta will be considered later (p. 193).

In any Greek state, when an eromenos was old enough to serve as a
soldier (and at Athens this liability began at 18, though only within
the frontiers of Attica for the age-group 18-19) erastes and eromenos
could find themselves fighting the same battle; the desire of the erastes
to excel in the eyes of his eromenos was a spur to his courage (cf. Pl.
Smp. 178e-179a). If the eromenos responded to the sentiment of the
erastes with love and admiration, the eromenos, for his part, wished to
live up to the example set by the erastes; that was *his* spur to courage.
As we saw in the case of Harmodios and Aristogeiton (p. 41), who
killed the brother of the Athenian tyrant Hippias in 514 B.C. and
passed into Athenian tradition as a supreme example of devotion to
liberty at the price of life,[14] erastes and eromenos could dedicate
themselves to a joint enterprise requiring the utmost heroism.
Anecdotes illustrative of this accumulated, some of them mythological
in character, e.g. (Neanthes of Kyzikos F1) the story that when an
oracle demanded a human sacrifice of Athens Kratinos, a beautiful
youth, offered himself as the victim, and his erastes Aristodemos
sacrificed himself as well (possibly Pl. *Smp.* 179e-180a contributed to
this story). We cannot however dismiss all anecdotes of this type as
romantic fictions of the post-classical period. Some were contained in a
work on eros written by Herakleides Ponticus in the late fourth century
B.C., e.g. (fr. 65) the plot of Khariton and his paidika Melanippos
against Phalaris, tyrant of Akragas, and the pardon they received
because the tyrant's heart was moved by their courage under torture
(cf. the tradition that Aristogeiton withstood fearful torture [Aristotle
Constitution of Athens 18.5f.]). Plutarch's story (*Dial.* 760e-1a) that the
high regard of the men of Khalkis for homosexual eros arose from the
encouragement and inspiration given to their ally, Kleomakhos of
Pharsalos, by his eromenos in the preparation for battle (Kleomakhos
lost his life) was drawn, though the names of the protagonists were not

14. Thuc. vi 54.1 plays down the political importance of the act of Harmodios and
Aristogeiton, as arising fortuitously from a love-affair, but he does not say anything
derogatory about the love-affair itself.

the same, either from Aristotle or from Aristoteles of Khalkis.

In Elis and Boiotia erastes and eromenos were posted beside each other in battle (Xen. *Smp*. 8.32). Both states, that is, exploited an aspect of the homosexual ethos for military purposes. About Elean military organisation we know no more, but the 'Sacred Band' of Thebes, formed *c*. 378, was composed entirely of pairs of homosexual lovers;[15] it was the hard core of the Boiotian army, a formidable army at all times, throughout the middle period of the fourth century, and at Khaironeia in 338, where Philip II of Macedon crushed Greek opposition, it died to a man. A certain Pammenes, a Theban military commander, advocated this type of pairing as a principle of military organisation (Plu. *Dial*. 761a), and it was a practice at Thebes (*ibid.*), when an eromenos came of age, for his erastes to make him a present of armour. When Epameinondas fell in battle at Mantineia in 362, his current eromenos Asopikhos died beside him; an earlier eromenos, Kaphisodoros, was destined to become the most formidable Theban fighter of his day (*ibid* 761d). Xenophon's passing reference (*Anab*. vii 4.8) to the valour displayed by Episthenes in a company selected on the criterion of beauty (cf. p. 51) shows that the Thebans of the 370s were not the first to exploit the anxiety of men to show off their prowess to the young and handsome. Here we seem to catch a historical development actually in process, and it is in a non-Dorian ambience. A Spartan erastes and eromenos might find themselves close together in the battle-line, and it might even be contrived that they should do so – when the Spartan commander Anaxibios sought death in battle to atone for his military carelessness, his paidika stayed with him to the end (Xen. *Hell.* iv 8.39) – but it was not part of Spartan military organisation that they should deliberately be posted side by side (Xen. *Smp*. 8.35).

(v) Social and military organisation.

The peculiarity of Spartan and Cretan society was the segregation of the male citizen population into messes and barracks (Aristotle *Politics* 1271^a 40-2^{b}4, Xen, *Lac*. 5.2, Plu. *Lyc*. 12.1), and – certainly at Sparta; cf. Xen. *Lac*. 6.1, Plu. *Lyc*. 15-17 – the quite deliberate withdrawal of authority from fathers of families and its transference to the oldest male age-group and those to whom responsibility for the various age-groups of boys, adolescents, youths and men was delegated. Spartan society as a whole was permanently organised like an army in training (cf. Plu. *Lyc*. 24.1). Since it has been observed in our own day (to say nothing of Euboulos fr. 120 [p. 135]) that segregation of males into armies, ships or prisons promotes homosexual behaviour, there is an *a priori* argument

15. On the chronology cf. Dover (1965) 9-15.

for an exceptional degree of such behaviour in Sparta and Crete. Yet the behaviour of the inhabitants of a barracks in the middle of a town is not the same as that of an expeditionary force in a desert, and one of the variables upon which the validity of the argument turns is the attitude of a given military society towards women. The Spartans valued any individual of either sex to the extent to which he or she contributed to the maintenance of Spartan power over a subject population and in confrontation with other states, and this meant that in their eyes the best woman was the healthiest mother of the healthiest children. With this attitude, which affected men and women alike, went a much greater public exposure and freedom of movement for women than was normal in the Greek world (Plu. *Lyc.* 14-15.1; cf. Ar. *Lys.* 79-84); it entailed physical training and athletic and musical contests, from which male spectators were not excluded, so that the 'shamelessness' of Spartan women was a matter for adverse comment at Athens (Eur. *Andromache* 595-601). The young Spartan was not involved, as he grew up, in a simple opposition between sexual love for women and sexual loyalty to the males of his own unit. A Spartan could in fact enter into four relationships: first, loyalty to the males of his age-group, with whom he competed for recognition of his male virtues and with whom he may (for all we know) have had frequent and casual homosexual relations; secondly, the much more intense erastes-eromenos relationship, as elsewhere in the Greek world; thirdly, marriage; and fourthly, if there is anything in the evidence of Hagnon (p. 188), an erastes-*eromenē* relationship with an unmarried girl, consummated anally.[16] Overt recognition of the fourth of these relationships constitutes an element in which Sparta seems to have differed from other states.

Members of a closed and secretive community are apt to meet by simple, confident denial any allegation by outsiders that the community misbehaves.[17] If Spartans in the fourth century B.C. unanimously and firmly denied that their erastai and eromenoi ever had any bodily contact beyond a clasping of right hands, it was not easy for an outsider even at the time to produce evidence to the contrary, and for us it is impossible. Secretiveness was built into the Spartan way of life (cf. Thuc. v 68.2); according to Plu. *Lyc.* 15.8 a young married Spartan, living with his age-group, was expected to conceal utterly his visits after dark to his wife.[18] Athenians no doubt

---

16. The Thessalian (non-Dorian) term for an eromenos was *aitās* (Theokritos 12.14); Alkman (fr. 34) used *aitis* in the sense 'pretty girl'.

17. Cf. the anecdote (Plu. *Lyc.* 15.17f.) about a Spartan's denial that any Spartan ever committed adultery.

18. This may be the model for the prescriptions in Pl. *Laws* 841a-e about the need for shame and secrecy in all sexual relations.

prided themselves on their smartness in 'knowing' that any Spartan would present his buttocks to anyone for the asking (Theopompos F225 says much the same of the Macedonians, adding the shocking fact that they do it even after their beards have grown). Anyone today who is sure he knows what the people of a remote culture 'must have done' is at liberty to express his assurance, and we are naturally tempted to believe that a society such as Sparta, capable of great cruelty and treachery, was guilty also of hypocrisy; but an alliance between ignorance and partisanship is a poor foundation for historical hypotheses.

The Homeric epics are composed in a language which, although a highly artificial amalgam, is basically Ionic in its phonology and largely Ionic in its morphology also; and of the various places which claimed to be Homer's native land the Ionian island of Chios has the oldest and strongest claim. The epics narrate events believed to have occurred in what we would call 'the twelfth century B.C.', and the Greek world as they present it – a world which, like epic language, is an amalgam – contains cultural, technological and political elements which must have survived in tradition (presumably a tradition of narrative poetry) from the fourteenth and thirteenth centuries B.C. Since there is no overt homosexuality at all in these epics, neither enshrined in the traditional ingredients nor imported by the Ionian culture which generated the poems as we now have them (cf. p. 196), it is reasonable enough to look for the point of origin of Greek homosexuality neither in the Bronze Age nor in Ionia, and the Dorians suggest themselves as that point of origin in so far as they moved down into southern mainland Greece at the end of the Bronze Age and forced a large-scale migration of Greek-speaking peoples, notably the Ionians, eastwards across the Aegean. At least one question is begged by this hypothesis, for if the Dorians were not already differentiated by the overt practice of homosexual relations when they first arrived in southern Greece – if, that is to say, it began at a point in time later than the establishment of the pattern of ethnic groupings with which we are familiar in the archaic period – it could just as well have begun in a non-Dorian as in a Dorian region. We come back to the Dorians, in that case, solely on the strength of the link between military organisation and homosexuality, and the chronological order of the Trojan War, the Dorian Invasion and the composition of the *Iliad* ceases to have any bearing in itself on the history of homosexuality.

It might be more helpful to consider the order in which direct evidence for homosexuality is to be found in different times and places during the archaic period. The graffiti of Thera, a Spartan colony, may go back well into the seventh century B.C., but the paucity of relevant evidence leaves much room for disagreement on their date,[19] and if I am right in interpreting them as essentially frivolous (p. 123), those of them which allege or proclaim that X buggered Y do not help us at all to date the emergence of socially acceptable homosexuality among the Dorians or anyone else. There are no homosexual elements discernible in the iambic and elegiac poetry which flourished in the middle of the seventh century and is known to us through fragments and citations from the Ionians Kallinos and Arkhilokhos and the Spartan Tyrtaios; the absence (so far) of homosexuality from Arkhilokhos may be significant, since he is notably uninhibited in his description of heterosexual behaviour, and so may the lack of any reference in later erotic literature (e.g. Plutarch's *Dialogue on Love*) to Tyrtaios in connection with homosexual eros among the Spartans for whom, and about whom, he composed.[20] Strong evidence for female homosexuality appears in the Lesbian poetry of Sappho in the early part of the sixth century B.C., and language strongly suggestive of female homosexuality makes a virtually simultaneous appearance in Sparta (cf. p. 179) in the *partheneia* of Alkman. Sappho's Lesbian contemporary Alkaios is described by Cicero (*Tusculan Disputations* iv.71) as 'singing of the love of youths'. Not one of the extant fragments of Alkaios supports this generalisation; but the total percentage of Alkaios which we possess is so small that we can blame chance for our loss, and instead of imagining that Cicero may have confused Alkaios with Anakreon or that he may have meant 'the love felt by youths for girls' we must note that Horace *Odes* i 32.9-11 is much more precise: Alkaios 'sang of Lykos, beautiful with his dark eyes and dark hair'. The earliest expression of male homosexual eros in poetry is therefore non-Dorian, and so is all its expression in the arts for the rest of the sixth century: the earliest scenes of homosexual courtship on Attic black-figure vases (on C42 cf. p. 94) are contemporary with Solon fr. 25:

> when in the delicious flower of youth he falls in love with a boy (*paidophilein*), yearning for thighs and sweet mouth,

19. Cf. Jeffery 318f.

20. On the date of Theognis cf. p. 10 n. 16; the homosexual poetry in the Theognidean corpus may be its latest ingredient in date. Tyrtaios's reference (fr. 10.27-30) to the beauty of a young male is modelled on Hom. *Il.* xxii 71-3, and makes the point that it is shameful to see an old man dying of wounds on the battlefield, but appropriate that the young should suffer wounds and death. It is of particular interest that Tyrtaios describes the beautiful youth as '*eratos* to women' (cf. p. 43) but as *thēetos*, i.e. attracting attention as admirable or remarkable, to men.

a couplet which raised some eyebrows in later times, since Solon was revered at Athens as a lawgiver and upright moralist. In the generation after Solon the Ionian lyric poets Ibykos and Anakreon include among their erotic poems some which are addressed to eromenoi, e.g. Ibykos fr. 288, Anakreon frr. 346 and 357 (cf. Maximus of Tyre 37.5 on the various eromenoi of Anakreon).

It will be seen from the evidence cited and discussed that there can be no question of tracing the diffusion of homosexual eros from Sparta or other Dorian states. We can only say that its social acceptance and artistic exploitation had become widespread by the end of the seventh century B.C. Ephoros gives us a glimpse of its peculiarly formal evolution in Crete; terminology affords evidence that it was possible in classical Athens to regard it as characteristically Spartan and possible somewhere, at some time, to regard it as especially conspicuous at Khalkis; Xenophon and Plato's *Symposium* tell us that its most direct and uninhabited expression was to be observed in Elis and Boiotia; Plato at the end of his life criticises its exceptionally entrenched position in the society of Sparta and of Crete. The extent of the period summarised in this paragraph is two and a half centuries, eight generations, and regrettable though it may seem to those who would like the shape of the past to be bold and simple, we are probably confronted with a phenomenon which varied not only from place to place but also from time to time.

B.   Myth and History

The statement (p. 194) that there is no overt homosexuality in Homer is not in conflict with *Il.* xx 231–235:

> And Tros begot three noble sons, Ilos and Assarakos and godlike Ganymede, who was the most beautiful of mortal men; him the gods carried off, to be wine-pourer for Zeus because of his beauty, that he might be among the immortals.

(Cf. *Il.* v 265f., where Zeus is said to have given fine horses to Tros in recompense for Ganymede.) If the original form of the Ganymede legend represented him as eromenos of Zeus, Homer has suppressed this important fact. If the legend had no erotic element, we may wonder why beauty (as distinct from zeal and a steady hand) is a desirable attribute in a wine-pourer, but it should not be impossible for us, even after a prolonged immersion in the ambience of Greek homosexuality, to imagine that the gods on Olympos, like the souls of men in the Muslim paradise (Koran 76.19), simply rejoiced in the beauty of their servants as one ingredient of felicity. The earliest surviving testimony to Zeus's homosexual desire for Ganymede is Ibykos fr. 289, where the ravishing (*harpagē*) of Ganymede is put into the same context as the rape of Tithonos by Dawn (who did not want a wine-pourer). The *Hymn to Aphrodite* 202-206 draws heavily on *Il.* v 265f. and xx 231-235 but makes Zeus himself the ravisher of Ganymede and goes on (218ff.) to speak of Dawn and Tithonos.[1]

Homer, as Aiskhines i 142 remarks, nowhere speaks of an erotic relationship between Achilles and Patroklos. We would reasonably attribute the poet's silence to the absence of any erotic element from the relationship as he envisaged it, but to Aiskhines, as to other Greeks of the classical period, the extravagance of Achilles' emotion when Patroklos is killed, combined with the injunction of Patroklos that when Achilles too dies their ashes should be interred together, signified homosexual eros, and Aiskhines treats Homer's reticence as a sign of cultivated sensitivity. The mainstay of the erotic interpretation of the central motif of the *Iliad* was undoubtedly Aiskhylos's trilogy *Myrmidons, Nereids* and *Phrygians* (or *Ransoming of Hektor*), about which Phaidros in Pl. *Smp.* 180a has this to say:

> Aiskhylos is talking nonsense in saying that Achilles was in love with Patroklos. Achilles was more beautiful not only than Patroklos but than all the heroes, and his beard was not yet grown; moreover, he was much younger than Patroklos, as Homer says.

Phaidros is right in saying that Homer represents Achilles as younger than Patroklos (*Il.* xi 786), yet he does not discard the erotic interpretation of the story; for him Achilles is the eromenos who so honoured his erastes Patroklos that he was ready to die in avenging him. Aiskhylos seems to have used at some points a directness of expression which characterised the earlier part of the fifth century; this appears in fr. 228, where Achilles addresses the dead Patroklos:

> And you felt no compunction for (*sc.* my?) pure reverence of (*sc.* your?) thighs – O, what an ill return you have made for so many kisses!

Again in fr. 229 we read 'god-fearing converse[2] with your thighs' (cf. p. 70).

1. Cf. Sichtermann (n.d.) 15-18, Kunze 38f.

2. *Homūliā*, 'association', 'intercourse', 'dealings', as in Aristotle, *Politics* 1272[a] 23-26, quoted on p.186. Hagnon uses the cognate verb *homūlein*, of Spartan dealings with virgin girls (I misquoted in Dover [1964] 37). On the other hand, the writer of [Dem.] lxi feels

Aiskhylos was never afraid to modify inherited myth (some of his modifications fared better in later generations than others) but he is nowhere as explicit – as a tragic dramatist, he could not explain himself *in propria persona* to his audience – as Pindar in *Olympian Odes* 1, composed for Hieron, tyrant of Syracuse, in 476. Pindar is there dealing with the myth of Pelops, which, in the form in which he inherited it, said: Tantalos, having been entertained by the gods, invited them to his house for a banquet, and to test their omniscience killed, cooked and served up his own son Pelops; Demeter alone ate some of the meat; the other gods, knowing well what had happened, brought Pelops to life and gave him a shoulder of ivory to replace what Demeter had eaten. To Pindar the idea that the gods should tuck into human food is revolting, and he refuses to countenance it (52); he declares that he will tell the story of Pelops 'in opposition to earlier (*sc.* poets)' (36), and in this new story Pelops disappears not because he has been cooked but because Poseidon, in love with his white shoulder (25-7), has ravished him (40-5):

> Then he of the Shining Trident carried you off, overcome in his heart by desire, and transported you in a golden chariot to the lofty home of Zeus, who is honoured everywhere; whither in later time Ganymede also came, to serve Zeus in the same way.

When Pelops' beard grows (67f.) he returns to earth, and, needing the help of Poseidon if he is to win Hippodameia as his bride, he reminds the god of 'the fond gifts of Aphrodite' and asks for a favour in return (75f.).

This passage is the most daring and spectacular 'homo-sexualisation' of myth that we have; Pindar's gods are too refined to digest anything but ambrosia, but never so insensitive that their genitals cannot be aroused. It may well be that the late sixth and early fifth centuries, the generation of the men who (like Aiskhylos) defeated the Persians, witnessed a more open, headstrong, sensual glorification and gratification of homosexuality than any other period of antiquity. The late fifth century probably knew this; it had the art and poetry of Aiskhylos's day as evidence, and if in the contest between Right and Wrong in Aristophanes' *Clouds* it seems to us that Right, the champion of the good old days, is curiously concerned with boys' genitals, we must remember that he is looking at the manners and life-style of boys in the 420s through the eyes of an old-fashioned

---

able to use these words (e.g. §§ 3, 17, 20) of ostensibly 'platonic' converse between a boy and his admirers.

erastes, for whom shyness, modesty, discretion and respect for grown-ups (whatever their intention) greatly enhance the charm with which hard exercise, exposure to the elements and conscientious learning of traditional musical skills invest a boy.

In Xen. *Smp.* 8.31 Socrates denies that Homer intended any erotic element in his portrayal of Achilles and Patroklos, and he cites other pairs of comrades in legend, such as Orestes and Pylades, or Theseus and Peirithoos, who 'are celebrated not for sleeping together but because they admired each other for their accomplishment of the noblest achievements in joint endeavour'. Socrates' picture of heroic legend is correct, but he lived in an age when legend owed its continued hold on the imagination at least in part to the steady importation of homosexual themes.[3] The Boiotians turned Iolaos, the comrade-in-arms of Herakles, into his eromenos, and in Aristotle's time (fr. 97) the tomb of Iolaos was a sacred place where erastai and eromenoi exchanged pledges of mutual love and loyalty. Ibykos (fr. 309) made Rhadamanthys the eromenos of Talos (nephew of Daidalos). The Hellenistic poets, notably Phanokles (frr. 1, 3-6) took the process further; Zenis of Chios, and made Minos fall in love with Theseus (F1) in Kallimakhos *Hymn to Apollo* 49 Apollo is described as 'fired with eros for the youthful Admetos'. The most bizarre of these developments was the portrayal of Herakles by a minor epic poet Diotimos (Athenaios 603d) as performing his labours in thrall to Eurystheus because Eurystheus was his paidika (one sees here the reflex of anecdotes [e.g. Konon (F1.16)] about the perilous tasks imposed on erastai by un-relenting eromenoi). Hylas, the eromenos of Herakles whose seizure by water-nymphs is the subject of Theokritos 13, is the squire of Herakles as the story is told by Apollonios *Argonautica* i 1187-1357, and on present evidence it is not possible to trace an erotic relationship between him and Herakles further back than Theokritos.

It is one thing to see how, when and why an existing legend was given a homosexual character, but quite another when we are confronted by an important homosexual myth of which the antecedents are unknown to us. This is the case with the myth of Khrysippos, the subject of a tragedy of that name produced by Euripides in 411-409 and (about the same date) of a brief narrative in Hellanikos (F157). He was the son of Pelops, and Laios, the father of Oedipus, overcome with desire for his extraordinary beauty, carried him off – the first of

3. Cf. the warning of Kroll (1921) 903 against dating homosexual myths too early. The analysis of homosexual attitudes underlying the treatment of myths by individual poets is quite a different matter; cf. Devereux (1967) 83 on Bakkhylides 5.155-75 and (1973) 113-47 on Deianeira in Sophokles' *Trachiniae*.

mankind, according to Euripides' presentation of the story, to fall in love with a person of his own sex (hence Plato's reference to 'the rule as it was before Laios' in *Laws* 836c). We know that Aiskhylos produced a *Laios*, the first play of an Oedipus tetralogy, in 467; we do not know whether the rape of Khrysippos figured in it, and no trace of the rape of Khrysippos can be identified with assurance before Euripides.[4] The subject is used by vase-painters (two vase-painters, to be precise) in southern Italy in the fourth century, but has not yet been identified in any earlier picture.[5]

Laios, the mythical Theban hero,[6] thus became in Greek tradition the 'inventor' of homosexuality. The Greek habit of attributing all innovation to a named god or culture-hero or individual figure of the mythical or semi-mythical past[7] – or, on occasion, to a named community at a point in past time – strikes us as naive when the 'invention' is (e.g.) shelter or religion, or artificial when the invention of inventors becomes an intellectual game, but the impossibility of discovering who was actually the first person to (e.g.) cook meat before eating it does not alter the fact that there was a point in space and a moment in time at which an individual person deliberately cooked meat for the first time in the history of the world.[8] Whether the same discovery was made independently in other places at later times is a separate issue. The Greeks had the right end of the stick, at least, in regarding innovation as having precise location. It seemed self-evident that most 'inventions' – building houses, for example – were adopted and diffused because they improved human life, and if we could ask ancient Greeks why homosexual eros, once invented, caught on so quickly, widely and deeply, practically all of them (I exclude some philosophers and most cynics) would reply rather as if we had asked them the same question about wine:

4. But cf. Lloyd-Jones 120-4 on the fifth-century antecedents of Euripides' play; Keydell 146f.

5. Cf. *IGD* III 3.16-18.

6. Plu. *Pelopidas* 19.1 mentions (only to reject it) a belief which linked the story of Laios with the exceptional homosexuality of the Thebans. According to Aristotle, *Politics* 1274^{a}31ff., the Thebans regarded their legislator Philolaos as having been erastes of a young Olympic victor, Diokles; Philolaos was Corinthian (and Corinth was Dorian), but we do not know at what stage, or where, the erotic element entered the tradition.

7. Cf. Kleingünther, especially 25, 143f. on Pindar and 45-65 on Herodotos.

8. Equally, there must have been a moment at which a chimpanzee for the first time put a sliver of wood into an ants' nest to extract ants; observers in Japan a few years ago came very close to seeing the first moment at which a monkey washed a potato in seawater before eating it and so established a habit in a community of monkeys (cf. Wilson 170).

enjoyment of *both* females *and* males affords a richer and happier life than enjoyment of *either* females *or* males.[9] This does not, however, go very far to explain why they developed homosexual eros much more elaborately and intensely than other peoples, or why its elaboration took certain forms rather than others.

Whether any anthropologist, sociologist or social historian initially ignorant of the Greeks but supplied with a succession of data which did not include any manifest evidence of homosexuality could say after a certain point 'It necessarily follows that overt homosexuality was strongly developed in such a society', I do not know, and the experiment is hardly practicable, for a social scientist not already aware that homosexuality was a conspicuous feature of Greek life will not easily be found. The best we can do is first, to make the reasonable assumption that Greek homosexuality satified a need not otherwise adequately satisfied in Greek society, secondly, to identify that need, and thirdly, to identify the factors which allowed and even encouraged satisfaction of the need by homosexual eros in the particular form which it took in the Greek world. It seems to me that the need in question was a need for personal relationships of an intensity not commonly found within marriage or in the relations between parents and children or in those between the individual and the community as a whole. The deficiencies of familial and communal relationships can be derived ultimately from the political fragmentation of the Greek world. The Greek city-state was continuously confronted with the problem of survival in competition with aggressive neighbours,[10] and for this reason the fighter, the adult male citizen, was the person who mattered. The power to deliberate and take political decisions and the authority to approve or disapprove of social and cultural innovation were strongly vested in the adult male citizens of the community; the inadequacy of women as fighters promoted a general devaluation of the intellectual capacity and emotional stability of women; and the

---

9. Cf. Hdt. i 135 on the readiness of the Persians to adopt *eupatheiai*, 'enjoyments', 'comforts', almost 'good-time activities', from other peoples; 'and indeed they have sexual intercourse with boys, having learned this from the Greeks'. Xen. *Cyr*. ii 2.28, a joke put into the mouth of the Persian Kyros, presupposes that acquisition of an eromenos is 'the Greek way'. Phanokles fr. 1.7-10 attributes the death of the legendary Orpheus at the hands of Thracian women to his having been the first to preach in Thrace the superiority of homosexual to heterosexual eros.

10. Cf. the words of the Cretan in Pl. *Laws* 626a on the 'undeclared war' which exists between every city and every other city, and the totally illusory nature of what is called 'peace'. Marrou 26-33 treats homosexual eros as evolving (and, in the classical period, already degenerating) from the ethos of a warrior-community; I would prefer to say that the warrior-community provided one favourable condition for the evolution.

young male was judged by such indication as he afforded of his worth as a potential fighter. Sparta and Crete alone went to the length of constructing a society in which familial and individual relationships were both formally and effectively subordinated to military organisation; elsewhere varied and fluctuating degrees of compromise between the claims of community, family and individual prevailed.[11] Males tended to group themselves together for military, political, religious and social purposes to a degree which fell short of welding them into a totally efficient fighting-machine but was nevertheless enough to inhibit the full development of intimacy between husband and wife or between father and son.[12]

Erastes and eromenos clearly found in each other something which they did not find elsewhere. When Plato (*Phdr.* 255b) said that the eromenos realises that the love offered by his erastes is greater than that of all his family and friends put together, he was speaking of an idealised, 'philosophical' eros, and yet he may have been a little closer than he realised to describing the everyday eros which he despised. Indeed, the philosophical *paiderastiā* which is fundamental to Plato's expositions in *Phaedrus* and *Symposium* is essentially an exaltation, however starved of bodily pleasure, of a consistent Greek tendency to regard homosexual eros as a compound of an educational with a genital relationship. The strength, speed, endurance and masculinity of the eromenos − that is to say, his quality as a potential fighter − were treated (and I offer no opinion on the unexpressed thoughts and feelings of erastai) as the attributes which made him attractive. The Spartans and Cretans went a stage further in professing to have much more regard for qualities of character than for bodily beauty (Ephoros F149; cf Plu. *Agis* 2.1, on the achievement of Agis, as a lame boy, in becoming the eromenos of Lysander). The erastes was expected to win the love of the eromenos by his value as an exemplar and by the patience, devotion and skill which he displayed in training the eromenos. At Sparta (Plu. *Lyc.* 22.8) the educational responsibility of the erastes was so interpreted that he bore the blame for a deficiency in courage manifested by his eromenos. 'Education' is the key-word in Xenophon's evaluation of a chaste homosexual relationship (*Lac.* 2.13, *Smp.* 8.23), and Spartan terminology ('breathe into …', 'inspire' [Aelian *Varia Historia* iii 12, Hesykhios ε 2475] = 'fall in love with …', and *eispnēlos* or *eispnēlās* [Kallimakhos fr. 68 Pfeiffer, Theokritos 12.13] = 'breather-into' = 'erastes') points to a notion that the erastes was able to transfer qualities from himself into his eromenos.[13] On

11. Cf. *GPM* 156-60, 288-310.
12. Cf. Devereux (1967) 78f., Slater 53-64 (questioned in part by Pomeroy 95f.).
13. Cf. Ruppersberg. Bethe 465-74 (cf. Devereux [1967] 80) considers the possibility

growing up, in any Greek community, the eromenos graduated from pupil to friend, and the continuance of an erotic relationship was disapproved, as was such a relationship between coevals. Homosexual relationships are not exhaustively divisible, in Greek society or in any other, into those which perform an educational function and those which provoke and relieve genital tension. Most relationships of any kind are complex, and the need for bodily contact and orgasm was one ingredient of the complex of needs met by homosexual eros.[14]

The modern sentiment which I have heard expressed, more than once, in the words 'It's impossible to understand how the Greeks could have tolerated homosexuality' is the sentiment of a culture which has inherited a religious prohibition of homosexuality and, by reason of that inheritance, has shown (until recently) no salutary curiosity about the variety of sexual stimuli which can arouse the same person or about the difference between fundamental orientation of the personality and episodic behaviour at a superficial level. The Greeks neither inherited nor developed a belief that a divine power had revealed to mankind a code of laws for the regulation of sexual behaviour; they had no religious institution possessed of the authority to enforce sexual prohibitions. Confronted by cultures older and richer and more elaborate than theirs, cultures which none the less differed greatly from each other, the Greeks felt free to select, adapt, develop and – above all – innovate.[15] Fragmented as they were into tiny political units, they were constantly aware of the extent to which morals and manners are local. This awareness also disposed them to enjoy the products of their own inventiveness and to attribute a similar enjoyment to their deities and heroes.

---

that injection of semen by the erastes into the eromenos was believed to transfer virtue; there are anthropological parallels, and some striking evidence from clinical psychology (Karlen 420, 424, 435, 482).

14. The story (Plu. *Dial.* 762c and *Alcibiades* 4.5f.) that an erastes of Alkibiades, insolently robbed of half his gold and silver drinking-vessels by his drunken eromenos in front of guests, exclaimed at the kindness of Alkibiades in leaving him the other half, suggests the possibility that on occasion eros satisfied an eromenos's need to be cruel and a kind of religious need on the part of the erastes (a blend of Job with Pollyanna) to grovel and insist that bad fortune is good.

15. Cf. Devereux (1967) 72-7 on the strikingly 'adolescent' character of Greek culture. The prolongation of undifferentiated sexual exuberance into adult life was one aspect of this.

Addenda

I omitted to discuss (because I could not explain) two passages of Aristophanes which refer to homosexual rape as an expression of dominance. (i) *Ach.* 591f. Dikaiopolis is mocking the fully-armed Lamakhos: 'If you're such a mighty man, come on, bare my knob!' (*lit.*, 'Why didn't you bare my knob?' On the idiom cf. Kühner-Gerth i 165) 'You're well enough armed'. (ii) *Knights* 963f. Kleon and the Sausage-seller are competing for the confidence of Demos: – 'If you believe him, it's your fate to become a bag' (cf. Henderson 212) – 'And if you believe *him*, to have your foreskin pulled right back to your bush!' These passages become intelligible if the assumption is that the erastes handles the penis of the eromenos during anal copulation; cf. Straton (*Palatine Anthology* xii 7), comparing girls unfavourably with boys: 'They're all so dull from behind, and the main thing is, you've nowhere to put a roaming hand'. This helps to explain why the erastes touches the penis of the eromenos in courtship (pp. 94-6), trying to break down resistance by the most direct stimulus and promising reward (a point relevant to p. 100 and p. 125 n. 1). It raises afresh the question of convention and inhibition in vase-painting (pp. 96-9), and it suggests a certain reluctance to face facts in Xen. *Smp.* 8.21 (p. 52).

I overlooked a Cretan bronze plaque of the seventh century B.C. (Boardman [1973] fig. 47) in which a man carrying a bow faces, and grasps the forearm of, a youth (cf. pp. 93f.) who carries a wild goat over his shoulders. Both man and youth wear short tunics, which expose the genitals of the latter alone (cf. pp. 130f.). Whether the scene portrays courtship, dispute or neither, I do not know. The fact that it is Cretan must be taken into account in connection with the argument of p. 195; so must the emphasis given by inlay to the pubic hair in an ivory statuette of a youth, of similar date, from (non-Dorian) Samos (ibid., fig. 32).

P.17 n. 31: Professor Thomas Gelzer has reminded me, in connection with '*paidika*', of 'my playthings', in the sense 'my lover', Ar. *Eccl.* 922. P. 183n. 37: the point was made by M. Campbell, *Museum Criticum* viii/ix (1973/4) 168f.

List of Vases

The vases listed here are those mentioned in the book. By no means all of them portray homosexual behaviour or bear erotic inscriptions; a great many vases which do portray such behaviour or do bear such inscriptions are not listed.

Column I gives the index-number by which reference is made in the book, and column II the page-references. Column III gives the location of the vase (where this is known) and column IV references to standard works and (selectively) recent illustrations.

In Column III the following collections are to be understood unless otherwise specified:- Adolphseck: Landgraf Philipp von Hesse; Altenburg: Staatliches Lindenau-Museum; Amsterdam: Allard Pierson Museum; Berkeley: University of California; Berlin: Staatliche Museen; Bonn: Akademisches Kunstmuseum; Boston: Museum of Fine Arts; Brussels: Musées Royaux; Cambridge: Fitzwilliam; Cleveland: Museum of Art; Compiègne: Musée Vivenel; Frankfurt: University; Geneva: Musée d'Art et d' Histoire; Hamburg: Museum für Kunst und Gewerbe; Hannover: Kestner; Harvard: Fogg; Heidelberg: University; Karlsruhe: Badisches Landesmuseum; Leiden: Rijksmuseum van Oudheden; Leipzig: University; Leningrad: Hermitage; London: British Museum; Munich: Antikensammlungen; New York: Metropolitan Museum; Oxford: Ashmolean; Oxford (Miss.): University of Mississippi; Paris: Louvre; Ruvo: Jatta; Vienna: Kunsthistorisches Museum; Würzburg: Martin von Wagner; Zürich: University. Others: 'National Museum', failing which, the only or principal archaeological museum.

ATTIC BLACK-FIGURE (SIXTH CENTURY B.C.)

B6	115	Athens 15499	*ABV* 39 (Sophilos, no. 16); *Par* 18; Boardman (1974) no. 26.
B12	96	London B600.28	*ABV* 67 (cf. Manner of the Heidelberg Painter); *Par* 27.
B16*	78, 92, 96	Copenhagen 5180	*ABV* 69 (Painter of the Boston Circe-Acheloos, no. 5).
B20	70	Oxford (Miss.?)	*ABV* 70 (Sandal Painter, no. 1).
B24	97	Florence 4209	*ABV* 76, 682 (Kleitias, no. 1); *Par* 29; Boardman (1974) no. 46.
B28	125	Athens, Acropolis 611	*ABV* 82 (Nearchos, no. 1); *Par* 30.
B31	97, 103 n.85	New York 26.49	*ABV* 83, 682 (id., no. 4); *Par* 30; Boardman (1974) no. 50.
B35	131	Leipzig T4225f,h	*Par* 35, 40 (Castellani Painter; cf. *ABV* 94); *CVA* DDR 2, plates 9.6, 9.9.
B39	134	Rome, Conservatori 119	*ABV* 96 (Tyrrhenian Group, no. 21); *Par* 37.
B49	102	Munich 1432	*ABV* 102 (id., no. 98); *Par* 38; *EG* 76.
B51*	100, 115, 135	Munich 1431	*ABV* 102 (id., no. 99); *CVA* Germany 32, plates 316.1f., 317.1.
B53*	78, 135	Heidelberg inv. 67/4	*ABV* 102 (id., no. 101); *Par* 39; *CVA* Germany 31, plates 143f.
B60	100, 106 n.100		*Par* 41 ('Philadelphia market'; cf. *ABV* 105, Near the Tyrrhenian Group).
B64	95	Paris, Bibl. Nat. 206	*ABV* 109 (Lydos, no. 27).
B65*	95	Nicosia, Cyprus Museum C440	*ABV* 109 (id., no. 28); *Par* 44.
B76*	70, 92	Rome, Vatican 352	*ABV* 134 (Group E, no. 30).
B79	94	Berlin 3210	*ABV* 151, 687 (Amasis Painter, no. 21); *Par* 63; Boardman (1974) no. 87.
B80*	70, 71, 128	Würzburg 265	*ABV* 151, 687 (id., no. 22); *Par* 63.
B84	92	Paris A479	*ABV* 156, 688 (id., no. 80); *Par* 65.
B90	152	Boston 10.651	*ABV* 157 (id., no. 86); *Par* 65; Boardman (1974) no. 82; *EG* 82.
B94	114, 117	Palermo	*ABV* 675 (cf. 161).
B98	120	Rhodes 10527	*ABV* 162 (Eucheiros, Potter, no. 1).
B102	78, 95	Würzburg 241	*ABV* 169, 688 (Phrynos Painter, no. 5); *Par* 70; Boardman (1974) no. 124.
B107	92, 96	Oxford 1929. 498	*Par* 72 (Sokles Painter, no. 2); cf. *ABV* 172f.
B108	122	Paris F38	*ABV* 174 (Taleides Painter, no. 7); *Par* 72.

B109	116	Harvard 60.332	*ABV* 175 (id., no. 8); *Par* 73.
B114*	98		*Par* 73 ('London market'; cf. *ABV* 175).
B118	97, 139 n.6	London B410	*ABV* 181 (Tleson, Potter, no. 3); *Par* 75.
B120	152	Athens 1045	*ABV* 186 (Kleisophos).
B122	97	New York 17.230.5	*Par* 78 (Oakeshott Painter, no. 1; cf. *ABV* 188); Boardman (1974) no. 118.
B126	97		*ABV* 188 (Little-master cups, signed, name uncertain, no. 2).
B130	78, 98	Berlin 1773	*ABV* 198 (Painter of the Boston Polyphemos, no. 1); *Par* 80.
B134	100	Athens Acr.1639	*ABV* 198, 689 (id. [?], no. 2); *Par* 80.
B138	97	Munich 2016	*ABV* 199 (cf. Painter of the Boston Polyphemos).
B142	91	Paris CA3096	*Par* 82 (Group of Courting Cups, no. 1; cf. *ABV* 199ff.).
B146	91	Paris F139	*Par* 82 (id., no. 10; cf. *ABV* 199f.).
B152	94	Naples Stg. 172	*ABV* 203, 689 (Kallis Painter, no. 1).
B154	97	Paris, Bibl. Nat. 343	*ABV* 206 (Krokotos Painter [Group of Walters 48.42]); *Par* 93.
B158	97	Paris F133	*ABV* 208 (Durand Painter, no. 2); *Par* 98.
B166	94	Paris C10352	*Par* 82 (Group of Courting Cups, no. 9; cf. *ABV* 211).
B170	78	Paris C10363	*Par* 82 (id., no. 14; cf. *ABV* 211).
B176	130	Hannover 1961.23	*ARV* (not *ABV*) 122 (Painter N, no. 7); *CVA* Germany 34, plate 17.4.
B178	97	Berlin 1671	*ABV* 226 (BMN Painter, no. 2); Marcadé 109.
B186	93	Boston 99.156	*ABV* 239 (Affecter, no. 11); *Par* 110.
B190	92	Bologna PU189	*ABV* 245 (id., no. 67).
B194	93	New York 18.145.15	*ABV* 247, 715 (id., no. 90); *Par* 111.
B202	117	Munich 1575	*ABV* 256, 1617 (Lysippides Painter, no. 16).
B214	117	Boston 01.8058	*ABV* 263 (Related to the Lysippides Painter, no. 6).
B218	116	London B339	*ABV* 264 (Group of London B339, no. 1).
B219	133	London, Bomford coll.	Boardman (1974) no. 177; id. (1976).
B220	122 n.33	Leiden xv e 28	*ABV* 266, 691 (Antimenes Painter, no. 1); *Par* 117.
B222	115f.	London B336	*ABV* 266 (id., no. 3).

B226	130	London B266	*ABV* 273 (id., no. 118).
B242*	135	Munich 1509	*ABV* 285 (Group of Bologna 16, no. 1); *CVA* Germany 37, plate 418.
B250*	78, 92, 95f., 98	London w39	*ABV* 297 (Painter of Berlin 1686, no. 16); Boardman (1974) no. 136; Schauenburg (1965) 863f. & fig. 10; *EG* 79.
B254	92	London B253	*ABV* 308 (Swing Painter, no. 68).
B258	6, 106 n.100	Paris F51	*ABV* 313 (Painter of Louvre F51, no. 1); *Par* 136.
B262	92, 94	Providence (R.I.), School of Design 13.1479	*ABV* 314 (id., no. 6).
B266	92	New York 56.171.21	*ABV* 321 (Medea Group, no. 2); *Par* 141.
B267	78, 92	London B262	*ABV* 321 (id., no. 3).
B271*	70, 95, 99	Munich 1468	*ABV* 315 (cf. Painter of Cambridge 47, no. 3); *CVA* Germany 32, plate 343.
B283	119	Madrid 10920	*ABV* 332 (Priam Painter, no. 17); *Par* 146.
B287	97	Rome, Villa Giulia 3550	*ABV* 375 (Leagros Group, no. 201).
B295	128, 130	Paris, Bibl. Nat. 322	*ABV* 380 (id., no. 296); *Par* 164.
B299	93	New York 26.60.29	*ABV* 384 (Acheloos Painter, no. 17); *Par* 168.
B302	96	London w40	*ABV* 384 (id., no. 20); Boardman (1974) no. 211.
B310	130	Paris, Bibl. Nat. 320	*Par* 171 (cf. *ABV* 389, Chiusi Painter).
B318	117	London B631	*ABV* 423, 697 (Charinos, Potter).
B322	118, 119 n.2	Munich 2447	*ABV* 425 (cf. Class of London B632).
B326	119	London B507	*ABV* 426 (Keyside Class, no. 9).
B330	152	Athens 1045	*ABV* 186, 432 (Kleisophos).
B334	93	Copenhagen 8385	*Par* 179 (Class of London B524, no. 12; cf. *ABV* 438).
B336	97	Munich 1525	*Par* 192 (cf. *ABV* 443); *CVA* Germany 37, plate 400.2.
B338	94	Rhodes 13472	*ABV* 449 (Painter of Rhodes 13472, no. 1); *Par* 195.
B342*	70, 95	Boston 08.31i	*ABV* 454 (cf. Painter of the Nicosia Olpe, no. 1); Vermeule 11, plate 4.6.
B346	152	Maplewood, Noble	*Par* 198 (Painter of Munich 1842; cf. *ABV* 454).
B354	97	Munich, private	*ABV* 469 (Cock Group, no. 71).

B358	118, 120		*Par* 220 (cf. *ABV* 481f., Doubleens).
B362	97	Rome, Villa Giulia	*ABV* 495 (Class of Athens 581, no. 149).
B366	97	Bucarest 0461	*Par* 241 (Class of Athens 581 [ii]; cf. *ABV* 503f.).
B370*	128, 132f.	Athens 9690	*ABV* 505 (Painter of Athens 9690, no. 1); Metzger (1965) plate XXVII.
B378	97	Capua, Museo Campano inv. 163	*ABV* 707 (Manner of the Haimon Painter, no. 502bis [*ABV* 559]).
B382	77	Mainz, University 91	*Par* 289 (Painter of Elaious I, cup type B; cf. *ABV* 576).
B386	133	Berlin 2095	*ABV* 610, 711 (Group of Berlin 2095, no. 1); Marcadé 103.
B394	128, 152	Frankfurt VF β 310	*ABV* 631 (Essen Group, no. 1); *CVA* Germany 30, plate 55.3.
B398	133	Paris, Bibl. Nat. 333	*ABV* 646 (Late Cups; Leafless Group, no. 203).
B406	98, 122		*ABV* 664 ('once Lord Guildford'); *Par* 317.
B410	114, 117	Munich	*ABV* 664.
B418	114 n.11	Rome, Conservatori	*ABV* 671; *CVA* Italy 36, plate (III H) 28.3f.
B422	114, 117	Compiègne 978	*ABV* 674.
B426	94	New York 41.162.32	*ABV* 676, 714; *Par* 319.
B430	118	Lyon 75	*ABV* 677.
B434	116	Naples RC187	*ABV* 678.
B442	118	Paris F283	*ARV* (not *ABV*) 1584.
B450	92, 100	Copenhagen Chr. viii 323	*CVA* Denmark 3, plate 101.1.
B454	116	Copenhagen Chr. viii 961	*CVA* Denmark 3, plate 117.5.
B458	95, 98	Copenhagen, Ny Carlsberg 13966	*CVA* Denmark 8, plate 324.1b.
B462*	127	Paris F314	*CVA* France 2, plate (III He) 8.2.
B470*	130	Paris AM1008	*CVA* France 5, plate (III He) 29.3, 30.3.
B474	130	Paris, Bibl. Nat. 185	*CVA* France 10, plate 57.5.
B478	6	Paris, Bibl. Nat. 308	*CVA* France 10, plate 87.15.
B482	78, 98	Paris F85bis	*CVA* France 12, plate (III He) 79.6.
B486*	70, 78, 98	Sèvres, Musée Céramique 6405	*CVA* France 13, plate 15.7.
B494*	133	Paris C11251	*CVA* France 19, plate 157.4.
B498	130	Paris E665	*CVA* France 19, plate 164.4.
B502*	70, 78, 92	Munich 2290a	*CVA* Germany 9, plate 140.8.
B510	95	Heidelberg inv. S148	*CVA* Germany 31, plate 163.1.
B516	100	Leipzig T3359	*CVA* DDR 2, plate 31.1f.

B518	77, 100	Leipzig T3362	*CVA* DDR 2, plate 32.1f.
B522	97 n.70	London C820	*CVA* Great Britain 2, plate (III He 10.4.
B526	70	Athens 501	*CVA* Greece 1, plate (III Hg) 5.1f.
B534	98	Rome, Villa Giulia 1932	*CVA* Italy 3, plate (III He) 50.13.
B538*	98	Bologna PU 239	*CVA* Italy 7, plate (III He) 44.3.
B542	134	Bologna 1434	*CVA* Italy 7, plate (III He) 11.4.
B554	97	Tarquinia	*CVA* Italy 26, plate (III H) 34.2.
B558	95	Parma C120	*CVA* Italy 45, plate (III H) 2.1.
B562	134	Ferrara inv. 159	*CVA* Italy 48, plate (III H) 41.2.
B566	94	Leiden 1965/11/2	*CVA* Netherlands 3, plate 24.2.
B570	133	Oslo, Etnografisk-museum 11074	*CVA* Norway 1, plate 22.4.
B578	94	Barcelona 420	*CVA* Spain 3, plate 9.1b.
B582	131	Zürich inv. 2472	*CVA* Switzerland 2, plate (III H 16.12.
B586	100	Boston 80.621	*CVA* USA 14, plate 40.2, 4.
B588	134	Boston 97.205	*CVA* USA 14, plate 41.1, 3.
B589	134	Boston 1970.69	*CVA* USA 14, plate 42.2.
B592	92, 99	Leningrad 1440	Beazley (1947) 203 no. a 15 Schauenburg (1965) 859f., fig. 7f.
B594	96	Boston 08.32c	Beazley (1947) 204 no. a 17 Vermeule 10, plate 6.1.
B598*	78, 96	Boston 08.292	Beazley (1947) 208 no. a 41 Vermeule 10, plate 5.1f.; *EG* 80f.
B610	93, 96	Berlin 1947	Beazley (1947) 209f.
B614	92, 146	Boston 08.30d	Beazley (1947) 212 no. β 10 Vermeule 10, plate 6.4.
B622	92	Orvieto	Beazley (1947) 214 no. β 13.
B634*	77	Berlin 1798	Beazley (1947) 218 no. γ 13.
B646	116 n.14, 120 n.28	Paris F358	Beazley (1950) 315.
B650	120		Caskey and Beazley iii 1.
B658	133	Athens Acr. 1623a	Graef and Langlotz i 172, plate 85.
B662	101	Athens Acr. 1669ab	Graef and Langlotz i 176, plate 85.
B666	100	Athens Acr. 1684a	Graef and Langlotz i 177, plate 85.
B670	100	Athens Acr. 1685a	Graef and Langlotz i 177, plate 85.
B676	100	Athens Acr. 1913	Graef and Langlotz i 192, plate 90.
B678	131	Berlin 1684	Licht iii 73.
B686	75	Rome, Villa Giulia	Mingazzini plate 33.1.
B694	101	Rome, Villa Giulia	Mingazzini plate 89.2.
B695	132	Florence 3897	Pickard-Cambridge plate IV.
B696	86	Athens 1121	Schauenburg (1965) 855f., fig. 6.
B697	119	Munich, Bareiss	Schauenburg (1969) 42, plates 1-3.
B702	99	Boston 08. 31f	Vermeule 11 plate 6.5.

BOEOTIAN (MAINLY BLACK-FIGURE: SIXTH AND FIFTH CENTURIES B.C.)

BB8	152	Thebes R50.265	*ABV* 30 (Boeotian Imitators of the KX Painter, no. 8)
BB16*	71, 128	Heidelberg 190	*CVA* Germany 10, plate 27.4.
BB20	97	Heidelberg inv. s148	*CVA* Germany 31, plate 163.1.
BB24*	102	Berlin 3364	*CVA* Germany 33, plate 197. 4.
BB28	129	Tübingen, University S/10.1361	*CVA* Germany 36, plate 51.3f.
BB40	133	Hamburg inv. 1963.21	Hoffmann (n.d.) 19, no. 12.
BB48	120	Private	Rolfe 89-101.
BB60	118	Athens 11554	Wolters 201f.

CORINTHIAN (SIXTH CENTURY B.C.)

C4	132	Corinth KP 2372	Seeberg (1971) 40, no. 211*bis.*
C10	128	Paris E632	Seeberg 45, no. 226; *IGD* no. I, 6.
C15	135 n.23	Paris H30	*CVA* France 12, plate (III Cc) 7, 16, 18, 22.
C19*	135 n.23	Paris inv. AM1566	*CVA* France 12, plate (III Ca) 28.7.
C22	135	Paris inv. AM1569	*CVA* France 12, plate (III Ca) 28.15.
C24	135	Paris inv. AM1571	*CVA* France 12, plate (III Ca) 28.24.
C28*	135 n.32	Leipzig T315	*CVA* Germany 14, plate 32.2.
C32*	135	Leipzig T4763	*CVA* Germany 14, plate 32.5.
C40	135	Warsaw 199241	*CVA* Poland 5, plate 35.7.
C42	94, 195	Oxford 1966.1011	[Beazley] (1967) 29, no. 71, plate VI.
C44	128	Athens 571	Collignon and Couve plate 23.
C52	128f.	Berlin	Pfuhl (1955) plate 17.
C56	132f.	Corinth IP1708	Pickard-Cambridge 306, plate Xb.
C58	132	Oslo, Jensen	Pickard-Cambridge 307, plate Xc.
CC62	106, 134 n.20	Paris E640	Robertson (1959) 80.
C66	128f.	Boston 13.96	Seeberg (1967) 25-9, plate IIb.
C70	152	Munich	Sieveking and Hackl fig. 176.
C74	86,99		Sotheby's 43, no. 107.
C78	100		Vorberg (1932) 112.

AEGEAN ISLANDS AND ASIA MINOR (SIXTH CENTURY B.C.)

CE10	132	Oxford 1924.264	*CVA* Great Britain 9, plate (IId) 10.24; Boardman (1958).
CE20	97	Athens	Brendel fig. 7.
CE28	127	London A1311	Cook 20, plate 11a.
CE33*	78, 94	Heraklion	Richter plate VIIIb; Schefold plate 27b.
CE34*	93f., 173	Thera	Richter plate VIIIc.
CE36	100	Würzburg 354	Rumpf plate 43.
CE37	100	Madrid 10909	Rumpf plate 44.

LAKONIAN (SIXTH CENTURY B.C.)

CP4	127	Paris Campana 44	*CVA* France 1, plate (III Dc) 7f.; Lane 146f., plate 42a.
CP12	127	Oxford	Lane 131, plate 34c.
CP16	100, 128, 152	Sparta	Lane 137, plates 39a, 40.
CP20	127	London B3	Lane 150, plate 46a.

ETRUSCAN AND ITALIOTE BLACK-FIGURE (SIXTH CENTURY B.C.)

CW8	134	Paris, Bibl. Nat. 172	Ducati plate 14f.
CW12	102	Würzburg	Vorberg (1932) 182.
CW16	86, 93, 99		Vorberg (1932) 463.

ATTIC RED-FIGURE AND WHITE-GROUND (*c.* 530-430 B.C.)

R4	127	Berlin 2159	*ARV* 3, 1617 (Andokides Painter, no. 1); *Par* 320.
R6	71, 127 n.5	Bologna 151	*ARV* 4, 1617 (id., no. 10); *Par* 320; *CVA* Italy 33, plate (III H) 95.3.
R8	70	Paris F203	*ARV* 4 (id., no. 13); Boardman (1975) no. 4.
R12	70f., 127	Warsaw 142463	*ARV* 10, 1618 (Goluchów Painter, no. 1); *Par* 321.
R16	79, 126	Paris G103	*ARV* 14, 1619 (Euphronios, no. 2); *Par* 322.
R20	70f.	Leningrad 644	*ARV* 16, 1619 (id., no. 14); *Par* 322.
R23	130	Munich 2620	*ARV* 16f., 1619 (id., no. 17); *Par* 322.
R27*	75, 96	Gotha 48	*ARV* 20 (Gotha Cup); *Par* 322; Boardman (1975) no. 51.
R31	122	Athena, Agora P7901	*ARV* 1559 (cf. 20, Gotha Cup).
R35	93, 117	Brussels A717	*ARV* 20, 1619 (Smikros, no. 1); *Par* 322.
R39	130	Berlin 2278	*ARV* 21, 1670 (Sosias Painter, no. 1); *Par* 323.
R44	103, 120 n.24	Paris C10784	*ARV* 23 (Phintias, no. 3).
R46	128	Leningrad inv. 1843	*ARV* 23 (id., no. 5).
R48	130	Athens 1628	*ARV* 25 (Phintias, Potter, no. 1).
R50	114	Oxford 333	*ARV* 1602 (cf. 26)
R52	5, 116	Munich 2907	*ARV* 26, 1620 (Euthymides, no. 1); *Par* 323; Boardman (1975) no. 33.
R55*	70f., 78	Munich 2309	*ARV* 27, 1620 (id., no. 4); *Par* 323; Boardman (1975) no. 34.
R57	71	Turin 4123	*ARV* 28, 1620 (id., no. 11); Boardman (1975) no. 36.
R59*	96	Paris G45	*ARV* 31 (Dikaios Painter, no. 4); *Par* 324.

R62	96, 131 n.12, 131 n.23, 171	Brussels R351	*ARV* 31 (id., no. 7); Boardman (1975) no. 46.
R70	117	Berlin 1966.20	*Par* 508 (cf. Near the Dikaios Painter, *ARV* 32).
R78	114, 116	Leningrad 615	*ARV* 1594 (cf. 33-5, Pioneer Groups: Sundry); *Par* 507.
R82*	86, 94, 118	New Haven, Yale 163	*ARV* 36 (cf. Gales Painter).
R86	70, 120	Bonn 73	*ARV* 48 (cf. Eye-cups, no. 162).
R90	116	New York 10.210.18	*ARV* 54 (Oltos, no. 7); *Par* 326.
R94	132	Boston 08.31d	*ARV* 56 (id., no. 23); Vermeule 14, plate 11.3.
R102	78	Tarquinia RC6848	*ARV* 60, 1622 (id., no. 66); *Par* 327.
R110	120 n.24, 121	Naples 2617	*ARV* 65 (id., no. 108).
R112	93 n.61	Bologna inv. D.L.8	*ARV* 65 (id., no. 113).
R114	102		*ARV* 66 (id., no. 121).
R125	116 n.15	London E37	*ARV* 72, 1623 (Epiktetos, no. 17); *Par* 328.
R132	102, 117	Leningrad inv. 14611	*ARV* 75 (id., no. 60); Boardman (1975) no. 71.
R136	130	Oxford 520	*ARV* (id., no. 84); *Par* 328; Boardman (1975) no. 76.
R140	130	London E137	*ARV* 78 (id., no. 95); Boardman (1975) no. 78.
R144	93	Athens 17303	*ARV* 80, 1624 (Manner of Epiktetos, no. 12).
R148	97	Palermo V651	*ARV* 85 (Skythes, no. 21).
R152	70, 102, 146	Paris G14	*ARV* 85 (Pedieus Painter, no. 1); *Par* 330.
R156	101f., 127	Paris G13	*ARV* 86 (id.); Marcadé 138f.
R160	119	Paris C11224	*ARV* 89 (Euergides Painter, no. 20).
R164	116	New York 09.221.47	*ARV* 91 (id., no. 52).
R168	6, 130	Athens 1430	*ARV* 95 (id., no. 122).
R169	130	Laon 371060	*ARV* 95 (id., no. 123); *Par* 330.
R171	133	Oxford 1966.447	*Par* 330 (id., no. 136).
R173	97, 118	Brussels Cinq. R260	*ARV* 97 (Manner of the Euergides Painter, no.10).
R177*	133	Rome	*ARV* 108 (Kachrylion, Potter, no. 29).
R189*	106 n.100	Warsaw 198514	*ARV* 113 (Thalia Painter, no. 4); *Par* 332.
R192	101, 127	Berlin 3251 + Florence I B49	*ARV* 113, 1626 (id., no. 7); Boardman (1975) no. 112.
R196*	79, 95f., 120	Berlin 2279	*ARV* 115, 1626 (Peithinos, no. 2); *Par* 332; *EG* 92f.
R200*	86, 94	Bologna 436	*ARV* 118 (Epidromos Painter, no. 11).

R204	114	London E25	*ARV* 1577 (cf. 117f.).
R207*	173	Tarquinia	*Par* 333 (cf. *ARV* 120; Apollodoros, no. 9*bis*); *EG* 111.
R208	120 n.24		*ARV* 120, 1627 (id., no. 12); *Par* 333.
R210	79	Munich inv. 8771	Boardman (1975) no. 115 (Cf. *ARV* 119, the Elpinikos Painter).
R212	102, 132	London E815	*ARV* 125 (Nikosthenes Painter, no. 15).
R216	130	Boston 24.453	*ARV* 129 (Pamphaios, Potter, no. 28).
R219*	72	Athens 1409	*ARV* 130 (id., no. 31); *Par* 333.
R223*	86, 99, 101f., 127, 176 n.9	Boston 95.61	*ARV* 132 (Nikosthenes, Potter); Vermeule 12, plate 9; Boardman (1975) no. 99; *EG* 86.
R227	102	Boston 08.30a	*ARV* 135 (Wider Circle of Nikosthenes, Potter); Vermeule 13, plate 10.1.
R231	127	Warsaw 198059	*ARV* 1628 (cf. 136, Poseidon Painter, no. 3); *CVA* Poland 6, plate 7.3.
R235	71, 128 n.7	Altenburg 233	*ARV* 137 (Aktorione Painter, no. 1).
R239	120 n.26	Copenhagen 127	*ARV* 138 (Charops Painter, no. 1).
R243*	87, 120, 127	Turin 4117	*ARV* 150, 1628 (cf. Manner of Epileios Painter); *CVA* Italy 40, plate (III I) 3.2.
R247	101, 118	Durham (N.C.), Ruestow	*Par* 336 (cf. *ARV* 148-51, Manner of Epileios Painter).
R251	120	New York 06.1021.166	*ARV* 153 (Painter of Berlin 2268, no. 1); *Par* 336.
R255	106 n.100	Geneva I 529	*ARV* 154 (id., no. 7); *Par* 336.
R259*	133	Berlin 2320	*ARV* 157 (id., no. 84).
R261	70	London E6	*ARV* 166 (Pheidippos, no. 11); *Par* 337; Boardman (1975) no. 80.
R263	131	Rome, Villa Giulia 50448	*ARV* 167 (Bowdoin-Eye Painter, no. 7).
R265	135, 152	Brussels R259	*ARV* 169 (Scheurleer Painter, no. 7); Boardman (1975) no. 84.
R267	127	Munich 2586	*ARV* 169 (Near the Scheurleer Painter, no. 1).
R275	131	Paris G73	*ARV* 170, 1630 (near Scheurleer Painter and near Bowdoin-Eye Painter).
R279	93	Oxford 1911.616	*ARV* 173 (Ambrosios Painter, no. 1).
R283*	94	Rome, Villa Giulia 50458	*ARV* 173 (id., no. 5).

R291	152	Boston 08.31b	*ARV* 174 (id., no. 22); Vermeule 14, plate 11.2.
R295*	96	New York 07.286.47	*ARV* 175, 1631 (Hegesiboulos Painter); Boardman (1975) no. 126.
R299	114	Havana, Lagunillas	*ARV* 1570 (cf. Painter of Agora Chairias Cups, 176f.).
R303*	71	Berlin 2269	*ARV* 177 (Kiss Painter, no. 1); *Par* 339; Boardman (1975) no. 123; *EG* 89.
R305*	70	Oxford (Miss.)	*ARV* 177 (id., no. 3); *Par* 339.
R309	71	Würzburg 507	*ARV* 181 (Kleophrades Painter, no. 1); *Par* 340; Boardman (1975) no. 129.
R310	119	Würzburg 508	*ARV* 182, 1631 (id., no. 5); *Par* 340.
R311	119	New York 13.233	*ARV* 183, 1632 (id., no. 13); *Par* 340.
R313*	70	Tarquinia RC4196	*ARV* 185, 1632 (id., no. 35); *Par* 340; Boardman (1975) no. 133.
R315	126	London E441	*ARV* 187 (id., no. 57); Boardman (1975) no. 137.
R317	132	Paris G57	*ARV* 188 (id., no. 65).
R321	70	Naples 2422	*ARV* 189, 1632 (id., no. 74); *Par* 341; Boardman (1975) no. 135.
R322	92	Rome, Villa Giulia 50384	*ARV* 189, 1632 (id., no. 75).
R326	127 n.6	Munich 2310	*ARV* 197, 1633 (Berlin Painter, no. 6).
R328*	126	Würzburg 500	*ARV* 197, 1633 (id., no. 8); *Par* 342; Boardman (1975) no. 145.
R329*	127 n.6	Munich 2311	*ARV* 197, 1633 (id., no. 9).
R332	70, 127 n.6	Munich 2313	*ARV* 198 (id., no. 12).
R336*	70, 75 n.23	London E267	*ARV* 199 (id., no. 28).
R340	70	Zürich ETH 17 (418)	*ARV* 202 (id., no. 85); *CVA* Switzerland 2, plate 23.3.
R344	5	Rome, Villa Giulia 50755	*ARV* 204 (id., no. 111).
R348*	70f., 78f., 92f., 125	Paris G175	*ARV* 206, 1633 (id., no. 124); *Par* 342.
R351	79	Paris G192	*ARV* 208, 1633 (id., no. 160); *Par* 343; Boardman (1975) no. 155.
R352	133	Munich 2304	*ARV* 220 (Nikoxenos Painter, no. 1); *Par* 346.
R356	146	Boston 95.19	*ARV* 220 (id., no. 5).
R358	122 n.32	Munich 2381	*ARV* 221 (id., no. 14); Boardman (1975) no. 163.
R361	92, 100	Tarquinia	*ARV* 224 (Akin to the Nikoxenos Painter, no. 7); *EG* 107.

R365	70	Munich 2306	*ARV* 225 (Painter of Munich 2306, no. 1).
R367	126	Hamburg 1966.34	*Par* 347 (Eucharides Painter, no. 8*ter*); Boardman (1975) no. 165.
R369	118	Paris G136	*ARV* 231 (id., no. 78).
R373*	125	Tarquinia RC2398	*ARV* 236 (Chairippos Painter, no. 4).
R377	121	Paris G54 *bis*	*ARV* 246 (Painter of the Munich Amphora, no. 8).
R381	5	London E261	*ARV* 248 (Diogenes Painter, no. 2); Boardman (1975) no. 194.
R383	78	Paris, Niarchos	*ARV* 250 (Syleus Painter, no. 18); Boardman (1975) no. 197.
R385	146	London E350	*ARV* 256 (Copenhagen Painter, no. 2).
R387	71	London E442	*ARV* 257 (id., no. 9); Boardman (1975) no. 201.
R391	93	Bologna PU283	*ARV* 260 (Syriskos Painter, no. 8); Boardman (1975) no. 203.
R405	92f.	Naples 3152	*ARV* 275 (Harrow Painter, no. 60).
R406*	70, 93	Vienna 3737	*ARV* 275 (id., no. 61).
R414*	102, 132f.	Paris, Petit Palais 307	*ARV* 279 (Flying-Angel Painter, no. 2); Boardman (1975) no. 176.
R416	133	Athens, Agora P27396	Lang no. 29.
R418	92	Rome, Villa Giulia 50462	*ARV* 284 (Matsch Painter, no. 3).
R422*	128	Paris G234	*ARV* 286, 1642 (Geras Painter, no. 16).
R426	122	London E718	*ARV* 306 (cf. Painter of Würzburg 517).
R430	127	London E296	*ARV* 309 (Tithonos Painter, no. 6).
R434	100	London E816	*ARV* 315 (Near the Eleusis Painter, no. 2); Brendel plate 22; Boardman (1975) no. 219.
R438	117	Paris G25	*ARV* 316 (Proto-Panaitian Group, no. 5).
R442	133	Brussels A723	*ARV* 317 (id., no. 15).
R446	128	Oxford (Miss.)	*ARV* 320 (Onesimos, no. 10).
R450	131	Boston 01.8020	*ARV* 321 (id., no. 22); *Par* 359; Bowra (1957) plate 56b.
R454*	72	Paris G291	*ARV* 322 (id., no. 36); Ginouvès plate XIII.39.
R455*	71	Basel, Antikenmuseum BS439	*ARV* 323 (id., no. 56); *Par* 359; Boardman (1975) no. 230.
R456*	127	Boston 95.29	*ARV* 324, 1645 (id., no. 65); von Lücken plate 56.6.
R458*	70, 116, 127	Schwerin 725 (1307)	*ARV* 325 (id., no. 73); *Par* 359; *CVA* DDR 1 plate 18.2.

R462*	131, 135	Munich, Bareiss 229	*Par* 360 (id., no. 74*ter*).
R463	6, 95, 116	Boston 63.873	*Par* 360 (id., no. 74*quater*).
R465	120	Boston 10.179	*ARV* 327f. (id., no. 110); *Par* 359.
R467	125	Vienna 1848	*ARV* 329 (id., no. 128).
R471*	72	Brussels A889	*ARV* 329, 1645 (id., no. 130); *Par* 359; Boardman (1975) no. 224.
R472*	72	Copenhagen, Thorvaldsen 105	*ARV* 329 (id., no. 131).
R474	120	Berlin 2322	*ARV* 329, 1645 (id., no. 134).
R476	70, 106 n.98, 117, 120 n.24	Oxford (Miss.)	*ARV* 331 (Manner of Onesimos, no. 20); *Par* 361.
R478	118	Berlin 2316	*ARV* 1559f. (cf. 333, Manner of early Onesimos).
R480	94	Berlin (East) 2325	*ARV* 335 (Antiphon Painter, no. 1); *Par* 361; Boardman (1975) no. 239.
R484	118	Erlangen, University 454	*ARV* 339 (id., no. 49).
R486	79	Orvieto inv. 585	*ARV* 339 (id., no. 51).
R490	100f.		*ARV* 339 (id., no. 55); Boardman (1975) no. 241.
R494*	70, 118	Hannover 1958.57	*ARV* 356 (Colmar Painter, no. 51); *Par* 363; *CVA* Germany 34, plate 31.5.
R496	78, 118	Oxford 300	*ARV* 357 (id., no. 69); *Par* 363; Boardman (1975) no. 236.
R498*	118, 130	Hannover 1964.5	*ARV* 359 (Painter of the Louvre Komoi, no. 26); *Par* 364; *CVA* Germany 34, plates 31.3, 35.2.
R502*	92, 98	Mykonos	*ARV* 362 (Triptolemos Painter, no. 21).
R506	101f.	Tarquinia	*ARV* 367 (id., no. 93); *EG* 114.
R507	101, 118	Tarquinia	*ARV* 367 (id., no. 94); Boardman (1975) no. 302; *EG* 115.
R514	71, 116	London E68	*ARV* 371, 1649 (Brygos Painter, no. 24); *Par* 365; *EG* 63.
R518	101	Florence 3921	*ARV* 372 (id., no. 31); *EG* 97-9.
R519	93, 152	Würzburg 479	*ARV* 372, 1649 (id., no. 32); *Par* 366.
R520*	92 n.59, 95f., 98	Oxford 1967.304	*ARV* 378 (id., no. 137); *Par* 366; Boardman (1975) no. 260.
R521	127, 130	Paris G156	*ARV* 380, 1649 (id., no. 172); *Par* 366.
R525	134	Leningrad 680	*ARV* 382, 1701 (id., no. 191).
R527	75, 78	Gela	*ARV* 384 (id., no. 219); *Par* 366.
R528	135	Corpus Christi College, Cambridge	*ARV* 402, 1651 (Foundry Painter, no. 12); *Par* 370; Boardman (1975) no. 261.

R529	92	Leningrad 663	*ARV* 403 (id., no. 25).
R531	135	Berlin 3757i	*ARV* 404 (Manner of the Foundry Painter, no. 11).
R539	96	Paris G278 +Florence ZB27	*ARV* 407 (Briseis Painter, no. 16).
R543*	100	Tarquinia	*ARV* 408 (id., no. 36); *EG* 112.
R545*	100	Oxford 1967.305	*ARV* 408 (id., no. 37); *Par* 371; Boardman (1975) no. 272.
R546	78	Boston 63.1246	*Par* 373 (Dokimasia Painter, no. 34*quater*); Boardman (1975) no. 274.
R547*	92	Hillsborough (Ca.), Hearst	*ARV* 421 (Painter of Paris Gigantomachy, no. 83).
R551	120 n.24	Paris G131	*ARV* 1566 (cf. 425-9, early Douris).
R555	130	Vienna 3695	*ARV* 429, 1653 (Douris, no. 26); *Par* 374.
R559	120 n.26	Athens 1666	*ARV* 1567f. (cf. 429, Douris).
R563	126	Boston 98.930	*ARV* 431 (id., no. 45); *Par* 374.
R565	135	Rome, Vatican	*ARV* 432, 1653 (id., no. 53).
R567	123 n.38	Paris G115	*ARV* 434, 1653 (id., no. 74); *Par* 375.
R569	96, 117	Christchurch (N.Z.), University College	*ARV* 438 (id., no. 138).
R571	70	New York 23.160.54	*ARV* 441, 1653 (id., no. 186).
R573*	96, 98	Munich 2631	*ARV* 443 (id., no. 224).
R574	93	Boston 95.31	*ARV* 443 (id., no 225); *Par* 375; *EG* 103.
R577*	100, 116	Boston 1970.233	*ARV* 444 (id., no. 241); Buitron 107; Boardman (1975) no. 297.
R581	131	London E768	*ARV* 446 (id., no. 262); *Par* 375; Boardman (1975) no. 299.
R585	127	Athens 15375	*ARV* 447, 1653 (id., no. 274).
R589	92f.	London E51	*ARV* 449, 1653 (Manner of Douris [II], no. 4); *Par* 376.
R593	102, 133		*ARV* 450 (id., no. 22).
R595	122 n.34	Richmond (Va.)	*ARV* 450 (id., no. 24).
R603*	75, 98	Boston 13.94	*ARV* 1570 (Style related to Douris); Vermeule plate 12.5; *EG* 102.
R607	132f.	Rome, Villa Giula 50404	*ARV* 1565 (cf. 456, Magnoncourt Painter).
R619	96, 118	New York 06.1152	*ARV* 463 (Makron, no. 52); Marcadé 87.
R623	94	Gotha 49	*ARV* 467 (id., no. 119); *Par* 378.
R627	92f., 96	London E61	*ARV* 468, 1654 (id., no. 145).
R628	93, 117	New York 12.231.1	*ARV* 468, 1654 (id., no. 146).
R630	96	Paris G143	*ARV* 469 (id., no. 148).
R632	92	Oxford 1966.498	*ARV* 469 (id., no. 152); *Par* 378.

R634	75	Vienna 3698	*ARV* 471, 1654 (id., no. 193).
R636	6	Berlin 2292	*ARV* 471 (id., no. 195); *CVA* Germany 21, plate 90.2.
R637*	92, 117	Munich 2655	*ARV* 471 (id., no. 196).
R638	92, 125	Rome, Villa Giulia 916	*ARV* 471 (id., no. 197).
R651*	95	Boston 08.31e	*ARV* 478 (id., no. 306); Vermeule 14, plate 12.1.
R655	146	Athens, Acropolis 560	*ARV* 479 (id., no. 336).
R659*	71, 78	Paris G416	*ARV* 484, 1655 (Hermonax, no. 17); *Par* 379; Boardman (1975) no. 354.
R663	93	St. Louis, Washington Univ. 3271	*ARV* 488 (id., no. 77).
R667	43 n.10, 75, 130	Munich 2413	*ARV* 495, 1656 (Painter of Munich 2413, no. 1); *Par* 380.
R671	70	Warsaw 142310	*ARV* 500 (Deepdene Painter, no. 32).
R675	126	Paris G164	*ARV* 504, 1657 (Aegisthus Painter, no. 1); *Par* 381.
R680	127, 132	Adria B114+	*ARV* 505 (id., no. 9).
R682*	71, 93	Vienna, Univ. 551a	*ARV* 505 (id., no. 13).
R684*	5, 75, 93	Cambridge 37.26	*ARV* 506 (id., no. 21); *Par* 381.
R688	71	Cleveland 30.104	*ARV* 516 (Cleveland Painter, no. 1); *CVA* USA 15, plates 23.3f., 24.1f.
R690	117, 120 n.27	London E318	*ARV* 530 (Alkimachos Painter, no. 20); *Par* 383.
R691	117, 120 n.27	Naples 3125	*ARV* 530 (id., no. 21).
R692	71, 93	Leningrad 611	*ARV* 530 (id., no. 26).
R693	93	Boston 10.185	*ARV* 550, 1659 (Pan Painter, no. 1); *Par* 386; Boardman (1975) no. 335.
R695	132	Berlin (East) inv. 3206	*ARV* 551 (id., no. 10); *Par* 386; Marcadé 107; Boardman (1975) no. 342.
R699*	129, 130	Athens 9683	*ARV* 554 (id., no. 82); *Par* 386; Bowra (1957) plate 60; Boardman (1975) no. 336.
R701	70	Munich 2417	*ARV* 556 (id., no. 101); *Par* 387.
R705	79	Adolphseck 51	*ARV* 557 (id., no. 119).
R712*	70	Harvard 60.346	*ARV* 563 (Pig Painter, no. 8); Boardman (1975) no. 321.
R716	70, 75, 125	Cleveland 24.197	*ARV* 564 (id., no. 18); *Par* 389; *CVA* USA 15, plate 28.1f.; Boardman (1975) no. 320.
R720	92	New York 41.162.86	*ARV* 564 (id., no. 24).

R728	92	Adolphseck 41	*ARV* 566 (Manner of the Pig Painter, no. 6).
R729	132	Athens	*ARV* 567 (id., no. 7); *Par* 390.
R733	70	Milan C316	*ARV* 569 (Leningrad Painter, no. 40); *CVA* Italy 51, plate (III I) 2.1.
R737	70, 131	Warsaw 142290	*ARV* 571 (id., no. 76); *Par* 390.
R741	94	London E264	*ARV* 579 (Oinanthe Painter, no. 1); *Par* 392.
R742	117	London E182	*ARV* 580 (id., no. 2); *Par* 392.
R750*	71	Madrid 11038	*ARV* 586 (Earlier Mannerists [viii], Undetermined, no. 46).
R752	127 n.4	Athens, Agora P8892	*ARV* 587 (id., no. 63); Lang no. 34.
R754	130	London E467	*ARV* 601 (Niobid Painter, no. 23); *Par* 395.
R758*	92	Vienna 652	*ARV* 636 (Providence Painter, no. 10).
R762	97	Munich 2335a	*ARV* 637 (id., no. 34).
R766	118	Berlin 2334	*ARV* 646 (Oionokles Painter, no. 5).
R770	78, 93, 131	London E297	*ARV* 647 (id., no. 13).
R774	152	London E302	*ARV* 652 (Nikon Painter, no. 2).
R778	120	London E289	*ARV* 653 (Charmides Painter, no. 6).
R779	117	Paris C10764	*ARV* 653 (id., no. 7).
R783*	70	Boston 00.356	*ARV* 741 (cf. Carlsruhe Painter); *Par* 413.
R789	92	Leningrad 712	*ARV* 784 (Painter of Munich 2660, no. 27).
R791*	92	Oxford 517	*ARV* 785 (Euaichme Painter, no. 8); Boardman (1975) no. 373.
R795	94	Geneva I519	*ARV* 792 (Euaion Painter, no. 49); *CVA* Switzerland 1, plate (III I) 10.3f.
R797	94	Florence 3946	*ARV* 792 (id., no. 51).
R801	93	Boston 95.28	*ARV* 816 (Telephos Painter, no. 1); *Par* 420; Boardman (1975) no. 379.
R805	70	Warsaw 142313	*ARV* 821 (Boot Painter, no. 4); *Par* 421.
R813	70	Berkeley 8.3225	*ARV* 822 (id., no. 24).
R817	92	Altenburg 271	*ARV* 832 (Amphitrite Painter, no. 31).
R821	134	Berlin 1960.2	*ARV* 861, 1672, 1703 (Pistoxenos Painter, no. 12); *Par* 425; *CVA* Germany 22, plate 105.3.
R825	116	Rome, Villa Giulia 50329	*ARV* 872 (Manner of the Tarquinia Painter, no. 26).
R829*	71, 78, 93	Basel, Cahn 9	*ARV* 874 (Painter of Florence 4021, no. 3).

R833*	70, 78, 92f.	Ferrara T212B	*ARV* 880, 1673 (Penthesilea Painter, no. 12); *Par* 428.
R837	134	Ferrara T18C	*ARV* 882, 1673 (id., no. 35); *Par* 428.
R841	5	Boston 03.815	*ARV* 887, 1673 (id., no. 145); *Par* 428.
R843	93	Leningrad inv. 4224	*ARV* 889 (id., no. 166).
R845	131	New York 07.286.36	*ARV* 890, 1673 (id., no. 173); *Par* 428.
R847	75, 78, 83	New York 28.167	*ARV* 890, 1673 (id., no. 175).
R851*	92	Bologna 384	*ARV* 903 (Veii Painter, no. 57).
R853	92	Florence 74356	*ARV* 904 (id., no. 59); *Par* 429.
R861	120	Oxford 1929.466	*ARV* 911 (Painter of Bologna 417, no. 73); *Par* 430.
R863	92	Florence 77922	*ARV* 911 (id., no. 75); *Par* 430.
R867*	92	Florence 9626	*ARV* 953 (Angular Painter, no. 47); *Par* 433.
R871	131	Munich 2469	*ARV* 971 (cf. Class of the Seven Lobster-Claws); *Par* 435.
R875	75, 92	Berkeley 8.4581	*ARV* 974 (Lewis Painter, no. 31).
R879	130	Schwerin 716 (1277)	*ARV* 976 (Zephyros Painter, no. 4); *CVA* DDR 1, plate 34.3.
R887	117	Athens 1923	*ARV* 995 (Achilles Painter, no. 119).
R890	117	Athens 1963	*ARV* 995, 1677 (id., no. 122); *Par* 438.
R894	130	Athens 1818	*ARV* 998, 1677 (id., no. 161); *Par* 438.
R898	102, 127	Paris C9682	*ARV* 1029 (Polygnotos, no. 16); Marcadé 143; *EG* 126f.
R902	119 n.22, 152	Boston 00.346	*ARV* 1045 (Lykaon Painter, no. 7); *Par* 444; *IGD* no. III.1.28.
R904	116	Naples Stg. 281	*ARV* 1045 (id., no. 9).
R912	75, 93, 118	Paris, Bibl. Nat. 846	*ARV* 1050, 1679 (Pantoxena Painter, no. 1); *Par* 444.
R913	118	Boston 10.224	*ARV* 1050 (id., no. 2); *Par* 444.
R917	70, 146	Munich 2411	*ARV* 1501f., 1680 (Group of Polygnotos, no. 18).
R918	117	Boston 95.21	*ARV* 1052, 1680 (id., no. 19).
R922	119	New York 22.139.11	*ARV* 1083, 1682 (Cassel Painter, no. 5).
R926	71, 120	Bologna 261	*ARV* 1089 (Painter of the Louvre Centauromachy, no. 28).
R928	93 n.61	Florence inv. 4012	*ARV* 1101 (Ariana Painter, no. 9).
R930	70	Vienna 2166	*ARV* 1111 (Painter of Tarquinia 707, no. 1); *Par* 452.
R932	152	London 1923.10-16.10	*ARV* 1112 (Orestes Painter, no. 5); *Par* 452; *IGD* no. III.1.8.

R934*	93	Frankfurt VF β413	*Par* 453 (cf. *ARV* 1115, 1683; Hephaistos Painter, no. 31*bis*).
R938	70	Paris G4549	*ARV* 1128 (Washing Painter, no. 106).
R942	125	Oxford 308	*ARV* 1139 (Manner of Hasselmann Painter, no. 5).
R946	72, 120	Munich 2415	*ARV* 1143, 1684 (Kleophon Painter, no. 2).
R950	121	Munich 2361	*ARV* 1145 (id., no. 36); *Par* 456.
R954*	87, 99	London F65	*ARV* 1154 (Dinos Painter, no. 35).
R958*	71f.	Bonn 78	*ARV* 1171 (Polion, no. 4); *Par* 459.
R962	128	New York 25.78.66	*ARV* 1172 (id., no. 8); *Par* 459.
R966	125, 127	Madrid 11365	*ARV* 1174, 1685 (Aison, no. 1).
R970*	87 n.49, 101, 127	Berlin F2414	*ARV* 1208, 1704 (Shuvalov Painter, no. 41). *Par* 463; *EG* 124f.
R978	125	Berlin 2728	*ARV* 1275 (cf. Codrus Painter, no. 4).
R990	146	London E719	*ARV* 1560.
R994	114	Athens, Agora P5160	*ARV* 1561.
R997	115, 120 n.27	Heidelberg	*ARV* 1579.
R999	120	Hamburg 1963.2	*ARV* 1593, 1699 (no. 37); *Par* 507.
R1000	120 n.24		*ARV* 1593 (no. 45, 'lost').
R1005	120	Athens 1226	*ARV* 1601.
R1006	120	Athens, Agora P10948	*ARV* 1601.
R1007	120	London E548	*ARV* 1601.
R1015	114		*ARV* 1605 ('once Chiusi').
R1017	120 n.30		*ARV* 1607 ('once Mastrillo').
R1019	117	Paris, Bibl. Nat. 508	*ARV* 1610.
R1023	117, 120	Rome, private	*Par* 523.
R1027*	130	Copenhagen Chr. viii 56	*CVA* Denmark 4, plate 162.1b.
R1031	117, 130	Copenhagen, Ny Carlsberg 14628	*CVA* Denmark 8, plate 336.1b.
R1039	116	Compiègne 1106	*CVA* France 3, plate (III Ib) 13.9f, 15.1.
R1047*	70, 127, 131	Frankfurt VF β402	*CVA* Germany 30, plate 59.2.
R1053	10, 116 n.15	Athens 1357	*CVA* Greece 1, plate (III Ic) 3.1.
R1055	131	Athens 1431	*CVA* Greece 1, plate (III Ic) 3.5.
R1067	70, 127	Rhodes	*CVA* Italy 10, plate (III Ic) 6.3.
R1071*	102	Siracusa inv. 20065	*CVA* Italy 17, plate (III I) 7.1f.
R1075	128	Siracusa inv. 23508	*CVA* Italy 17, plate (III I) 14.1.
R1079	96	Milan CMA265	*CVA* Italy 31, plate (III I) 3.1.
R1087	133	Milan HA C316*bis*	*CVA* Italy 51, plate (III I) 3.2.
R1091	120 n.24, 125	Amsterdam, Scheurleer inv. 21	*CVA* Netherlands 2, plate (III Ib) 7.1-3.
R1095	93	Barcelona 4201	*CVA* Spain 3, plate 17.3.

R1099	130	Barcelona 4237	*CVA* Spain 3, plate 25.7.
R1103	130	Geneva inv. 16.908.1939	*CVA* Switzerland 1, plate 9.2.
R1107	70	Berkeley 8/5	*CVA* USA 5, plate 31.1a.
R1111	125	Oxford (Miss.)	*CVA* USA 6, plate 23.2.
R1115	70, 125	New York L2625	*CVA* USA 8, plate 46.1c.
R1119	72, 125	Bryn Mawr, College P.205	*CVA* USA 13, plate 10.1.
R1123	122	Athens, Agora P7690	Beazley (1947) 222, no. 16.
R1127*	87, 99	Berlin	Brendel fig. 20.
R1135*	71	Athens Acr. 188	Graef and Langlotz ii 14, plate 9.
R1137	72	Athens Acr. 226	Graef and Langlotz ii 18, plate 12.
R1139	146	Athens Acr. 676	Graef and Langlotz ii 62, plate 112.
R1141	128	Athens Acr. 1073	Graef and Langlotz ii 92, plate 83.
R1143	75	Munich 2686	Greifenhagen (1957) 23, fig. 18.
R1147	120 n.30		Klein 4, 169.
R1151	101, 135	Athens	Marcadé 137; *EG* 122.
R1155	105	Private	Schauenburg (1975) 103.
R1159	133	Boston 08.31c	Vermeule 11, plate 11.5.
R1163	102		Vorberg (1932) 409.
R1167	87		Vorberg (1932) 447.

ATTIC RED-FIGURE (LATE FIFTH AND FOURTH CENTURIES B.C.)

RL2	70, 78	Florence 81947	*ARV* 1312 (Meidias Painter, no. 2); Charbonneaux fig. 327.
RL4	72	London 98.7-16.6	*ARV* 1333 (Nikias Painter, no. 1).
RL13	78 n.30, 131	Naples 3240	*ARV* 1336, 1704 (Pronomos Painter, no. 1); *IGD* no. II.1.
RL14	77 n.29	Ruvo 1501	*ARV* 1338 (Talos Painter, no. 1); Charbonneaux fig. 38.
RL16	118, 120	Ferrara T412	*ARV* 1348 (Painter of Ferrara T412, no. 1).
RL20	151	Bologna 329	*ARV* 1410 (Meleager Painter, no. 21).
RL28	126	Munich 2398	*ARV* 1446 (Pourtalès Painter, no. 3).
RL32	72	Athens 12592	*ARV* 1447 (Painter of Athens 12592, no. 3).
RL35	77	London E424	*ARV* 1475, 1695 (Marsyas Painter, no. 4); Charbonneaux fig. 381.
RL40	122	Oxford G141-48	Beazley (1927) 352f.
RL41	77	New York 25.190	Charbonneaux fig. 378.
RL44	130	Berlin 2688	*RCA* 59, plate II.1.
RL52	78	Leningrad 1891.818	*RCA* 120, plate IX. 2.
RL56	130, 151	Paris G507	*RCA* 131, plate XV.4.
RL60	93	Manchester University	*RCA* 141, plate XIX.4.
RL64	72	New York 24.97.5	*RCA* 203, plate XXVII.4.
RL68	96	Naples H2202	*RCA* 363, plate XLVIII.2.

RL72	132	Vienna 924	Metzger (1965) 88, plate XXXIV.

ITALIOTE AND SICELIOTE RED-FIGURE (LATE FIFTH AND FOURTH CENTURIES B.C.)

RS8	130	Compiègne	*CVA* France 3, plate 28.3.
RS12*	72	Karlsruhe B136	*CVA* Germany 8, plate 66.1.
RS13	72	Karlsruhe B134	*CVA* Germany 8, plate 66.3.
RS16	72	Karlsruhe B41	*CVA* Germany 8, plate 69.1.
RS20*	72	Karlsruhe B2425	*CVA* Germany 8, plate 73.5.
R24	130	Altenburg 272	*CVA* Germany 18, plate 85.1.
RS26*	70, 72	Schwerin 720	*CVA* DDR 1, plate 45.2f.; *LCS* 68 (Lucanian, no. 337), plate 31.5f.
RS27	72	Schwerin 703	*CVA* DDR 1, plate 49.1; *LCS* 165 (Lucanian, no. 919).
RS28	72	Milan HA C231	*CVA* Italy 51, plates (IVD) 1.1, 2.2f.
RS30	128	San Francisco, de Young 226/24866	*CVA* USA 10, plate 24.2; *LCS* 34 (Lucanian, no. 114).
RS31	72	Paris K710	Charbonneaux fig. 350.
RS32	72	Ruvo 1088	Charbonneaux fig. 357.
RS36	132	Vienna 942	*LCS* 28 (Lucanian, no. 98), plate 8.5.
RS44	130	Paris, Bibl. Nat. 442	*LCS* 36 (Lucanian, no. 136).
RS48	130	New York 91.1.466	*LCS* 49 (Lucanian, no. 251), plate 20.3.
RS52	72	Taranto 8263	*LCS* 55 (Lucanian, no. 280); Charbonneaux figs. 347f.
RS56	72	London F184	*LCS* 58 (Lucanian, no. 289), plate 28.1f.
RS60	72	Taranto, private	*LCS* 60 (Lucanian, no. 302), plate 29.6.
RS64	72	Reggio di Calabria 7004	*LCS* 64 (Lucanian, no. 315), plate 30.2.
RS68	72	Taranto 50938	*LCS* 66 (Lucanian, no. 325), plate 31.1.
RS69	72		*LCS* 66 (Lucanian, no. 326), plate 31.2.
RS73	72	Taranto 52535	*LCS* 67 (Lucanian, no. 336), plate 31.4.
RS77	72	Madrid 32681	*LCS* 73 (Lucanian, no. 371), plate 34.3.
RS81	70	Bari 6327	*LCS* 96 (Lucanian, no. 502), plate 47.3f.
RS85	72	Compiègne 1023	*LCS* 101 (Lucanian, no. 529), plate 52.1.
RS89	72	Bari 6264	*LCS* 102 (Lucanian, no. 535), plates 51.8, 53.1.
RS97	151	London F179	*LCS* 113 (Lucanian, no. 582), plate 58.

RS101	72	Naples 1761	*LCS* 167 (Lucanian, no. 927); Charbonneaux fig. 354.
RS109	72	Dublin 960.1	*LCS* 214 (Campanian, part 1, no. 74), plate 84.6.
RS113	72	Cambridge GR 14/1963	*LCS* 236 (Campanian, part 2, no. 63), plate 93.4.
RS121	130	London F211	*LCS* 258 (Campanian, part 2, no. 211), plate 103.1f.
RS129	72	Naples 856	*LCS* 497 (Campanian, part 4, no. 412), plate 192.
RS133	72	London F473	*LCS* 597 (Sicilian, no. 82), plate 232. 3f.
RS137	72	Gela 9163	*LCS* 619 (Sicilian, no. 232), plate 243.6.
RS141	128	Bari 3899	*PhV* 27, no. 18; *IGD* no. IV.26.
RS147	128	Harvard, McDaniel	*PhV* 30, no. 24; *IGD* no. IV.16.
RS151	128	Leningrad inv. 299	*PhV* 33, no. 31; *IGD* no. IV.22.
RS159	71	Santa Agata dei Goti	*PhV* 44, no. 59; *IGD* no. IV.33.
RS163	71	Rome, Vatican U19	*PhV* 46, no. 65; *IGD* no. IV.19.
RS171	71	Naples Rgaua 13	*PhV* 62, no. 115; *IGD* no. IV.32.
RS175	128	Ruvo 1402	*PhV* 68, no. 135; *IGD* no. IV.12.
RS179	152	London 1917.12-10.1	*IGD* no. III.1.11.

Bibliography

This list includes all works to which reference has been made in the footnotes. It is not a definitive bibliography of Greek sexual life, still less of the history of homosexuality.

Armstrong, A.H., 'Platonic Eros and Christian Agape', *Downside Review* lxxix (1961) 105-21.

Beattie, A.J., 'Sappho Fr. 31', *Mnemosyne* S. IV ix (1956) 103-11
   id., A Note on Sappho Fr. 1', *CQ* N.S. vii (1957) 180-3

Beazley, J.D., *Attische Vasenmaler des rotfigurigen Stils* (Tübingen 1925)
   id., 'Some Inscriptions on Vases', *AJA* xxxi (1927) 345-53, xxxiii (1929) 361-7, xxxix (1935) 475-88, xlv (1941) 593-602, liv (1950) 310-22, lviii (1954) 187-90, lxi (1957) 5-8, lxiv (1960) 219-25
   id., 'The Antimenes Painter', *JHS* xlvii (1927) 63-92.
   id., 'Two Inscriptions on Attic Vases', *CR* lvii (1943) 102f.
   id., 'Some Attic Vases in the Cyprus Museum', *Proceedings of the British Academy* xxxiii (1947) 195-244
   id., *Attic Black-Figure Vase-Painters* (Oxford 1956)
   id., *Attic Red-Figure Vase-Painters*, second edition (Oxford 1963)
   id., *Paralipomena: Additions to* Attic Black-Figure Vase-Painters *and* Attic Red-Figure Vase-Painters (Oxford 1972)

[Beazley, J.D.] *Ashmoleán Museum Catalogue of Sir John and Lady Beazley's Gifts to the Ashmolean Museum 1912-1966* (London 1967)

Beazley, J.D., and Payne, H.G.G., 'Attic Black-Figured Fragments from Naucratis', *JHS* xlix (1929) 253-72

Bethe, E., 'Die dorische Knabenliebe', *RM* N.F. lxii (1907) 438-75

von Blanckenhagen, P.H., 'Puerilia', in *In Memoriam Otto F. Brendel: Essays in Archaeology and the Humanities* (Mainz 1975) 44-6

Blegen, C.W., 'Inscriptions on Geometric Pottery from Hymettus', *AJA* xxxviii (1934) 10-28

Boardman, John, 'A Greek Vase from Egypt', *JHS* lxxviii (1958) 4-12
   id., *Greek Art* (second edition, London 1973)
   id., *Athenian Black-Figure Vases* (London 1974)
   id., *Athenian Red-Figure Vases: the Archaic Period* (London 1975)
   id., 'A Curious Eye-Cup', *AA* 1976 281-90

Boardman, John, Dörig, J., Fuchs, W., and Hirmer, M., *The Art and Architecture of Ancient Greece* (English translation, London 1967)

Boardman, John, and La Rocca, E., *Eros in Grecia* (Milan 1975)

den Boer, W., *Eros en Amor: Man en Vrouw in Griekenland en Rome* (The Hague 1962)

Bowra, C.M., *The Greek Experience* (London 1957)

id., *Greek Lyric Poetry*, second edition (Oxford 1961)

Brendel, O.J., 'The Scope and Temperament of Erotic Art in the Greco-Roman World', in Bowie, T., *et al.*, *Studies in Erotic Art* (New York and London

Buitron, Diana M., *Attic Vase-Painting in New England Collections* (Cambridge, Mass. 1972)

Caskey, L.D., and Beazley, J.D., *Attic Vases in the Museum of Fine Arts, Boston* (Oxford 1931-1963)

Charbonneaux, J., Martin, R., and Villard, F., *Classical Greek Art 480-330 B.C.* (English translation, London 1972)

Chase, G.H., 'An Amphora with a New Kalos-name in the Boston Museum of Fine Arts', *HSCP* xvii (1906) 143-8

Collignon, M., and Couve, L., *Catalogue des vases peints du Musée National d'Athènes* (Paris 1902-1904)

Cook, R.M., 'Fikellura Pottery', *ABSA* xxxiv (1933/4) 1-98

Degani, E., 'Arifrade l' anassagoreo', *Maia* xii (1960) 190-212

Delcourt, Marie, *Hermaphrodite* (English translation, London 1961)

id., *Hermaphroditea* (Brussels 1966)

Denniston, J.D., *Greek Particles*, second edition (Oxford 1954)

Deubner, L., *Attische Feste* (Berlin 1932)

Devereux, G., 'Greek Pseudo-homosexuality and the "Greek Miracle"', *Symbolae Osloenses* xlii (1967) 69-92

id., 'The Nature of Sappho's Seizure in fr 31 LP as Evidence of her Inversion', *CQ* N.S. xx (1970) 17-31

id., *Ethnopsychanalyse complémentariste* (Paris 1972)

id., *Tragédie et poésie grecque: études ethnopsychanalitiques* (Paris 1973)

Dickinson, R.L., *Human Sex Anatomy*, second edition (London 1949)

Diels, H., 'Alkmans Partheneion', *Hermes* xxxi (1896) 339-74

Dover, K.J., 'Notes on Aristophanes' *Acharnians*', *Maia* N.S. i (1963) 6-25 [= Dover 1963a]

id., 'The Poetry of Archilochos', *Entretiens de la Fondation Hardt* x (1963) 183-222 [= Dover 1963b]

id., 'Eros and Nomos', *BICS* xi (1964) 31-42

id., 'The Date of Plato's *Symposium*', *Phronesis* x (1965) 2-20

id., 'Aristophanes' Speech in Plato's *Symposium*', *JHS* lxxxvi (1966) 41-50

id., *Lysias and the Corpus Lysiacum* (Berkeley and Los Angeles 1968)

id., 'Classical Greek Attitudes to Sexual Behaviour', *Arethusa* vi (1973) 59-73 [= 1973a]

id., 'Some Neglected Aspects of Agamemnon's Dilemma', *JHS* xciii (1973) 58-69 [= Dover 1973b]

id., *Greek Popular Morality in the Time of Plato and Aristotle* (Oxford 1975)

Ducati, P., *Pontische Vasen* (Berlin 1932)

Dugas, C., *Les Vases attiques à figures rouges* = *Exploration archéologique de Délos* xxi (Paris 1952)

Fehling, D., *Ethologische Ueberlegungen auf dem Gebiet der Altertumskunde* (Munich 1974)

Ferri, S., 'Sui vasi greci con epigrafi "acclamatorie"', *Rendiconti della Regia Accademia dei Lincei*, cl. sci. mor., S. VI xiv (1938) 93-179

Flacelière, *Love in Ancient Greece* (English translation, New York 1962)

Fränkel, Charlotte, *Satyr- und Bakchennamen auf Vasenbildern* (Halle 1912)

Fraenkel, Eduard, 'Neues Griechisch in Graffiti (I) *Katapugaina*' *Glotta* xxxiv (1955) 42-5

Friis Johansen, K., 'Fragmente Klazomenischer Sarkophage in der Ny Carlsberg Glyptotheke', *Acta Archeologica* vi (1935) 167-213

Furtwängler, A., and Reichhold, K., *Griechische Vasenmalerei* (Munich 1904-32)

Gentili, B., 'Il "letto insaziato" di Medea e il tema dell' *adikia* a livello amoroso nei lirici (Saffo, Teognide) e nella *Medea* di Euripide', *Studi classici e orientali* xxi (1972) 60-72

id., 'La Ragazza di Lesbo', *QUCC* xvi (1973) 124-8

Giangrande, G., 'Anacreon and the Lesbian Girl', *QUCC* xvi (1973) 129-33

Ginouvès, R., *Balaneutiké* (Paris 1962)

Gould, John, *The Development of Plato's Ethics* (Cambridge 1955)

id., 'Hiketeia', *JHS* xciii (1973) 74-103

Gould, T.F., *Platonic Love* (London 1963)

Gouldner, A.W., *Enter Plato* (London 1967)

Graef, B., and Langlotz, E., *Die antiken Vasen von der Akropolis zu Athen* (Berlin 1925-33)

Greifenhagen, A., *Eine attische schwarzfigurige Gattung und die Darstellung des Komos im sechsten Jahrhundert* (Königsberg 1929)

id., *Griechische Eroten* (Berlin 1957)

Guarducci, Margherita, 'Due o più donne sotto un solo manto in una serie di vasi greci arcaici', *MDAI (Athen. Abt.)* liii (1928) 52-65

Guthrie, W.K.C., *History of Greek Philosophy* (Cambridge 1962–)

Harrison, A.R.W., *The Law of Athens* (Oxford 1968-71)

Hauschild, H., *Die Gestalt der Hetäre in der griechischen Komödie* (Leipzig 1933)

Henderson, J., *The Maculate Muse: Obscene Language in Attic Comedy* (New Haven and London 1975)

Herter, H., *De dis atticis Priapi similibus* (Bonn 1926)

id., *De Priapo* (Giessen 1932)

id., 'Phallophorie', *RE* II xix (1938) 1673-81

id., 'Phallos', *ibid.*, 1681-1748

Hoffmann, H., *Vasen der klassischen Antike* (Hamburg, n.d.)

id., 'Hahnenkampf in Athen. Zur Ikonologie einer attischen Bildformel', *Revue Archéologique* 1974, 195-220

Hopfner, T., *Das Sexualleben der Griechen und Römer*, i pt. 1 (Prague, 1938)

Hoppin, J.C., *A Handbook of Attic Red-Figured Vases* (Cambridge, Mass. 1919)

Hyland, D.A., '*Ἔρως, Ἐπιθυμία* and *Φιλία* in Plato', *Phronesis* xiii (1968) 32-46

Immerwahr, H., 'An Inscribed Terracotta Ball in Boston', *Greek, Roman and Byzantine Studies* viii (1967) 255-66

Innis, Anne C., 'The Behaviour of the Giraffe', *Proceedings of the Zoological Society of London* cxxxi (1958) 245-78

Jacobsthal, P., *Ornamente griechischer Vasen* (Berlin 1927)

Jeffery, L.H., *The Local Scripts of Archaic Greece* (Oxford 1961)

Kaimakis, D., *et al.*, 'Vier literarische Papyri der Kölner Sammlung', *ZPE* xiv (1974) 29-38

Karlen, Arno, *Sexuality and Homosexuality* (London 1971)

Keydell, R., 'Peisandros (13)', *RE* II xix (1937) 146f.

Klein, W., *Die griechischen Vasen mit Lieblingsinschriften*, second edition (Leipzig 1898)

Kleingünther, A., *Prōtos euretēs = Philologus* Supplbd. xxvi. I (1933)   )

Knox, A.D., 'On Editing Hipponax: a Palinode?', *Studi Italiani di Filologia Classica* xv (1939) 193-6

Kretschmer, P., *Die griechische Vaseninschriften* (Gütersloh, 1894)

Kroll, W., 'Knabenliebe', *RE* xxi (1921) 897-906
   id., 'Lesbische Liebe', *RE* xxiii (1924) 2100-2

Kühner, R., *Ausführliche Grammatik der griechischen Sprache*, revised by Gerth, B. (Hanover and Leipzig 1898-1904)

Kunze, E., 'Zeus und Ganymedes, eine Terrakottagruppe', *Hundertstes Winckelmannsprogramm der archäologischen Gesellschaft zu Berlin* (Berlin 1940) 25-50

Lagerborg, R., *Die Platonische Liebe* (Leipzig 1926)

Lane, E.A., 'Lakonian Vase-Painting', *ABSA* xxxiv (1933/4) 99-189

Lang, Mabel, *Graffiti in the Athenian Agora* (Princeton 1974)

Lefkowitz, Mary R., 'Critical Stereotypes and the Poetry of Sappho', *Greek, Roman and Byzantine Studies* xiv (1973) 113-23

Licht, H., *Sittengeschichte Griechenlands* (Dresden 1925-28)

Lipsius, J.H., *Das attische Recht und Rechtsverfahren* (Leipzig 1905-1915)

Littman, R.J., 'The Loves of Alcibiades', *TAPA* ci (1970) 263-78

Lloyd-Jones, Hugh, *The Justice of Zeus* (Berkeley, Los Angeles and London 1971)

von Lücken, G., 'Die Schweriner Onesimos-Schale', *Wissenschaftliche Zeitschrift der Universität Rostock* xvi (1967) 485-90

Lullies, R., *Die Typen des griechischen Hermen* (Königsberg 1931)
   id., 'Neuerwerbungen der Antikensammlung in München', *AA* 1957 373-416

Lullies, R., and Hirmer, M., *Greek Sculpture*, second edition (English translation, New York 1960)

Marcadé, J., *Eros Kalos* (Geneva 1962)

Marcovich, M., 'Sappho Fr. 31: Anxiety Attack or Love Declaration?', *CQ* N.S. xxii (1972) 19-32

Marrou, H.I., *History of Education in Antiquity*, third edition (English translation, London 1956)

Masters, W.A., and Johnson, V.E., *Human Sexual Response* (London 1966)

Mead, Margaret, *Male and Female* (London, 1949)

Merkelbach, R., 'Sappho und ihr Kreis', *Philologus* ci (1957) 2-29
  id., 'Aischines 1.20', *ZPE* xvi (1975) 145-8
Metzger, H., *Les Représentations dans la céramique attique du IVe siècle* (Paris 1951)
  id., *Recherches sur l'imagerie athénienne* (Paris 1965)
Milne, Marjorie, and von Bothmer, D., '*Katapugōn katapugaina*', *Hesperia* xxii (1953) 215-24
Mingazzini, P., *Vasi della collezione Castellani* (Rome 1930)
Montuori, Mario, 'Su Fedone di Elide', *Atti dell' Accademia Pontaniana* N.S. xxv (1976) 1-14
Moss, Cynthia, *Portraits in the Wild* (London 1976)
Nagy, G., 'The White Rocks of Leukas', *HSCP* lxxvii (1973) 137-77
Napoli, M., *La Tomba del Tuffatore* (Bari 1970)
Neumann, G., *Gesten und Gebärden in der griechischen Kunst* (Berlin 1965)
Neumann, Harry, 'Diotima's Concept of Love', *AJP* lxxxvi (1965) 33-59
Nilsson, M.P., 'Kallisteia', *RE* x 1674
Nygren, A., *Agape and Eros* (English translation, London 1953)
Oehler, J., 'Gymnasium', *RE* xvii (1912) 2003-26
Page, Denys, *Alcman: the Partheneion* (Oxford 1951)
  id., *Sappho and Alcaeus* (Oxford 1955)
Pfuhl, E., *Malerei und Zeichnung der Griechen* (Munich 1923)
  id., *Masterpieces of Greek Drawing and Painting* (English translation, London 1955)
Pickard-Cambridge, A.W., *Dithyramb, Tragedy and Comedy*, second edition, revised by Webster, T.B.L. (Oxford 1962)
Pomeroy, Sarah B., *Goddesses, Whores, Wives and Slaves: Women in Classical Antiquity* (London 1975)
Reynen, H., 'Philosophie und Knabenliebe', *Hermes* xcv (1967) 308-16
Richter, G.M.A., *Korai: Archaic Greek Maidens* (London 1968)
Richter, G.M.A., and Hall, L.F., *Red-Figured Athenian Vases in the Metropolitan Museum of Art* (New Haven 1936)
Rist, J.M., *Eros and Psyche = Phoenix* Suppl. 6 (Toronto 1964)
Robertson, (C.) Martin, *Greek Painting* (Geneva 1959)
  id., '"Epoiesen" on Greek Vases: Other Considerations', *JHS* xcii (1972) 180-3
Robin, L., *La Théorie platonicienne de l'amour* (Paris 1908)
Robinson, D.M., 'The Villa of Good Fortune at Olynthos', *AJA* xxxviii (1934) 501-10
Robinson, D.M., and Fluck, E.J., *A Study of the Greek Love-names* (Baltimore 1937)
Rodenwaldt, G., 'Spinnende Hetären', *AA* 1932 7-22
Rolfe, J.C., 'An Inscribed Kotylos from Boeotia', *HSCP* ii (1891) 89-101
Rumpf, A., *Chalkidische Vasen* (Berlin and Leipzig 1927)
Ruppersberg, A., '*Eispnēlas*', *Philologus* N.F. lxx (1911) 151-4
Schaal, H., *Griechische Vasen aus Frankfurter Sammlungen* (Frankfurt am M. 1923)
Schauenburg, K., 'Iliupersis auf einer Hydria des Priamosmalers', *MDAI*

(*Röm. Abt.*) lxxi (1964) 60-70

id., 'Erastes und Eromenos auf einer Schale des Sokles', *AA* 1965 849-67

id., 'Herakles bei Pholos', *MDAI (Athen. Abt.)* lxxxvi (1971) 43-54

id., '*Eurumedōn eimi*', *MDAI (Athen. Abt.)* xc (1975) 07-122

Schefold, K., *Myth and Legend in Early Greek Art* (English translation, London 1966)

Schneider, L.M., 'Compositional and Psychological Use of the Spear in Two Vase-Paintings by Exekias: a Note on Style', *AJA* lxxii (1968) 385f.

Schreckenburg, Hans, *Ananke: Untersuchungen zur Geschichte des Wortgebrauchs* (Munich 1964)

Seeberg, A., 'Hephaistos Rides Again', *JHS* lxxxv (1965) 102-9

id., 'A Boston Fragment with a Prisoner', *BICS* xiv (1967) 25-35

id., *Corinthian Komos Vases* = *BICS* Suppl. xxvii (1971)

Semenov, A., 'Zur dorischen Knabenliebe', *Philologus* N.F. lxx (1911) 146-50

Sichtermann, H., *Ganymed: Mythus und Gestalt in der antiken Kunst* (Berlin n.d.)

id., 'Hyakinthos', *Jahrbuch des deutschen archäologischen Instituts* lxxi (1956) 97-123

id., 'Zeus und Ganymed in frühklassischer Zeit', *AK* ii (1959) 10-15

Sieveking, J., and Hackl, R., *Die königliche Vasensammlung zu München*, i (Munich 1912)

Slater, P.E., *The Glory of Hera* (Boston 1968)

Sotherby's Sale Catalogue 26 Nov. 1968

Stibbe, C.M., *Lakonische Vasenmaler des sechsten Jahrhunderts v. Chr.* (Amsterdam and London 1972)

Symonds, J.A., *A Problem in Greek Ethics* (London 1908)

Taillardat, J., *Les Images d'Aristophane* (Paris 1965)

Talcott, Lucy, 'Vases and Kalos-names from an Agora Well', *Hesperia* v (1936) 333-54

Tarbell, F.B., 'A Supposedly Rhodian Inscription Re-examined', *CP* xii (1917) 190f.

Trendall, A.D., *Phlyax Vases*, second edition = *BICS* Suppl. xix (1967) [= Trendall 1967a]

id., *The Red-Figured Vases of Lucania, Campania and Sicily* (Oxford 1967) [= Trendall 1967b]

Trendall, A.D., and Webster, T.B.L., *Illustration of Greek Drama* (London 1971)

Treu, M., *Von Homer zur Lyrik: Wandlungen des griechischen Weltbildes im Spiegel der Sprache*, second edition (Munich 1968)

Tripp, C.A., *The Homosexual Matrix* (New York 1975)

Trudgill, Eric, *Madonnas and Magdalens* (London 1976)

Vanggaard, T., *Phallós* (English translation, London 1972)

Vermeule, Emily T., 'Some Erotica in Boston', *AK* xii (1969) 9-15

Vlastos, Gregory, *Platonic Studies* (Princeton 1973)

Vorberg, G., *Ars Erotica Veterum* (Stuttgart 1926)

id., *Glossarium Eroticum* (Stuttgart 1932)

Wankel, H., 'Aischines 1.18-20 und der neue Kölner Papyrus', *ZPE* xvi (1975) 69-75

Webster, T.B.L., *Potter and Patron in Classical Athens* (London 1972)

Wender, Dorothea, 'Plato: Misogynist, Paedophile and Feminist', *Arethusa* vi (1973) 75-90

West, D.J., *Homosexuality Re-examined* (London 1977)

West, M.L., 'Alcmanica', *CQ* N.S. xv (1965) 188-202

  id., 'Melica', *CQ* N.S. xx (1970) 205-15

  id., *Studies in Greek Elegy and Iambus* (Berlin 1974)

Westwood, G., *A Minority: a Report on the Life of the Male Homosexual in Great Britain* (London 1960)

Willetts, R.F., *The Law Code of Gortyn* = *Kadmos* Suppl. i (1967)

Wilson, E.O., *Sociobiology* (Cambridge, Mass, 1975)

Wolters, P., 'Eingeritzte Inschriften auf Vasen', *MDAI* (*Athen. Abt.*) xxxviii (1913) 193-202

Zinserling, V., 'Physiognomische Studien in der spätarchaischen und klassischen Vasenmalerei', *Wissenschaftliche Zeitschrift der Universität Rostock* xvi (1967) 571-5

Index of Greek Texts
and Documents

Index of Greek Words

General Index